Protesters on Trial

A Volume in the
Crime, Law, and Deviance
Series

Steven E. Barkan

Protesters on Trial

Criminal Justice in the Southern Civil Rights and Vietnam Antiwar Movements

Rutgers University Press

New Brunswick, New Jersey

The following materials are reprinted with permission:

> Chapter 2 is adapted from my article in *Social Forces* 58 (March 1980): 944–961, and minor portions of it appeared in my article in *Social Problems* 27 (October 1979): 19–37.
>
> Chapter 4 is adapted from my article in *American Sociological Review* 49, no. 4 (August 1984): 552–565.
>
> Chapter 6 is adapted from my article in *Social Problems* 24 (February 1977): 324–336.
>
> Chapter 8 is adapted from my article in *Social Problems* 31 (October 1983): 28–45.
>
> Portions of various chapters appeared in somewhat different form in my article in *Research in Law and Sociology*, ed. Steven Spitzer, vol. 3. New York: JAI Press, 1980.

Library of Congress Cataloging in Publication Data

Barkan, Steven E., 1951–
  Protesters on trial.

  (Crime, law, and deviance series)
  Bibliography: p.
  Includes index.
  1. Political crimes and offenses—United States.
2. Criminal justice, Administration of—United States.
3. Civil rights movements—Southern States.   4. Vietnamese
Conflict, 1961–1975—Protest movements—United States.
I. Title.   II. Series.
KF9390.B37   1985   306'.25   85–1980
ISBN 0–8135–1108–9

For my parents

Contents

	Preface	ix
	Acknowledgments	xi
One	Introduction: Political Trials and the Legal Process	1
Two	Political Trials, Resource Mobilization, and Social Control	10
Three	Criminal Justice in the Civil Rights Movement	28
Four	Legal Control of Civil Rights Protest Campaigns	58
Five	Criminal Prosecutions in the Vietnam Antiwar Movement	87

Contents

Six   *Pro Se* Defense in Vietnam Protest Trials   105

Seven   Radical Catholics and the Destruction of
              Draft Files   119

Eight   Jury Nullification in Vietnam Protest Trials   132

Nine   Conclusion: Social Movements and Political
              Justice   149

              Bibliography   159

              Index   191

Preface

My interest in political trials began with my own arrest in an antiwar sit-in at the Hartford, Connecticut, Federal Building in May 1972. My fellow protesters and I acted as our own attorneys in a three-day trial and attempted, with some success, to discuss the Vietnam War as much as possible. The jury could not agree on a verdict, as at least one or two jurors sympathized with our protest, and the government later dismissed the charges.

My unforgettable but often frustrating experience in the courtroom during those three days made me decide not to go to law school—much to the dismay of my parents—but instead to study the sociology of law in general and political trials in particular. In a senior paper on power relationships in the courtroom I drew on experience from my trial, as I did in my graduate master's thesis on *pro se* defense, or self-representation, in political trials. These beginning pieces evolved, almost inevitably, into the present work, grounded in the theory and empirical analysis of sociology but inspired by my own personal and political interest in the subject. I trust that this interest has served to invigorate the presentation rather than to bias the discussion.

The fields of criminology, law and society, and social movements have largely neglected the origins, dynamics, and consequences of political trials. This lack of attention to such trials impoverishes these fields in several ways. First, it limits our understanding of the criminal trial process that can be gained from examining cases with underlying political, social, and moral issues which defense teams try to make central to the proceedings. Second, it restricts our appreciation of both the response of the American legal system to political ferment and the implications of this response for various conceptions of law and power in American society. Finally, it limits our awareness of the impact of the many arrests, prosecutions, and trials of American protesters on the social movements to which they belong.

This book examines these and other matters, and presents the first comprehensive analysis of the "political justice" that characterized the Southern civil rights and Vietnam antiwar movements. In the former movement, the criminal justice system was used by Southern officials to harass civil rights activists. Arrests and prosecutions intimidated Southern blacks and their allies, and forced the movement to spend large amounts of time, energy, and money defending its members against criminal charges. There was little or no chance of winning acquittals at the trial level, owing to the hostility of the region to the movement's challenge to segregation; consequently, civil rights lawyers concentrated at the trial level on building proper records for appeals to the federal courts.

In the antiwar movement, the criminal courts offered greater opportunities for mobilization than was true in the South. Judges, prosecutors, and juries were not nearly as hostile. Judges sometimes allowed defense teams to discuss political and moral arguments in criminal trials, and juries were more willing than in the South to acquit, though not as often as the movement may have wished. The opportunities that the courts offered the antiwar movement led to dilemmas in choosing between technical or political arguments at the trial level.

The very different experience of the civil rights and antiwar movements in the criminal courts reflects the varied nature of political prosecutions and trials in other eras of American dissent as well. Although this book focuses on only two social movements, its analysis may guide future research on the use of legal procedure in the many different protest movements in the American past. This research will present a much more complete picture than is now available on the legal system in times of political protest and on the impact of arrest and prosecution on the struggle for power between social movements and their antagonists.

Acknowledgments

The research for the doctoral dissertation upon which this book is based was partially funded by Grant No. 78-NI-99-0067 from the Law Enforcement Assistance Administration, United States Department of Justice. Researchers undertaking such projects under government sponsorship are encouraged to express freely their professional judgment. Therefore, points of view or opinions stated in this book do not necessarily represent the official position or policy of the United States Department of Justice.

Any book is necessarily the product of many minds, and this one is no exception. The members of my dissertation committee—Forrest Dill, Charles Perrow, Terry Rosenberg, and Michael Schwartz—offered valuable advice and suggestions on the original manuscript. Richard Colvard also read the original manuscript, and his recommendations proved invaluable when I revised it after the Rutgers University Press editor-in-chief, Marlie Wasserman, encouraged me to submit it for her consideration. David Greenberg and an anonymous reviewer subsequently read the entire revision and made many useful suggestions. Susan McLaughlin typed the revision, and I am very grateful for her help.

At the Meiklejohn Civil Liberties Institute in Berkeley, California, I found many primary and secondary sources, and I am grateful to David Christiano, Phoebe Watts, and especially Carolyn Mohr and Ann Fagan Ginger, the institute's founder, for taking so much time to help me. The institute is an invaluable though unheralded depository of information for social scientists and legal scholars alike, and its efforts in the areas of civil rights and civil liberties are praiseworthy.

I also owe a debt to several people who have influenced my life and work in many ways. Norman Miller introduced me to the fascination of sociology and never stopped forcing me to think like a sociologist. Forrest (Woody) Dill was an inspirational advisor; all my work, including this book, benefited immeasurably from his careful advice and criticism. His tragic, untimely death in an auto accident in Au-

gust 1981 deprived my discipline of a true scholar and, more important, took away a good friend. On a more cheerful note, I would like
to thank the many members of the Department of Sociology and Social Work at the University of Maine for providing a warm, suppor-
tive environment for my teaching and research.

The influence of my parents, Morry and Sylvia Barkan, on my val-
ues and life is reflected in the pages that follow. That this book is
dedicated to them signifies my love and respect for their many years
of devotion. Barbara Tennent was a patient source of encouragement
while I worked on my dissertation. My debt to her for everything is
unpayable; I can only hope that this book successfully reflects her
own deep commitment to peace and social justice. David Tennent
Barkan came along during the last few months of my research and
writing. He robbed me of some sleep but gave me the joy of fa-
therhood. His brother, Joel, was born as I was revising the manuscript for publication, and he left me even more sleepless. I hope
both boys read this book when they get older, learn from it, and are
inspired by it.

Finally, I must not neglect the civil rights and antiwar activists
and lawyers about whom I write. Their brave efforts helped change
the course of a nation, for they refused to sit by silently in the face of
racist injustice at home and murderous adventurism abroad.

Protesters on Trial

Chapter One

Introduction: Political Trials and the Legal Process

Political protesters have faced criminal prosecution throughout American history. From the tax and mercantile protesters of the colonial era to the demonstrators against nuclear power and nuclear weapons of the 1970s and 1980s, tens of thousands of Americans have been arrested, tried, and often imprisoned for dissent. This use of the criminal justice system has affected the fortunes of many social movements. In several periods of protest, government officials and other antagonists have effectively used the legal system to intimidate protesters and tie up their time, money, and energy. During the First World War, for example, federal and state prosecutions of some two thousand socialists, anarchists, and labor radicals under laws that forbid virtually all criticism of the war stifled dissent and helped destroy the Industrial Workers of the World (iww) (Chafee, 1941). In other periods, though, the legal system has enabled insurgents to gain many important advantages. Colonial law and legal proceeedings, for example, proved a "creative force" (Teachout, 1981: 198) in the struggle against English rule.

Despite this rich history of "political justice" (Kirchheimer, 1961), sociologists and other scholars have paid little attention to the impact of legal procedure, and especially criminal prosecutions and trials, on social movements. To what degree, and under what conditions, may the law and legal order serve as vehicles of harassment of social movements or, conversely, aid their efforts to change the status quo? What legal, social, and political factors affect the outcomes of attempts by movements and their opponents to use the legal system for political ends? In the criminal court arena, what factors determine defense strategies in trials of political protesters? What are the consequences of such political trials for social movements? These and other questions often go unasked by social scientists and legal scholars.

This book examines how the legal system and, especially, the criminal courts were used during the Southern civil rights movement of the early 1960s and the Vietnam antiwar movement that soon followed.* The courts were intimately involved in both movements, making them especially attractive targets of analysis along the lines already suggested. Yet because the legal experience of the two movements differed remarkably, a comparative analysis of the roots and impact of the court actions that typified each protest effort is illuminating. Particularly interesting are the different defense strategies that characterized the criminal trials of protesters in the two movements, as well as the ramifications of these trials for the movements' efforts at social change.

The criminal court is not ordinarily a setting for the struggle between radical activists and their opponents. The overwhelming majority of criminal cases involve defendants accused of committing public order crimes such as drunkenness and disorderly conduct (Clinard and Quinney, 1973). In these cases, court proceedings lack the adversary quality assumed by traditional legal theory (see Mayers, 1964). Defense attorneys usually turn to plea bargaining to reduce the lengths of sentences. Prosecuting attorneys likewise resort to plea bargaining to ensure convictions and help dispose of large numbers of cases expeditiously. When a trial does take place—some 10 percent of the time (Jones, 1981)—the goal of the defense is an acquittal or at least a hung jury. No other issue is at stake. Similarly, the prosecutor's primary concern is to obtain convictions. Moreover,

---

* The data for this investigation came from a variety of primary and secondary sources pertaining to the two movements. I drew widely on secondary accounts of the legal experiences of both movements, as well as on periodicals and articles written by members of both movements. The Meiklejohn Civil Liberties Institute in Berkeley, California, provided many of the primary sources I used to study the civil rights movement. I also interviewed three attorneys who were active in civil rights efforts in the South; a few others declined to be interviewed. The many legal cases discussed in the book represent those I discovered that had some bearing on the themes of the book. Although I cannot prove that the cases constitute a representative sample of all criminal cases in the two movements, they do, I believe, give an accurate picture of the legal experiences, dilemmas, and concerns of protesters in both movements.

most trials rarely conform to the Perry Mason–style adversary or combat model where prosecutors and defense counsels vigorously contend the evidence. Instead, trials typically involve harmonious relations among the courtroom workgroup of judge and attorneys (Blumberg, 1967; Eisenstein and Jacob, 1977; Skolnick, 1967; Sudnow, 1965).

By contrast, in the political trial as a generic legal event, both sides have multiple goals and "widely different perceptions of what is relevant to the criminal proceedings" (Allen, 1974:61). But what exactly is a political trial? The term is as elusive as *political criminal* (Schafer, 1971; Turk, 1982), and, as Dorsen and Friedman (1973, 79) point out, "has become so value-laden that its usefulness as an analytic concept has been undermined." Thus some legal scholars and officials deny that political trials exist in the United States (for example, Karlen, 1971), while others claim that virtually any American trial involving a poor or minority defendant is a political one (see Dorsen and Friedman, 1973:78). Between these two extremes lies the work of scholars who distinguish political trials as cases in which criminal proceedings are used to protect or change the existing structure of political power (Becker, 1971; Belknap, 1981; Kirchheimer, 1961). This definition allows for many particular kinds of political trials; Becker (1971) identifies four types, while Belknap (1981) differentiates as many as six.

In an attempt to clarify this conceptual muddle, I distinguish in this book two broad categories of political trials that differ according to their origins in the struggle for power between social movements and their opponents. In the first category, the initiative rests with state officials who wish to legitimize efforts at controlling individuals or groups believed hostile to the prevailing political order. The prosecution that results corresponds to the familiar American usage of the term *political trial*. The criminal charges and prosecutions are viewed by defendants, their supporters, and many disinterested observers, if not by government officials, as trumped up, a fraudulent and even repressive abuse of the legal system. The state's goals in this kind of prosecution are often fourfold: to put the defendants behind bars; to force them to spend large amounts of time, energy, and money on their defense, rather than on other political pursuits; to discredit the movement to which they belong by labeling their conduct as criminal; and to frighten off supporters and potential sympathizers who may not wish a similar fate. Thus, even if the state does not achieve a conviction, it may still win in other ways by achieving one or more of its other goals of social control. As one of the acquitted defendants in the 1973 Gainesville Eight trial for conspiracy to disrupt the 1972 Republican National Convention asserted, " 'In spite of all this joy and elation, I can't forget that the government put me through fourteen months of hell'" (in Kifner, 1973: 8). Examples of this kind of political trial include the prosecutions of the two thousand World War I critics, the 1921 Sacco-Vanzetti case, and the 1949 trial of Communist party leaders for conspiring to use violence to overthrow the United States government.

In the second category of political trial, the initiation of criminal proceeding rests with persons who deliberately break the law for political reasons, that is, who commit civil disobedience. Often one of their reasons for breaking the law is to continue in court the "educational effect of the illegal act itself" (Hall, 1971:125) by attempting to discuss political and moral issues, and to engender publicity through the drama of courtroom proceedings. Other civil disobedients violate the law to create test cases for appeals to higher courts; they can be expected not to stray from the legal issues at hand. A fairly recent example was the arrest of United Farm Workers leader Cesar Chavez, who defied a court injunction against picketing at a melon field in Arizona (*San Francisco Chronicle*, 1978). A third type of civil disobedient performs the classic act of moral witness by breaking the law with the expectation and even desire of arrest while intending to plead guilty to the charges. Finally, a fourth kind may publicly break the law without really wanting to be arrested. If arrests do take place, the defendants may choose to fight the charges, as occurred in the spring of 1977 when California students conducted sit-ins to protest university investments in corporations operating in South Africa (Rodden, 1977).

Whether initiated by state officials or by civil disobedients, these two categories of political trials are obviously ideal types. The origins of many political prosecutions fall somewhere in between the two extremes, as when movement activists deliberately break a law that itself clearly violates constitutional guarantees of freedom of speech, freedom of assembly, and the like. The arrests and trials before the Civil War of abolitionists for helping fugitive slaves escape cut across both types. The prosecution of suffragist Susan B. Anthony in 1873 for voting in violation of federal law is another case that falls in between the two categories.

Two further caveats remain. This categorization distinguishes political trials according to their origins. Whether political and moral issues in fact arise at the trial itself is an empirical question that will be discussed in the following chapter. Thus I allow for a trial to be a political one even if it proceeds without any recognition at all of its origins in the challenge posed by protest movements. Further, I allow for a trial to be political if it involves defendants accused of committing conventional crimes, say, robbing a bank and shooting the guards, for political reasons. However different this crime is from nonviolent civil disobedience, the defendants remain political criminals (see Minor, 1975; Schafer, 1974; Turk, 1982), and their trials are thus political trials.

The political trial, then, must be understood as both a legal event and as a small battle in the larger struggle between social movements and their opponents. As a result, the political trial raises several fascinating questions for our understanding of the criminal trial process, the place of law in American society, and the impact of legal procedure on movements' attempts to change the status quo: to what extent are arrests and prosecutions of political protesters informed by legal standards and procedures as opposed to purely political considerations? how independent, if at all, are law and the courts from political considerations? do legal rules and procedures have anything more than a minimal influence in political prosecutions? are political trials in the United States events where law essentially becomes irrelevant?

These questions address an important debate in sociology and political science circles on whether courts should best be understood as closed systems or open systems. In the closed-system model, criminal and appellate proceedings are thought to be primarily legal in form and substance, and influenced only minimally, if at all, by external forces such as political considerations. The courtroom is thus treated as a private domain with few, if any, connections to the outside world (Bickel, 1962; Blumberg, 1967; Frankfurter, 1971; Weschler, 1959). In contrast, the open-system model treats courts as institutions deeply enmeshed in society (Eisenstein and Jacob, 1977; Jacob, 1973; Levin, 1977; Rossett and Cressey, 1976). Emphasizing both the way courtroom events are conditioned by outside forces and the external relevance these events have, the open-system model presents a picture of far greater tension and complexity than that posed by its closed-system counterpart.

The connections between courts and the outside community are perhaps most dramatically apparent in prosecutions of political dissenters. There, outside influences are at a maximum, affecting prosecutorial and defense strategy and shaping the verdict. The proceedings and outcomes usually have consequences for groups and policies far removed from the immediate courtroom setting.

At the same time, however, political trials remain legal encounters; legal rules and procedure condition the behavior of political trial participants and affect the outcome of the proceedings. Thus political trials differ in many ways from other kinds of conflict between protesters and state officials, even though the extent to which law and legality do guide such proceedings varies from movement to movement.

The political trial is an important event in the life cycle of social movements, a point that will be developed in the next chapter. Questions such as: under what conditions can law and the courts be used by social movements to achieve their goals? under what conditions can legal procedure be used by state officials to attack social movements? and, what is the actual impact of the use of legal procedure on the struggle between social movements and their opponents? tie the discussion directly to the study of law and social change. The degree to which law can be used as an instrument of social change is an issue of much controversy in the study of law and society (Evan, 1965). Scholars have examined the impact of law and legal procedure on social change in several areas, including the ability of law to regulate business behavior (Ball and Friedman, 1965), to prevent immoral behavior (Skolnick, 1968), and to desegregate schools (Greenberg, 1959). Many such works have questioned the capacity of courts and the law to bring about major social change. Others have looked more positively on the law in this regard. Nonet (1969), for example, studied the legalization of workers' compensation as a result of interest group pressure and political controversy, and concludes that law served there as a "politically effective instrument" (1969 : 246) in extending the rights and benefits of workers.

Most of the research on law and social change, however, has neglected the impact of legal procedure on social movements. Although several political scientists have examined the strategies of interest group litigation, and the factors that affect the incidence and outcome of such litigation (Cortner, 1968; Hahn, 1973; O'Connor, 1980; Vose, 1958, 1972), their work has not generally been informed by the broader social movement theory of sociologists (but see Handler, 1978). Further, in focusing on civil litigation, they have neglected the use of criminal procedure by and against social movements.

In looking at the impact of such political justice on social movements, the use of civil disobedience by many movements is of special interest. Although the literature on civil disobedience is voluminous (e.g., Allen, 1967; Cohen, 1971; Hall, 1971), it is primarily the product of political philosophers and legal scholars who have focused on the definition and justification of civil disobedience in a democratic society. Much less sociological attention has been devoted to the uses and consequences of civil disobedience, and to the ways in which its history and practice may advance knowledge of political protest and judicial behavior. Whatever the definition of civil disobedience agreed upon, it specifically involves the violation of some criminal law. Arrests and prosecutions of civil disobedients allow political and moral issues to enter dramatically into the affairs of the legal system. Every such intrusion creates tensions that expose the legal system to the possibility of especially penetrating analysis. For this reason, Schur (1968), in one of the first law and society texts, maintains that the study of law and social change would profit greatly from analysis of civil disobedience movements.

The questions I have asked so far indirectly address the pluralist-Marxist debate on the nature of law and criminal justice in American society. The debate intensified a decade ago with the advent of the "new" criminology (Taylor, Walton, and Young, 1973) and has focused on such issues as the origins of criminal laws (Chambliss, 1974); the history of juvenile delinquency legislation (Hagan and Leon, 1977; Platt, 1974); and arrest and sentencing patterns (Chambliss and Seidman, 1971; Chiricos and Waldo, 1975; Hagan, 1974; Michalowski and Bohlander, 1976).

The arguments are by now familiar (see Hopkins, 1975). Pluralists generally contend that society is composed of diverse interest groups whose goals sometimes conflict. The American polity is structurally open to efforts at change by all these groups (Dahl, 1956; see Gamson, 1975). The state and its legal system are said to act as impartial

referees over this conflict of interests (Auerbach, 1959; Greer and Orleans, 1964; Pound, 1943). Many Marxists, new criminologists, and
conflict theorists contend in opposition that the law and legal system instead reflect the interests of the ruling class and are tools by
which that class maintains the existing order and augments its power
(Michalowski and Bohlander, 1976; Quinney, 1974). More recently,
other Marxist critics (e.g., Sumner, 1979) have focused on the ideological nature of American law, contending that law "offers us truth,
magic, impartiality and merit whilst denying the filthy side of politics" (Sumner, 1979:277). This is a point that I will address more
fully in chapter 8.

As fuel for either side in the debate, it would be instructive to examine the operation and impact of the courts during times of social
movement unrest. By definition these movements challenge existing
social, political, and economic conditions. Does the legal system impartially process the conflict between protest groups and government and business interests? Are the police and courts merely tools
of social control? Curiously these questions have received little attention in the pluralist-Marxist debate. Although there are several
accounts of attempts to use the legal system as a means of repression, such as the prosecutions of the IWW and other radicals during
and after World War I (Peterson and Fite, 1957; Preston, 1963) and the
Smith Act trials of Communist party leaders in the 1940s and 1950s
(Belknap, 1978), their relevance for theories of law, power, and society has not been adequately explored (but see Wolfe, 1971).

In an important and rare attempt to assess the theoretical signifi-
cance of legal responses to political protest, Balbus (1973) examines
ghetto revolts in Chicago, Detroit, and Los Angeles in the 1960s.
Among other conclusions he argues that the legal responses to the
riots are best explained not as examples of outright repression, as, he
says, instrumental Marxists might maintain but, rather, as a complex function of the constraints on legal officials to preserve social
order; to maintain the organizational efficiency of the criminal justice system; and to legitimate the political and economic orders by
adhering to standards of "formal legal rationality." Although at least
one author (Trubek, 1977) has questioned Balbus's theory of legit-
imation and use of the term *formal legal rationality*, his demonstration of the influence of formal legal norms on legal responses to the
urban disorders remains compelling. This is a point Balbus reempha-

sizes and extends in the introduction to the paperback edition of his book (1977 : vi): "I demonstrate . . . that the response of American legal authorities to the black ghetto revolts—or, for that matter, to any other event—can only be understood if we come to appreciate the way in which the form or internal structure of the legal order powerfully conditions—even during periods of extreme 'crisis'—the range of possible responses that emanate from the authorities who operate within this form."

But in thus criticizing the simplification he sees in instrumental Marxism, Balbus goes too far in the other direction. As noted earlier in regard to the IWW and other World War I radicals, there have indeed been periods of extreme crisis in the American past where the desire of legal officials to adhere to formal legal norms was at best minimal. And although the form of the legal order constrained the legal response of authorities in the events Balbus studied, such constraints were much weaker in the South during the civil rights movement of the early 1960s. What needs to be examined, then, is the differential commitment to "formal legal rationality" that has characterized the response of government and legal officials to American social movements, as well as the degree to which the courts have aided or impeded the efforts of these movements.

Chapter Two

Political Trials, Resource Mobilization, and Social Control

Recently the study of social movements has moved beyond the limitations of traditional, social-psychological perspectives on collective behavior that emphasized the shared frustration and discontent with existing conditions from which social movements were said to arise (see Gurr, 1970, Gusfield, 1968, Smelser, 1962). This was a fairly static approach, failing for the most part to examine adequately the many dilemmas of strategies and tactics that movements often encounter. In contrast, recent works have taken a more dynamic approach to the study of social movements, examining among other issues the strategic problems of having to appeal to various constituencies (Lipsky, 1968), and the tactics used by state officials and business interests to control insurgent efforts (Jenkins and Perrow, 1977).

These developments reflect the resource mobilization approach employed in recent studies (McCarthy and Zald, 1977; Oberschall, 1973). In this view the aggregation and use of resources of many types are critical to the success of social movement efforts. Some of these resources, such as leadership or membership morale, relate to the internal, organizational needs of protest groups. Others, such as the support of sponsoring organizations, are external to the group and have figured prominently in this new perspective on social movements. As Lipsky (1968:1153) puts it, "The essence of political protest consists of activating third parties to participate in controversy in ways favorable to protest goals."

In this chapter I will direct attention to the civil and criminal courts as additional, third-party resources that may be activated to achieve or impede the goals of social movement organizations. Since courts are reactive in that they must await decisions by citizens or groups to invoke the judicial process (Black, 1973; Sarat and Grossman, 1975), litigation strategies aimed directly at mobilizing the law on behalf of social movements or their adversaries may have a significant impact on the struggle between the two. At the same time, social movements may take *indirect* advantage of litigation to mobilize important resources: they may capitalize on litigation efforts to rally their members, to extend their membership base, and to convince the public of the justness of their cause. Political prosecutions and trials as one form of social movement litigation are especially convenient mechanisms by which insurgent groups and state officials may seek to mobilize or limit important social movement resources.

The Potential and Limits of Social Movement Litigation

Litigation has often been considered a form of political action (Casper, 1972; Ginger, 1963; Hakman, 1972). An extensive body of literature describes the variety of strategies and tactics that organized interest groups may use to bring questions of public policy and politics before the appellate courts (Cortner, 1968; Truman, 1951; Vose, 1972); these techniques include the use of test cases and *amicus curiae* briefs (Krislov, 1963; Vose, 1958). Often such civil litigation is initiated by organizations acting as parts of larger social movements seeking to advance various social and political objectives. The National Association for the Advancement of Colored People (NAACP), for example, played a major role in achieving the 1954 Supreme Court school desegregation decision (Greenberg, 1959; Kluger, 1976).

But a major study (Handler, 1978) of civil suits undertaken by the environmental, consumer, civil rights, and welfare movements of the 1960s and 1970s found that they achieved only limited success and questioned the capacity of litigation to achieve these movements' goals: "In sum, social-reform groups find it difficult to obtain tangible results directly from law-reform activity. It can be accomplished, and numerous cases have been discussed where such results have been obtained, but, on the whole, special circumstances are needed. . . . Social-reform groups seek out the courts because they are weak and have lost in the political process, and there is only so much that courts can do by way of direct, tangible benefits" (Handler, 1978:209).

Studies of litigation in the lower civil courts (Wanner, 1974, 1975) and small claims courts (Sarat, 1976; Yngvesson and Hennessey, 1975) have also discounted the ability of litigation to benefit directly the "have-nots" (Galanter, 1974) in society. Focusing on the motivations and backgrounds of litigants in such courts, and the social, political, and legal conditions that promote or inhibit litigation (Blankenburg, 1975; Felstiner, 1974; Grossman and Sarat, 1975), these studies have found among other conclusions that individuals are more likely to be defendants than plaintiffs in civil and small claims actions, and to lose their cases as well. Although these works have not looked at social movements, the obstacles they describe also pose difficulties for protest groups and individual activists who become litigants.

It is axiomatic that protest and litigation are strategies employed by groups lacking the power and ability to achieve their goals through other political means (Cortner, 1968; Lipsky, 1968). Although adjudication does reduce power disparities between the disputing parties, the disparities nonetheless remain. Typically beset by a lack of both money and competent, committed attorneys, social movements often encounter great obstacles in obtaining favorable court rulings. For example, the Southern civil rights movement, as we shall see, suffered profoundly from the refusal of Southern white attorneys to defend civil rights activists and from the paucity of Southern black attorneys. Communist party leaders facing prosecutions in the 1940s and 1950s under the Smith Act also found it difficult to obtain counsel. Fearing for their practice or disagreeing with communist beliefs, most attorneys were not willing to defend Communist party leaders (Alexander, 1962; Belknap, 1978).

Other problems in mobilizing the courts work similarly against quick and effective rule changes that would benefit social movements as well as private individuals. The courts may simply not be sympathetic to claims presented by groups seeking to change existing conditions. The refusal of judges in the 1970s to stop construction of nuclear power plants was a major impetus for the occupation of plant sites by antinuclear civil disobedients (Gyorgy et al., 1979). Also, case overload in the courts leads to delays in adjudication and thus to delays in judicial redress, which, in turn, increases the monetary costs of litigation and diverts protest group attention and resources from other pursuits (Galanter, 1974; Handler, 1978). Various rules of judicial procedure such as standing and jurisdiction present similar obstacles to relatively powerless groups seeking legal change, as the experience of the environmental movement illustrates (Large, 1972). As we shall see, the rules of judicial procedure posed particularly serious stumbling blocks to attempts by the Vietnam peace movement to end the war through legal means. In trials of antiwar activists, judges typically invoked the rules of evidence to rule out extensive discussions of the war, the draft, and the defendants' motives in committing illegal acts of protest. Their appellate counterparts similarly invoked the "political question" doctrine in refusing to hear cases disputing the constitutionality of the war or the draft.

Courts also lack effective means of enforcing their decisions (Handler, 1978). As a result, the policies they implement may often face delays, especially in the face of significant opposition that can be overcome only through separate legal actions costing much time and money (Scheingold, 1974). The experience of the civil rights movement again bears this out; the resistance of Southern cities to court-ordered school desegregation was not easily surmounted (Greenberg, 1959).

Finally, victories won by litigation efforts may well turn out to be more symbolic than concrete, placating protest members while preserving existing conditions and lending legitimacy to the political system (Sarat and Grossman, 1975). By promising to turn claims of interest into claims of right (Friedman, 1975) within a judicial structure that limits the degree of change that litigation can promote, adjudication may deflect the energies of the powerless away from attempts to effect more fundamental changes in the political and economic orders.

This is not to claim that civil litigation is a futile pursuit, for the potential of social movement litigation ultimately depends on the goals and resources of the movement, the historical and political context in which it takes place, and the kinds of changes it seeks

(Handler, 1978). Certainly the civil rights movement found in the law a tool, however imperfect, for ending desegregation in schools and public facilities, and for extending the right to vote to blacks. But more far-reaching changes may be beyond the scope of the law. For example, since a right to economic equality is not included in the Constitution, the law offers little hope for directly ending poverty (cf. Scheingold, 1974).

Litigation and Resource Mobilization

Although the law and the courts may not offer much direct help to social movements, civil litigation may still make a valuable, *indirect* contribution to the mobilization of internal and external resources crucial for social movement success: "Under the right circumstances rights can be used as a catalytic agent of mobilization. Mobilization can, in turn, be useful for articulating demands and forging those demands into viable political options" (Scheingold, 1974:213).

The mobilizing effects of litigation stem largely from the legitimacy that judicial decisions confer on claims of interest when they rule them claims of right. Individuals then come to perceive their discontent as worthy of political attention. Their new sense of entitlement may strengthen feelings of legal and political competence, increase their expectations for change, and spur them into action (cf. Scheingold, 1974). As Friedman (1975:234) points out, "Vindication of rights feeds on its own success. Success in one claim encourages and reinforces more claims and gives others a model and hope of success." Thus civil litigation can significantly solidify a protest group's organizational base by increasing morale and attracting new supporters. It may also serve, as Handler (1978) emphasizes, to publicize and legitimate social movement claims among the public and target groups, two more groups to which protest groups must appeal (Lipsky, 1968). In this fashion decisions won in the courts may indirectly contribute to a redistribution of political power; Handler (1978) has found that the civil lawsuits launched by the civil rights, consumer, environmental, and welfare movements of the last two decades succeeded more often on the indirect rather than the direct level.

The Dynamics of Political Trials

The works on litigation and on social movements that have been noted here suffer from their neglect of political trials. In such trials the verdict may assume only secondary importance or else take on wider implications as the prosecution and defense seek to take symbolic advantage of the legal trappings surrounding the proceedings and the public forum they provide. Legal procedure becomes a dramatic means for the goals of resource mobilization and social control in political trials.

This use of courts for dramatic purposes has attended virtually every period of political protest in American history, yet only Kirchheimer (1961) and a few less well-known works (e.g., Allen, 1974; Becker, 1971; Freidman, 1970; Hakman, 1972; *New York Review*, 1970) have examined it in any worthy detail, though without reference to social movement theory.

In the previous chapter I located the origins of political trials in attempts to advance or impede the goals of social movements. Defense teams in such cases face unusually hard decisions as a result. Strategic choices must be made and tactical dilemmas resolved. The accused must decide whether to plead guilty or to contest the charges. If the latter, they must also decide whether their primary goal will be to win an acquittal and avoid imprisonment or a fine, or, instead, to use the proceedings as a forum to inform the jury and the public of the political circumstances surrounding the case. Depending on these decisions, defendants must also decide whether to base their defense on technicalities or on moral and political grounds, and whether they will be represented by counsel or act as their own attorneys. Some political defendants have gone so far as to engage in disruptive tactics in court by violating norms of trial procedure and etiquette (Antonio, 1972; Sternberg, 1972).

Political defendants and their lawyers often have several reasons for wishing to address moral and political issues in court. Some defendants strive to discuss such issues primarily to "maintain the integrity of their political and moral commitments" (Brick, 1971 : 1503). Civil disobedients, as noted earlier, may feel compelled by conscience to discuss in court their motives for becoming lawbreakers by choice. Still other defendants have felt it necessary to challenge the legitimacy of the state and its judiciary in order not to lend their implicit support to what they consider a "white-wash" (Friedman, 1970:168). They therefore refuse to stand by as the trial proceeds without discussion of the political circumstances surrounding the case. As one Vietnam antiwar defendant wrote, "'We cannot resist illegitimate authority in the streets only to bow politely before it in the courtroom'" (in Brick, 1971:1503).

Two other, perhaps more vital reasons underlying defense attempts to politicize the proceedings concern the jury and the press. These are treated in detail in separate sections below.

The Defense and the Jury

In order to fully understand and interpret the attitudes and strategy of defense teams in trials of political protesters, one must not underestimate the influence of the jury. Often defense teams try to introduce political or moral issues in order to convince the jury of the justness of the accused's beliefs and actions and the unfairness of the prosecution, hoping that the jury will be more likely to acquit as a result. For many political defendants, convincing the jury (in this fashion) may be the only hope for avoiding conviction and imprisonment. Judges usually resist such efforts at politicization, though, and thus may greatly reduce the chances of jury acquittals, as chapter 8 will illustrate.

Despite the barriers posed by the judge, the prospect of "reaching" the jury with political and moral arguments still has an enormous attraction for many political defendants. Although these defendants readily concede "reasonable skepticism about such a fairy-tale outcome" (Crow and Davidson, 1978:5), there is often the hope that the fairy tale may come true. As two Vietnam War opponents wrote of the jury acquittal in a conservative town of a group of defendants who had blocked an ammunition train in 1972, "No one can say with certainty that it will not happen again" (Crow and Davidson, 1978:6). In fact, the desire to convince the jury on political and moral grounds may be so strong that political defendants are apt to reject a potent technical defense in favor of an explicitly political one that may be more risky. As we shall see in chapter 5, for example, several draft resisters during the Vietnam War insisted on basing their innocence on antiwar arguments, although they were more likely to win their cases with technical defenses (Baskir and

Strauss, 1978). In the same vein, a defendant who had toppled a nuclear plant weather tower in 1974 was disappointed when the judge dismissed the charges on a technicality near the end of his trial: "'The whole point was to see if I could convince twelve people from Franklin County that I did the right thing to stop the nuke. I wanted them to decide. I didn't want to win on a technicality'" (in Wasserman, 1977:37).

When an acquittal or hung jury is achieved through a political defense, the accused and their protest movement typically consider the verdict to be a great victory, a sign that the public represented by the jury (Jacob, 1973) supports or is ready to support the movement's goals. The news media often view the verdict in the same manner. The result for protest group members is a great deal of optimism and increased morale, strenghtening one of the internal resources of insurgent groups. Even if the jury convicts, the defense may be encouraged by the length of time the jury deliberated. Thus a Quaker youth found guilty in 1974 for refusing to register for the draft by a jury that deliberated more than seven hours concluded, "'I really think the jury had to sit and struggle with their consciences. I am a little more confident that the people in this country are ready for a change because the jury was out for so long'" (in the *New York Times*, 1974:61).

A few fairly recent cases exemplify the sense of elation and encouragement engendered by acquittals in political trials. In the February 1978 case of six people who had conducted a sit-in to protest the University of California's nuclear weapons research programs, the defense succeeded in discussing its view of the political and moral ramifications of such programs. Its efforts won a quick jury acquittal, which one defendant hailed as "'our fantasy come true'" and another as "'the greatest vote of confidence the public could have given us'" (in Tides, 1978:3). A newsletter published by the defendants' weapons conversion project later observed, "We are tremendously encouraged by our effect on the jury, a truly representative cross-section of the community, as a sign that our support will continue to grow" (UC Nuclear Weapons Lab Conversion Project, 1978:1).

A similar reaction greeted the December 1977 acquittal of ninety-six people who had blocked the gates of the Trojan nuclear power plant in Oregon. Throughout the trial the defense was able to introduce expert testimony to support its argument that the blockade was necessary to prevent the greater harm posed by the continued operation of the plant. Although the judge later told the jury to ignore the testimony, it nonetheless acquitted the protesters on a technicality after five hours' deliberation. A juror later revealed that the acquittal would have come after only a few minutes had the judge not ruled out the nuclear-related testimony. Thus one defendant was quick to call the verdict "'a major victory, not only for the Trojan Decommissioning Alliance, but also for the worldwide opposition to nuclear power'" (in Trojan Decommissioning Alliance, 1978:15), and even the public relations director for the owner of the Trojan plant, the Portland General Electric Company, said the acquittal would probably "'create some enthusiasm'" (in Wasserman, 1978:138) for new occupations of atomic plant sites. Interestingly, a minor debate ensued over the proper interpretation of the jury's decision, as one Oregon newspaper claimed the technical ground on which the verdict was based meant that the acquittal was not really a verdict against nuclear power, while the prosecutor asserted that the jury was not representative of the surrounding community (*Oregon Times Magazine*, n.d.: 21).

Apart from the verdict and its wider implications, political defendants also hope that their efforts to discuss moral and other issues will prompt jurors and other trial participants to examine their own political beliefs and even join the protest movement. As two activists put it, "Twelve jurors, a judge, a bailiff, a court reporter, and a prosecutor will all have reactions; and we do not know how many people they may share them with" (Crow and Davidson, 1978:6). Though the chances of swaying a juror or other trial participant in this manner are of course slim, such attempts at conversion do sometimes succeed, extending the membership base of the protest movement and once again encouraging defendants and their supporters. In a fall 1976 case arising from an illegal protest of the Trident submarine, a juror who voted to convict nonetheless talked at length with defendants after the trial and the next day handed out anti-Trident leaflets at the school where she taught (Crow and Davidson, 1978). After the conclusion of the Oregon nuclear plant sit-in case discussed above, several jurors said it had convinced them of the dangers of nuclear power, and two decided to start a nuclear power study group (*Oregon Times Magazine*, n.d.). And in a 1969 trial of

Catholic clergy and laity who had destroyed draft files, one of the two prosecutors was moved to resign his position in order to work on civil rights litigation (Gray, 1970).

But so far as I have been presenting only half the picture. There have been many political trials and many periods of political protest where the public has been extremely hostile to protest goals and tactics. In such a hostile political climate, juries promise little or no hope for defendants. The World War I years were one such period, the early 1960s in the South another. In the former era, juries readily convicted defendants charged with violating laws forbidding virtually all criticism of that war. One judge from that period put it well (in Chafee, 1941 : 70): "'I have tried war cases before jurymen who were candid, sober, intelligent businessmen . . . but during that period they looked back into my eyes with the savagery of wild animals. . . . Men believed during that period that their only verdict in a war case . . . was a verdict of guilty.'"

Thus depending on such factors as the specific crimes alleged, the location of the trial, and the jurors' attitudes as representatives of the public toward the defendants' movement and the cause they espouse, attempts to sway jurors with moral or political arguments may very well be futile. Defense teams may still launch such attempts under these circumstances; however, they are more likely to do so when they perceive some chance of succeeding. Thus we may distinguish between social movements where juries are regarded as potential allies and those where they are considered steadfast foes. Political defenses designed to win jury sympathy should be more common in the former than in the latter. I shall be arguing in later chapters that the Vietnam antiwar movement falls into the first category of movement, and the civil rights protests into the second, with corresponding differences between the defense strategies and tactics common to each.

The Press and the Public

Another, perhaps even more important goal of defense attempts at politicization is to use the proceedings as a forum to educate and to convert the public, whose support is invaluable if protest ends are to be reached (see Lipsky, 1968). "'One does not look for justice in court,'" Father Philip Berrigan, a Vietnam-era activist has written. " 'One hopes for a forum to communicate ideals, convictions, anguish'" (in Allen, 1974 : 60). The goal here is one of "counter-condemnation" (Kirchheimer, 1961 : 233). Typically the defense seeks publicity in order to undermine public confidence in the fairness of political trials (cf. Schneir, 1971). It may also wish to win publicity to induce the judge and prosecutor to restrict possible efforts to characterize the defendants as threats to the public and to allow the defense itself to bring in political considerations it deems relevant. This pressure may minimize the severity of a sentence should the jury convict. Yet another goal of publicity is to help secure funds for the defense and win support for the movement to which the accused belonged (Lefcourt, 1971).

Favorable press coverage of the trial is essential if the defense is to appeal successfully to the public: "Like the tree falling in the forest, there is no protest unless protest is perceived and projected" (Lipsky, 1968 : 1151). Political trials are no different. To secure press attention, defense supporters frequently organize rallies and demonstrations. In some cases the accused and their attorneys will speak at these rallies or appear at press conferences. Often a defense support group will be formed to spread information about the case and to collect funds for the defense effort.

Inside the court, the defense may seek publicity by trying to discuss political and moral issues. Some defendants have also engaged in disorderly behavior to attract attention, while others, as we shall see in chapter 7, have acted as their own attorneys. While courtroom proceedings have always seemed to hold a certain fascination for Americans, a political trial where defendants and their attorneys forcibly confront judge and prosecutor with efforts at politicization becomes one of particularly high drama, arousing the public's interest. The presence of the jury—twelve people sitting in judgment of their fellow citizens—adds to the tension. Thus, even where defendants and their attorneys do act with proper decorum, their efforts to raise political and moral issues may still receive considerable press attention, as recent trials of antinuclear power activists have shown. Samuel Lovejoy's trial for toppling the nuclear plant weather tower received extensive coverage in western Massachusetts (Wasserman, 1977), while the expert testimony on the dangers of nuclear radiation in the Trojan plant case in Oregon won major attention in news media throughout the state (Stein and Hott, 1978).

Conversely, defense decisions to concentrate on the charges rather than on political and moral issues may make for more boring proceedings, reduce press coverage, and otherwise impede goals that political defendants may have. Chapter 6 will treat this dilemma of defense strategy in greater detail.

These remarks presuppose that the news media are likely to devote favorable or at least neutral coverage to the proceedings and that segments of the public may become sympathetic if they read and hear such coverage. But depending on a variety of factors, including the accused's character and notoriety, the location of the trial, and the political climate, the press and public may well be hostile. In such circumstances, the defense may be less likely to introduce political and moral issues, perceiving the futility of winning favorable publicity through such efforts. Thus we may again distinguish between social movements where favorable and effective publicity deriving from political trials is possible, and those where it is not; the categories are, of course, ideal types.

Defense Strategy: Further Considerations

There are yet other factors that political defendants and their attorneys consider in deciding on a conventional or political defense. Depending on the nature and seriousness of the charges, the defense team may decide to argue on technicality of the law and evidence, or even to plead guilty in the first place. The more potent a technical defense, the more pressure to conduct one, regardless of the seriousness of the charges. Similarly, pleas of guilty may avoid the time and expense of a trial, win a lighter sentence, or, in the case of some civil disobedients, reaffirm their commitment to the rule of law. Thus some defense teams in political prosecutions either plead guilty or present technical arguments, despite the influence that the jury and the press often hold.

Thus a dilemma grips defense efforts in political prosecutions. To try to convert jurors or win press publicity through a political defense may increase the chances of acquittal in some cases but enhance the chances of conviction in those cases where technical arguments would prove more effective. At the same time, conducting technical defenses in these cases may increase the chances for acquittal but result in less press coverage. The ideal, of course, may be to combine a technical and political defense, but that is not so easily done.

The tension posed by the attractiveness of a technical defense was reflected in the legal experience of some fifty members of California's Abalone Alliance who trespassed in August 1977 onto the site of the Diablo Canyon nuclear power plant. When the first nine defendants were tried a month later, a few of them wanted to proceed with a political defense but were persuaded by their attorneys that technical grounds—namely, that the fence enclosing the site did not have the requisite number of no trespassing signs—would be more likely to win an acquittal. The defense also waived its right to a jury, feeling that a judge would better understand its technical arguments (Drysdale, 1978). Subsequently, however, the judge found the defendants guilty.

Finding this case politically unsatisfying and dismayed at the guilty verdict, the remaining defendants hired a new attorney and were determined that in the next trial they would attempt to raise the nuclear power issue along with the technical grounds that had failed previously, all before a jury. The beginning of the second trial was aborted, however, when it was discovered that one of the defendants was in fact an undercover sheriff, and the question of whether his presence undermined defense efforts was then argued in the appellate courts (Drysdale, 1978; Thompson, 1977).

One other factor affects the willingness of defense teams to politicize the proceedings. To mount such an effort takes a certain amount of fortitude as well as an ideological bent that views the courtroom as a proper setting for such tactics. Not all defendants and attorneys have such pluck, especially when politicization efforts may bring on contempt charges or other punishment, and not all think it proper to turn the courtroom into a political forum. The latter reservation is particularly characteristic of attorneys, whose training often predisposes them to defend on legalistic rather than political grounds, and who may be less radical than their clients. Chapter 7, which deals with *pro se* defense, explores further the repercussions of this point. Defendants also differ in the need they feel to present a political defense, apart from the influence of the jury and press and other tactical considerations. Thus we can again distinguish particular cases, as well as entire movements, on the basis of the desire and willingness of defendants and defense counsel to address political and moral issues in court. Defendants and attorneys in one trial may be more willing to discuss such issues than those in another. More generally, the accused and their lawyers in some movements may also be more ideologically inclined to attempt politicization than those in other movements. We shall see in succeeding chapters that the Vietnam antiwar period again falls into the former category of movement, and the civil rights protests into the latter.

The Prosecutor, the Judge, and Social Control

In any trial, the prosecutor and the judge affect the success of defense efforts to talk about political and moral issues. The prosecutor may object to all such efforts, and the judge may sustain these objections. Or both prosecutor and judge may give more latitude to the defense, though hardly ever as much as the defense desires. Though the trial is governed by the rules of evidence and other procedural guidelines, the judge has great discretion regarding the nature and extent of testimony that he or she allows, and judges who are sympathetic to the aims of political defendants may allow at least some discussion of issues the accused consider important. Samuel Lovejoy's trial for toppling the nuclear weather tower is illustrative. Lovejoy was fortunate in trying his case before one of the most liberal superior court judges in Massachusetts, who aided the self-represented defendant in the various stages of legal procedure. He allowed Lovejoy to take the witness stand for one and a half days and give his reasons for toppling the tower, though he refused to permit testimony by two expert witnesses, one on nuclear power and one on the history of civil disobedience (Wasserman, 1977). Elsewhere, however, antinuclear defendants have faced difficulties before more conservative judges. In New Hampshire, judges "have proven quite hostile and rude" (Light, 1978) to Clamshell Alliance attorneys and defendants, and have refused to allow nuclear-related testimony.

If the defense may try to take advantage of the jury and the press for purposes of resource mobilization, so may prosecutors seek to turn the public and the jury against the defendants (Dorsen and Friedman, 1973; Jackson, 1940). In 1886, for example, eleven well-known anarchists, all foreigners, were arrested for conspiracy to murder in the bombing of Haymarket Square in Chicago; not one was charged with actually throwing the bomb. In his opening statement to the jury, the prosecutor sought to put the defendants' political beliefs on trial as well: "'For the first time in the history of our country people are on trial for their lives for endeavoring to make anarchy the rule, and in that attempt for ruthlessly and awfully destroying life'" (in Morris, 1952:308). In his summation another attorney for the state likened the defendants' literary style to that of French communists and called the accused "'organized assassins'" (in Morris, 1952:317, 320).

Similar instances of prosecutorial efforts to discredit the accused and their movement abound. In the 1918 trial of socialist leader Eugene V. Debs for criticizing American participation in World War I, the prosecutor declared in his opening statement, "'This is the palpitating pulse of the sedition crusade'" (in Ginger, 1949:384). Thirty-three years later in the trial of Julius and Ethel Rosenberg, "Communism was mentioned so often during the proceedings that at times it threatened to become a separate issue" (Schneir and Schneir, 1965: 165). And a decade ago the jury in the Chicago Eight trial heard a familiar refrain when the prosecutor said in his opening statement that one defendant was "'calling for a revolution and insurrection'" (in Danelski, 1971:171).

Judges have also sometimes made similar comments or otherwise conducted trials in a manner prejudicial to the defense (Dorsen and Friedman, 1973). Rose Paster Stokes was tried in 1918 for violating the Espionage Act forbidding criticism of World War I with a letter to a newspaper. The judge admitted in evidence speeches made by the defendant for which she had not been indicted and then told the jury that they undermined the nation's welfare. He also denounced the Russian Revolution and said the defendant sympathized with it (Chafee, 1941:77). In the late 1960s, the conduct of Judge Julius Hoffman in the Chicago Eight case was also biased against the defense (Danelski, 1971; Kalven, 1970). The same was true of the conduct of the judge in the 1968 trial of Benjamin Spock and four others for conspiring to violate Selective Service laws (Jackson, 1974).

Thus we may distinguish political trials where prosecutors and judges sharply restrict defense attempts to discuss political and moral issues and themselves make comments prejudicial to the defense, and trials where these legal officials allow at least some discussion by the defense of issues it considers important. The same distinction between restrictive and lenient judges and prosecutors can be generalized to entire movements; in some movements judges and prosecutors may give greater latitude to the defense than in others, again reflecting the prevailing political climate. We shall see in later chapters that the Vietnam antiwar movement typified the first type, where defendants are sometimes allowed to discuss political issues, and the civil rights movement the second.

The Risks and Rewards of Political Trials

In despotic nations the outcome of political justice is usually a foregone conclusion. Dissidents are arrested and imprisoned summarily; if they do receive a trial, there are few, if any, procedural safeguards protecting the rights of defendants. Law is a direct instrument of state power, and concern for legality, or due process, rarely imbues the proceedings. The state-controlled press further aids in the effort to label the defendants' conduct as criminal. In democratic societies the situation is, of course, quite different. As Kirchheimer (1961) noted, political trials in such nations pose risks and uncertainties for all sides to the proceedings. On the one hand, conviction can remove the defendants from political action. The time, money, and energy they spend on their defense might be put to better use elsewhere; the fines and bonds they pay mean less money available for their protest goals. The public may accept the negative image of the accused and their cause that the prosecution presents in court. As noted earlier, arrests and trials of socialists and labor radicals during and after World War I almost always resulted in convictions. Ironically, even an acquittal may be interpreted as a sign of the justness and impartiality of the legal system, as happened after Angela Davis was found innocent in her trial several years ago (Major, 1973).

On the other hand, jurors may exercise their power to acquit with impunity. A sympathetic press may raise questions about the state's motive for prosecuting, and extensive media coverage may help to spread the message the defense tries to present in court, and swell the ranks and financial resources of the accused's protest movement. Finally, perhaps to a greater extent than is true in civil litigation, political trials may increase the morale of protest group members. As many political defendants and their supporters would attest, success in politicizing the proceedings, securing favorable press attention, avoiding convictions, or changing the beliefs of some of the jurors or other trial participants produces a sense of heady optimism and encourages renewed hopes and efforts for change. Obviously the converse is also true; a trial that succeeds in none of these goals may engender much frustration.

The civil disobedience trial of suffragist Susan B. Anthony suggests the mobilization potential of a political trial where the defense succeeds in spite of, or perhaps because of, a conviction. In November 1872 Anthony voted in violation of federal law. Her trial was held in Canandaigua, New York in June 1873. During the months preceding her trial, she gave more than fifty speeches in upstate New York, contending that the Fourteenth Amendment enfranchised women. Supreme Court Justice Ward Hunt presided over the trial and refused to let Anthony say a single word in her defense, ruling her incompetent as a witness. Later he ordered the jury to find her guilty. Finally the judge allowed Anthony to deliver a statement before sentencing that has since become famous, ending with the declaration, "I shall earnestly and persistently continue to urge all women to the practical recognition of the old revolutionary maxim, 'Resistance to tyranny is obedience to God.'" Anthony gained political victory in judicial defeat, since the judge's conduct of her trial and her stirring speech aroused sympathy and support throughout the country for the right of women to vote (Friedman, 1971).

In most trials of political activists, however, it is difficult to count precisely all the plusses and minuses that result for social movements and their opponents. Although acquittals may be considered defense victories, Angela Davis's trial illustrates how they may be interpreted ideologically in a manner favorable to the legal system. And while guilty verdicts can be considered defeats for protesters, they may still aid the mobilization of resources, as Anthony's case suggests. These problems in determining the consequences of political trials reflect more general difficulties in defining the success of social movement efforts (Gamson, 1975; Handler, 1978). With political prosecutions it seems best to take an eclectic approach, looking not only at verdicts but also at press coverage, public reaction, jury response, and the impact of the proceedings on financial and other resources important to social movements. In this manner we can judge the consequences that involvement with the criminal justice system has for the fortunes of social movements. Movements can thus be distinguished along a continuum ranging from complete mobilization by movements in the criminal justice system to complete control by state officials and other antagonists; the two poles are again ideal types. The civil rights movement, to which I now turn, represented the control end of the spectrum and the antiwar movement the mobilization end. Why this was so depended on many of the features discussed in this chapter.

Chapter Three

Criminal Justice in the Civil Rights Movement

For the Southern civil rights movement the legal system proved a mixed blessing. At the federal level, the Supreme Court, the Fifth Circuit Court of Appeals, and some district judges rendered many decisions favorable to the movement's aims. But at the state and local levels the law served as an effective instrument of social control. "Legal repression" is not too strong a term to use here (cf. Balbus, 1973), for many Southern communities experienced "a wholesale perversion of justice, from bottom to top, from police force to supreme court" (Lewis et al., 1966:289). The difficulties the movement encountered were in many ways similar to those confronting other movements. But in the South these problems were especially intense, owing to the particular historical and social context in which the civil rights effort found itself.

The Federal Courts

The numerous decisions of the United States Supreme Court involving civil suits and criminal prosecutions in the South have been discussed extensively (e.g., Casper, 1972) and thus will be considered here only briefly. Legal scholars have debated the merits of these cases (Rudman, 1963) and analyzed the legal doctrines upon which the Court based its opinions. Several writers have focused on the origins and impact of the 1954 *Brown v. Board of Education* decision that ordered the desegregation of Southern schools (Friedman, 1969; Kluger, 1976). The *Brown* decision culminated several decades of favorable Court decisions in civil rights cases handled by the NAACP Legal Defense and Educational Fund (LDF). By 1954 the LDF had won thirty-four of thirty-eight cases it had brought to the Court (Handler, 1978). Though the Court's ruling in *Brown* was thus not surprising, its consequences were profound. Change did not come quickly, however. For a decade Southern communities resisted school desegregation through a variety of evasive schemes (Casper, 1972; Greenberg, 1959), and by 1961 only 7 percent of Southern black students were attending integrated schools (Lomax, 1962). The indirect consequences of the Court's decision were probably far more important. By all accounts the effect of *Brown* in the South was "electric" (Lomax, 1962:74); it heightened morale among Southern blacks and civil rights leaders, increased their hopes for change, and helped lead to the protest campaigns that occurred later (Clark, 1969; Handler, 1978; Kamisar, 1969).

The Supreme Court continued to aid civil rights efforts in dozens of decisions arising from the public demonstrations and sit-ins that began after 1954, as civil rights forces won fifty-seven of sixty-one sit-in cases decided by the Court between 1957 and 1967 (Casper, 1972; Greenberg, 1968). Most of the Court's rulings in sit-in and demonstration cases, however, "generally sidestepped" (Casper, 1972: 175) First Amendment issues and certain Fourteenth Amendment matters. Instead the Court based its decisions on technical grounds relating to the defendants' peaceful conduct or to the enforcement by the state of laws requiring segregation (Bardolf, 1970; Bell, 1973). In *Garner v. Louisiana*, 368 US 157 (1961), for example, the Court unanimously overturned convictions for breach of peace in lunch counter sit-ins. Instead of deciding the constitutionality of lunch counter segregation, the majority opinion ruled that the defendants' conduct had not disturbed the peace or threatened to create such a disturbance by others (Rudman, 1963). In many such sit-in cases the United States solicitor general, Archibald Cox, urged the Court to rule for the demonstrators on narrow grounds, leading some civil rights attorneys to object to his stance (Casper, 1972).

In other cases the Supreme Court outlawed segregation in public parks, *Watson v. Memphis*, 373 US 526 (1963); interstate buses, *Boynton v. Virginia*, 364 US 454 (1960); public golf courses, *Holms v. Atlanta*, 357 US 879 (1955); airports, *Turner v. Memphis*, 369 US 762 (1962); and public libraries, *Brown v. Louisiana*, 383 US 131 (1966).

Thus in the Warren Court the civil rights movement found a powerful ally, the narrow grounds and inevitable slowness of its decisions notwithstanding. In the Fifth Circuit Court of Appeals that had jurisdiction over Florida, Georgia, Alabama, Louisiana, Mississippi, and Texas, the movement found another legal ally (Fingerhood, 1965). The Fifth Circuit ruled on many of the civil rights cases that eventually reached the Supreme Court, as well as others that did not reach the Court, and usually decided in favor of civil rights forces. As a result of such decisions, one civil rights attorney had called the actions of the Fifth Circuit in the early 1960s "beautiful, magnificent, heroic" (Ginger, 1979).

The federal district judges in the South proved more hostile to civil rights efforts. A few, such as Judge Frank M. Johnson of Alabama (Reed, 1965), often ruled in favor of the movement, but many others did not. Presiding in communities in which they had long lived, these judges approved the measures undertaken by Southern cities and states to evade school desegregation (Lusky, 1964; Peltason, 1961), and several of them enjoined civil rights picketing and demonstrations (Bell, 1973). One such judge, J. Robert Elliott, was appointed by President Kennedy to the federal bench in Georgia in 1962. Before he became a federal judge he had once said, "'I don't want these pinks, radicals and black voters to outvote those who are trying to preserve our segregation laws and other traditions'" (in Friedman, 1965:192). Another Kennedy appointee, William Cox of Mississippi, once remarked in a voting case, "'I am not interested in whether the registrar is going to give a registration test to a bunch of niggers on a voter drive'" (in Zinn, 1965:204).

It was thus to the Fifth Circuit Court and to the Supreme Court that the civil rights movement looked for justice. Most of the movement's members in the early 1960s generally accepted the legitimacy of the legal and political systems of the federal government, and sought in their legal actions to have the South act according to federal standards of freedom and justice. State appellate and supreme courts promised no real relief; typically they upheld convictions of protesters, only to be overturned at the federal level (Bardolph, 1970; Meltsner, 1964).

Although the civil rights movement did find some relief in the Warren and Fifth Circuit courts, only a small fraction of civil rights convictions in the criminal courts ever reached these higher courts for review. Those that did were decided one or more years after the original arrests. In the meantime, arrest, prosecution, and imprisonment had posed many difficulties for the movement, and even favorable Supreme Court rulings came too late to undo such damage. To thus concentrate on appellate review of civil rights cases, as most students of the legal aspects of the movement have done, is to ignore the serious consequences that criminal laws and criminal prosecutions created for the movement long before cases ever reached the United States Supreme Court. It is to such laws and prosecutions that I now turn, examining the obstacles they presented to the movement, and the strategies and tactics civil rights forces employed as a result.

Southern Laws

The Southern legal system was intimately involved with the civil rights movement at every turn, and it is impossible to fully understand and interpret the movement's life cycle, successes and failures, strategic and tactical dilemmas, and internal disagreements without also understanding the impact of law and the courts on the movement. The entire legal machinery of the South became a tool for social control of civil rights efforts. For example, shortly after lunch counter sit-ins started sweeping the South in February 1960, several state legislatures, notably those of Louisiana, Mississippi, Virginia, and Georgia, passed new laws designed to apply to the special characteristics of sit-ins. On 18 February 1960, the Georgia legislature enacted a trespass statute that made it illegal for a person to fail to leave the premises of another when so requested by the owner. The maximum sentence for violating this law was set at six months in jail, or a $1,000 fine, or twelve months in a work camp (*New South*, 1963). On 29 April 1960, the Mississippi legislature passed a breach of the peace law that applied to persons congregating in several kinds of public and private settings. The maximum penalty was set at four months in jail, or a $200 fine, or both. During debate on the statute, a member of the legislature objected that it violated the right of peaceful assembly, prompting one of the bill's sponsors to respond, "'You know what the bill's for. There's no need to talk about it'" (in Kunstler, 1961:352). A white-owned Jackson, Mississippi, newspaper called the measure a "'segregation bill'" and an "'anti sit-in bill'" (in Kunstler, 1961:352). Louisiana passed a similar law four weeks later.

Responding to the many telegrams, letters, and phone calls alleging civil rights abuses that were sent to the United States Department of Justice and the Federal Bureau of Investigation, another new Mississippi statute made it illegal to make false statements to any federal officials, though it did not define what was meant by "false." When law enforcement officials arrested two blacks under this statute for testifying in a federal court about voting discrimination, the Department of Justice acted to stop prosecution on the grounds that it was meant to harass the two defendants and other civil rights supporters (Lewis et al., 1966).

In some instances Southern prosecutors also invoked old antebellum and Reconstruction laws that had long been forgotten. Perhaps the most serious example of the use of such laws occurred in Americus, Georgia, in August 1963, when four members of the Student Nonviolent Coordinating Committee (sncc) who had been active in the area for some time were arrested on several charges, including one alleging a violation of an 1871 statute that made it a capital crime to incite blacks to "insurrection" (New South, 1963). The Supreme Court had held the law unconstitutional in 1937. Because the offense was punishable by death, the defendants were denied bail until November 1963, when a three-judge panel of the Fifth Circuit Court ruled the insurrection law unconstitutional (Student Voice, 1963). In October the prosecutor in the case had stated, "'The basic reason for bringing these charges was to deny the defendants, or ask the court to deny them, bond. We were in hopes that by holding these men, we would be able to talk to their lawyers and talk to their people and convince them that this type of activity is not the right way to go about it'" (in Lewis et al., 1966:290). The insurrection arrests slowed down civil rights activities in Americus, as residents were afraid of incurring similar charges. After the four were released by the federal court, the number of demonstrations increased (Roberts, 1965).

Despite the use of such felony charges, most arrests in the South were for misdemeanor offenses. Law still had some sway. The kinds of protests undertaken by civil rights activists did not readily lend themselves to felony charges, largely because of the absence of violence that characterized movement demonstrations. To have prosecuted too often for felony offenses in such circumstances might have increased the risks of reversals by federal courts and prompted Northerners and the federal government to view the arrests and prosecutions as especially unfair. Southern legal officials may have also felt bound by some degree of legality to lodge charges more applicable to the alleged offenses. In any event, the widespread use of misdemeanor charges did prove an effective method of legal harassment. Prosecutions of such charges forced the movement to spend large sums of money on bail, legal defense, and fines; incarcerated defendants before and after trials in Southern jails; and often helped prevent Southern blacks from taking part in various demonstrations.

Injunctions

One other form of legal action, the injunction, needs to be discussed before turning to the Southern criminal justice system. In the last half of the nineteenth century, American industry was wracked by labor disputes. Prosecution of workers on conspiracy charges for striking and other forms of union activity proved an ineffective means of social control. The trials that resulted were too protracted and costly for the state, and several times ended in jury acquittals, since it was difficult to prove the existence of an illegal conspiracy (Friedman, 1973). As a result, in the 1880s many companies and judges turned to the injunction, which proved to be "an especially deadly threat against labor" (Friedman, 1973:487; cf. Frankfurter and Greene, 1930). During strikes, companies would ask for injunctions, which were granted by judges without hearings and without the burdens of jury trials. Union activists who violated injunctions could be imprisoned. Perhaps the most famous such prisoner was Eugene V. Debs, who in 1894 violated an injunction prohibiting him from supporting the Pullman strike. A year later the Supreme Court unanimously upheld Debs's conviction. Thus the injunction was a powerful legal weapon that stifled labor protest. It could be granted quickly, and its scope could be made wide enough to prohibit almost every aspect of a strike. Recognizing this, the Democratic party platform of 1896 condemned "government by injunction as a new and highly dangerous form of oppression," and noted that judges were acting "simultaneously as legislators, judges and executioners" (Friedman, 1973:488).

During the civil rights movement some six decades later, the injunction again provided a legal mode of social control (*New South*, 1963). Granted several times by local and federal judges, sweeping injunctions limited or banned civil rights activity. Protesters who violated the injunctions were arrested. As a result, injunctions effectively impeded the movement in several cities, sometimes bringing all activities to a halt. One such injunction was granted by a federal court in December 1961 at the request of city officials in Baton Rouge, Louisiana, following a boycott and picketing of white merchants (Bell, 1973). In the spring of 1963, a state court injunction against a similar boycott seriously hampered civil rights forces in Jackson, Mississippi (Bell, 1973). The following chapter looks more closely at the legal experience of civil rights forces in cities such as Danville, Virginia, and Albany, Georgia, where civil rights groups suffered serious losses thanks to injunctions, arrests, prosecutions, and imprisonment.

The Criminal Justice System

Arrests, prosecutions, and jail terms were a daily threat to civil rights activists across the South. Over the years the news media, social scientists, and other observers have devoted a good deal of attention to the forms and impact of the direct action undertaken by the movement, emphasizing among other features its nonviolent character (e.g., Vander Zanden, 1963), and the sympathy aroused in the North by television and newspaper coverage of civil rights protests and the police and civilian brutality they often provoked (e.g., Meier, 1965; Obserschall, 1973; Sourian, 1978). The impact of the full involvement of the criminal justice system on the movement's protest campaigns has received far less attention.

As early as the celebrated 1955–1956 Montgomery bus boycott that propelled Martin Luther King, Jr., into national prominence, the law and the institutions of criminal justice began to play an important part in the development and outcome of civil rights protest. The boycott began, of course, with the December 1955 arrest of Rosa Parks for violating a segregation ordinance by refusing to move to the back of a city bus. Depending on many circumstances, arrests and trials can anger a social movement and spur its members into action, or they can intimidate a movement and dampen its enthusiasm for legal and illegal demonstrations and other forms of protest. Had Parks only been forced to leave the bus, as had happened several times before, "it probably could have been just another incident" (Parks, 1977:31). Instead her arrest galvanized the black community of Montgomery. Black leaders in the city had been waiting for an arrest of a "respectable" person to help start a bus boycott and decided that this would be the one. A one-day boycott called in response to Parks's arrest was to last 382 days; by the third month of the boycott, white merchants in the city had lost more than $1 million in sales because blacks were not riding the buses to their stores. Parks's conviction after a brief trial and fine of ten dollars and court costs only intensified the black community's effort. Thus, Ed Nixon, who had helped plan the boycott, considered the verdict a political victory: "They really did the thing that was best for us when they found her guilty" (Nixon, 1977:38).

The response of the white community came soon afterwards and relied on the use of law and the courts. Two December negotiating sessions between blacks and whites led nowhere. The mayor and city commissioners publicly joined the White Citizens Council, and in January 1956 the major announced what he called a "get-tough" policy. Two days later Martin Luther King was arrested for driving five miles an hour faster than the speed limit. However, a rally by local blacks at the jail led to his release on personal recognizance. The bombing of his house a few days later and his short speech from his front porch that calmed an angry crowd reached the American public through the news media and cemented King's role as leader of the Montgomery movement (Bennett, 1970).

Other forms of legal harassment proved effective. At the end of January, police began ticketing and arresting the drivers of vehicles that were part of the car pool that enabled the bus boycotters to get to work. People waiting for rides had to stand away from bus stops, so that drivers could not be arrested for operating illegal taxi services. Many blacks waiting for rides were threatened with arrest for vagrancy or hitchhiking. Police also wrote down the license plate numbers of boycott cars and intimidated in other ways as well:

> The tag numbers would be taken down by policemen, and then for other reasons you'd be harassed. Like, if you were out one night and you were at Gordon's Ice Cream Parlor . . . the police would see your car and know that you were one of the cars that were always involved in picking up the people. And then they'd just come in the place and ask who owned that car, and they'd say, "You're not parked close enough to the curb." They'd find something wrong to harass you about. (Martin, 1977:53)

Traffic arrests also tied up the funds of the Montgomery movement:

> The black folk knew that the movement did not have any money to pay for all this stuff [the car pool]. They were spending enough money on trying to get people out on bail bond if they got arrested. So people started giving you the nickel or the dime or whatever it was that they would give you for the bus, but not let nobody see it, so you could buy some gasoline. (Martin, 1977:55)

The police tactics made blacks afraid to continue driving in the car pool, forcing many people to walk (Lewis, 1970). As a result, the bus boycott almost ended within three months after it had begun.

In February 1956 the city intensified its use of the legal system for the purpose of social control, but this time did not succeed. On 21 February a county grand jury charged some one hundred boycott leaders, including almost all of Montgomery's black ministers, with violating a 1921 law that made it a misdemeanor to interfere with lawful business; the law had been enacted to impede unionization of steel mills in Birmingham (Raines, 1977). But these arrests unified the black community, as had the earlier arrests of Parks and King. The four-day trial of the boycott leaders resulted in a legal victory— conviction—for Montgomery but a moral victory for the black community, as the arrests and convictions received national press coverage.

Finally, in November 1956 city officials asked a state court to en- join the Montgomery Improvement Association, the group sponsor- ing the bus boycott, from operating an illegal transit system—the car pool. The city's request for an injunction "noticeably diluted the ardor of the black community" (Lewis, 1970:79). Had the injunction been granted, the movement would have suffered a serious, perhaps fatal blow. As King and other boycott leaders waited in court on 13 November for the judge's decision on the boycott injunction, they feared the worst. But word came that the Supreme Court had affirmed a lower court's declaration that the bus segregation statutes in Montgomery were unconstitutional; the original suit had been filed nine months earlier by four Montgomery blacks. The Supreme Court's ruling not only desegregated Montgomery buses; it also saved the boycott effort. As one black resident said upon hearing of the Supreme Court decision, "'God Almighty has spoken from Washington, D.C.'" (in Bennett, 1970:30).

The Montgomery bus boycott has been recounted in some detail to illustrate the impact of law and legal proceedings on its development. The Montgomery movement was able to capitalize on the arrests of Parks and King and the later ones of the boycott leaders. However, arrests and police harassment of car pool drivers seriously undermined the effectiveness of the boycott. Moreover, the injunction might have destroyed the boycott, had not the Supreme Court handed down a favorable ruling. The part played by law and legal authorities in the Montgomery effort was to be repeated in the South in the 1960s.

Legal Problems Confronting the Civil Rights Movement

The "direct action" phase of the movement is generally considered to have begun on 1 February 1960, when four black college freshmen in Greensboro, North Carolina, sat down at a Woolworth's lunch counter. They were refused service but remained at their seats until the normal closing time and returned to the counter on succeeding days. Word of their sit-in spread rapidly through the city, and they were joined on the second day by other Greensboro students. Publicized by the news media, these sit-ins attracted wide attention in the South, and within the next several weeks students in other cities conducted lunch counter sit-ins. Not long after, sit-ins were taking place at public parks, libraries, swimming pools, and movie theaters. As a result of the sit-ins, by September 1961 at least one lunch counter or restaurant had desegregated in 108 Southern cities (Bell, 1973).

These protest activities generated massive increases in police and court workloads. According to one estimate, within one and one-half years after the Greensboro sit-ins, 75,000 persons had taken part in some form of demonstration, and more than 3,600 arrests had taken place. In 1963 alone, some 20,000 were arrested (*New South*, 1963). Many were jailed for sit-ins, marches, rallies, and the like—actions for which they would probably not have been arrested outside the South. Others were arrested for traffic violations, loitering, and vagrancy, rather than for clear protest actions. Civil rights defendants and their attorneys never expected to receive justice in the Southern courts; nor were they to find it.

In any discussion of criminal prosecutions of civil rights activists and the problems they posed for the movement, the far-reaching racism of the South is the factor that underlies all other considerations. The experience of the movement in the courts was an inevitable outcome of the nature of the Southern criminal justice system. In this sense the fate of civil rights defendants was no different from that of Southern blacks in conventional criminal cases or in other legal encounters (Galphin, 1963; Myrdal, 1944; Sitton, 1962). But the civil rights movement and the passions it aroused intensified the difficulties encountered by movement defendants and their attorneys. Southern trial courts were often segregated; whites were required to sit on one side of the room, and blacks on the other, or sometimes in the back. Judges, prosecutors, court clerks, bailiffs, and jurors were typically white, and many were hostile to the aims of the civil rights movement. The justice handed out in the Southern trial courts was segregated as well, as civil rights defendants simply had little or no chance to win acquittals.

These and other factors affected defense strategy in criminal prosecutions. Although the trials of civil rights activists in the South were political trials that derived from the struggle for desegregation, they were largely devoid of explicit attempts to politicize the proceedings. In light of the advantages that political defenses may have for social movement activists, as seen in chapter 2, why were the civil rights trials so relatively quiescent?

Availability of Defense Attorneys

Attorneys are helpful for all kinds of litigants, whether the latter want to be in court or not. Their aid is of equal or greater importance in criminal proceedings involving social movement activists. Yet, as was true for communists prosecuted under the Smith Act, attorneys may be afraid or unwilling for ideological reasons to defend political protesters.

The lack of attorneys was a serious problem for the civil rights movement. Owing to decades of discrimination, the South had relatively few black attorneys; there were only eighty in 1963, and most of these lived in or near the larger cities (Carter, 1963). Fewer still were qualified to handle criminal cases raising constitutional issues, and not all of them were willing to take on such cases (Sitton, 1962). In Georgia, for example, there were several dozen black lawyers, but only a small handful were willing to represent civil rights clients (Moore, 1967). The white bar in the South, save for a very few attorneys, refused to defend civil rights clients; a survey of the United States Civil Rights Commission in 1963 indicated that in the previous eight years less than 3 percent of Southern white attorneys had defended civil rights protesters (Galphin, 1963). When, occasionally, one was appointed to do so by a judge, he would simply plead his client guilty or conduct a perfunctory defense. Thus the lack of civil rights attorneys for the movement made for difficulties across the South. Movement attorneys were extremely overworked and often had to travel several hundred miles a day to defend clients in different communities. Their non-civil rights practices suffered as a result, as, consequently, did their income. Some civil rights defendants simply could not obtain counsel, forcing them to plead guilty or conduct their own defense (cf. Holt, 1965; Pollitt, 1964).

A few examples will illustrate the depth of the problem. In Mississippi, only four attorneys, three of them black, took on civil rights cases. In the fall of 1961 an NAACP official in Greenville, Mississippi, was charged with breach of the peace for picketing white stores. He had to go without counsel since his trial was held the same day that the civil rights attorneys were occupied with three other trials occurring elsewhere in the state. The official thus had to pay a heavy fine and waive his right to appeal (Sitton, 1962). In Itta

Bena, Mississippi, fifty-seven blacks were arrested for breach of the peace when they marched to a deputy sheriff's home in June 1963 and asked for police protection during a voter registration campaign. The next day forty-five were tried without a lawyer, and an hour later were convicted and sentenced. The men received six months in jail and a $500 fine, while the women were sentenced to four months and a $200 fine (Lewis et al., 1966).

Even where attorneys were present, the sheer burden of defending so many clients led to legal problems that white authorities exploited. In the spring of 1961, for example, 303 Freedom Riders were arrested in Jackson, Mississippi, for breach of the peace upon entering segregated waiting room and facilities at the city's interstate bus terminal. The Jackson judge who was trying the cases refused to allow more than four out-of-state attorneys to assist in the defense of the protesters (Kunstler and Kinoy, 1964). The defense attorneys wished to try everyone together, or at least in large groups, to save the time and expense of individual trials. Instead the city decided to try them one or two at a time; at this rate trials of all the accused would have taken more than a year to complete. After the first few trials quickly ended in convictions and it became apparent that subsequent trials would end similarly, the remaining defendants pleaded guilty or *nolo contendere* (Kunstler, 1966; Lewis et al., 1966).

The lack of civil rights attorneys in the South prompted civil rights groups to call on Northern attorneys for assistance. Several did go to the South but faced problems in being allowed to represent clients. Most states have rules restricting practice by out-of-state attorneys, though these requirements are usually waived or easily surmounted. But many Southern communities enforced such rules. Some, for example, required that a lawyer from another state could defend a client only with a local attorney sitting at his or her side, wasting the time and energy of the few local attorneys who would do so. In the summer of 1963 in Danville, Virginia, a judge refused to allow out-of-state attorneys to defend civil rights clients unless they produced their certificates of admission to the bar. When one Boston lawyer did so, the judge nonetheless made her prove that Massachusetts allowed Virginia attorneys to practice in that state (Holt, 1965; Kunstler, 1966).

The LDF and the Guild

The NAACP Legal Defense and Educational Fund (LDF) did take on the cases of several thousand movement defendants through its network of cooperating Southern black attorneys. When cases deriving from arrests seemed constitutionally important, LDF's national office in New York City provided funds for bail and other legal expenses, as well as legal advice (Casper, 1972). But the aid and resources of LDF were not nearly enough for the movement's needs, and there were still too few cooperating attorneys in the South to begin with.

Moreover, the assistance of LDF presented civil rights forces in some areas with additional problems. Several writers (Oberschall, 1973; Turner 1970) have pointed to the influence that sponsoring organizations may have over movement tactics and strategy. Turner (1970), for example, notes the limitations imposed by potentially sympathetic groups from among the American middle and upper classes on the use by insurgents of coercive tactics. External groups exert their control by refusing to lend support to movement organizations unless certain conditions are met or, later, by threatening to withdraw such support. Thus the legal assistance offered by LDF had its drawbacks, for LDF lent its support only when it was guaranteed a large degree of control over litigation strategy.

In a typical case, one of LDF's several dozen cooperating attorneys in the South would handle the trial and the first appeal. If time were available and LDF willing, he or she would receive legal guidance and financial assistance from the New York staff of LDF; if the case promised to raise important constitutional issues, a staff attorney from New York might come down to the South to assist the local attorney. If a case finally reached the Supreme Court on appeal, LDF national office would handle all the litigation on that level. To assure that a proper record was made at the trial level for later appeal to the Court, LDF demanded that cooperating attorneys who received its funds and assistance follow its suggestions regarding trial strategy. As a result, local cooperating attorneys received "not only extensive support but also a good measure of direction and control" from the national LDF office (Casper, 1972:143) that dictated a cautious, "by the books" trial strategy aimed at winning cases on appeal.

The LDF approach to trial strategy reflected the legalistic method that had guided its litigation activity leading up to *Brown* in 1954. LDF had become technically independent of the parent NAACP in 1939 and by the early 1950s had its own budget, directors, and staff, but over the years both organizations had continued to work together closely, emphasizing appeals to the federal courts and the enactment of beneficial federal legislation (Meier, 1965). These emphases had been reflected in the direction of the NAACP since its inception. Working within the system and believing in the potential of American democracy, its "assumptions and strategy and tactics were essentially conservative" (Clark, 1966:51) and consist of what Bailey (1969) calls a "middle-class politics" strategy.

LDF's relatively cautious, legalistic approach and the control it demanded over cases in which it was involved sometimes posed difficulties for local cooperating attorneys and movement groups. In June 1963, some one hundred blacks in Danville, Virginia, had been arrested in various civil rights marches and demonstrations, and legal costs were mounting. Sam Tucker, a Virginia attorney who was the state's representative for LDF, told two local movement leaders that he thought LDF would pay all the fees for attorneys, court reporters, transcripts, briefs, and the like, and that the Virginia NAACP would provide funds for anything LDF would not underwrite (Holt, 1965). One of the movement leaders, Reverend Lawrence Campbell, asked Tucker, "Suppose we, the Movement, decide to demonstrate. Would we be bound to confer with the NAACP lawyers first?" Tucker replied, "It would be expected that some conferring would take place. Since the NAACP would be footing the bills, we would want to caution against anything unwise" (Holt, 1965:109). Then Campbell asked Tucker if NAACP attorneys would be willing to work with Len Holt, a black attorney from Norfolk, Virginia, who had already been defending Danville defendants and who had over the years taken issue with the NAACP's cautious, legalistic approach. He had been especially critical of the organization's reluctance, as he saw it, to undertake anything but school integration cases and its unwillingness to challenge courtroom segregation at every criminal trial. Tucker responded, "NAACP money can only go to NAACP lawyers, and Holt isn't in that category" (Holt, 1965:109). The Danville movement leaders turned down the NAACP offer of legal assistance.

LDF's approach to protest and legal defense had posed a similar problem for the Student Nonviolent Coordinating Committee (SNCC) the previous summer. Before that time, LDF had handled several arrests of SNCC field secretaries, and initially it had indicated it would take on any case that SNCC asked it to. But, according to Holt (1965), the number of calls from SNCC to LDF after arrests had occurred exceeded LDF's expectations and threatened its budget. LDF thus told SNCC to be less aggressive, that it had made its point and that it should allow the LDF caseload deriving from SNCC arrests to diminish before it undertook additional protests (Holt, 1965; Zinn, 1965).

This pressure by LDF prompted SNCC to ask the National Lawyers Guild for legal assistance, but new difficulties arose as a result, owing to the association of Guild members with the Communist party and other radical causes. The Guild was founded in 1936 by attorneys who were disenchanted with the hostility of the American Bar Association (ABA) to the New Deal. After World War II, Guild attorneys defended communists prosecuted under the Smith Act. Five Guild attorneys who represented Communist party leaders in the 1949 *Dennis* case were jailed for contempt for their actions during the trial. Several Guild members also belonged to the Party. As a result, the Guild came under increasing attack. The ABA board of governors banned Guild attorneys from ABA membership. In 1950 the House Un-American Activities Committee condemned the Guild as " 'the foremost legal bulwark of the Communist Party, its front organizations, and controlled unions'" (in Auerbach, 1976:234). In 1953 the United States attorney general charged that the Communist party dominated the Guild, and he tried to have the latter group placed on the government's list of subversive organizatons. Thus as the 1960s began, the Guild was still stigmatized by cold war hostility.

Consistent with its earlier representation of unpopular defendants, the Guild established the Committee to Assist Southern Lawyers (CASL) in February 1962, with the concomitant hope that Guild membership and financial assets would increase as a result. Under the direction of CASL, several attorneys and law students traveled to the South in the next two years to work with local attorneys in civil rights cases. The formation of CASL marked the first attempt by a lawyers' organization to aid Southern civil rights lawyers. In many ways the defense strategy of Guild attorneys and the local lawyers with whom they worked was more "imaginative," as one Guild member put it, (Ginger, 1979) than that of LDF. Guild attorneys typically challenged courtroom and jury segregation and, as we shall see, developed the technique of "removing" prosecutions to the federal courts. They were also more willing than LDF lawyers to file civil suits attacking segregation in areas other than the schools and to seek court injunctions against prosecutions for civil rights activities.

Thus, after LDF urged SNCC in the summer of 1962 to slow down its protests, SNCC was attracted to the Guild by its willingness to defend civil rights clients and by the kinds of strategies it advocated. It thus invited three Guild attorneys to address its annual convention later that summer. According to Holt (1965), one of the Guild members emphasized the importance of lawyers in political cases, while another "kept opening eyes" regarding the ways in which federal regulatory agencies and earlier labor cases could be used to assist civil rights efforts. One SNCC member asked the Guild attorneys, "'Why aren't the NAACP lawyers like you guys?'" (in Holt, 1965:90), and discussion with the Guild lawyers continued into the night. Two days later, the head of LDF, Jack Greenberg, arrived at the SNCC national office in Atlanta and said that he had been misunderstood, and that all SNCC cases would be handled by LDF (Holt, 1965; Zinn, 1965). SNCC accepted his offer.

But the rivalry between LDF and the Guild surfaced again a year later, when, in the fall of 1963, civil rights groups under the umbrella of the Council of Federated Organizations (COFO) in Mississippi staged a mock election with disenfranchised blacks as voters. To aid this effort, COFO brought 100 students from Yale and Stanford into the state. The increased civil rights activity engendered by the election led to increased arrests, which the three black attorneys in the state simply could not handle. LDF, which had been providing funds and legal advice, declined to send attorneys to Mississippi to help out. As a result, SNCC, which provided most of the COFO staff members, asked the Guild for assistance. When the Guild agreed, LDF finally sent down some attorneys (Holt, 1966).

Earlier LDF had been joined in its objections to Guild participation in Mississippi by other persons and groups. In the spring of 1963 heads of civil rights groups and various foundations met several times to discuss fund raising for civil rights efforts; the group was named the Council on United States Civil Rights Leadership. One of the council's members, the president of the Taconic Foundation, told James Forman, an SNCC leader, that he and other council members

were disturbed over SNCC's plans to accept the services of Guild attorneys. At two council meetings, Whitney Young, head of the Urban
League, urged the council to issue a statement saying that the civil
rights movement did not desire help by communists (Forman, 1973).

In the spring of 1964, as COFO was planning its intensive Mississippi Summer Project that would start a few months later, an LDF
official told SNCC that LDF would refuse to assist the project if COFO
accepted aid from Guild attorneys. In addition to losing LDF support,
SNCC also risked guilt by association with the Guild; the McCarthy
era was not yet a forgotten memory. Deciding, however, that Guild
attorneys had been helpful in the past and that COFO would need all
the legal assistance it could obtain, SNCC leaders refused to reject aid
from the Guild (Zinn, 1965).

Subsequently, COFO wrote Jack Greenberg of LDF that it would accept the services of all attorneys. Greenberg replied that LDF would
not assist COFO's Mississippi Summer Project but later stated that he
would come to orientation sessions for Northern student volunteers
for the project and ask each one to choose in advance between representation by the Guild or LDF. He also said that LDF would not represent any SNCC members in the future (Forman, 1973). During the
summer of 1964, COFO leaders attended a meeting with federal officials in Washington, D.C. Also present at the meeting was Arthur
Schlesinger, Jr., who said, " 'There are many of us who have spent
years fighting the Communists. We worked hard during the thirties
and forties fighting forces such as the National Lawyers Guild. We
find it unpardonable that you would work with them'" (in Forman,
1973 : 382). The issue of the Guild's involvement dominated the rest
of the meeting.

Another group that had been wary of Guild involvement in the
movement was the Congress of Racial Equality (CORE). After CASL
was formed in 1962, national CORE leaders had turned down the offer
of Guild assistance, "fearing that its identification as a Communist
front might damage the movement and believing that the dramatic
tactics of some of its lawyers were more often show than substance"
(Meier and Rudwick, 1973 : 271). Thus, when SNCC and COFO accepted the help of the Guild for its members in Mississippi, national
CORE did not, which left a CORE leader in the state "bitter" and "dis-
satisfied," owing to the need for legal help (Meier and Rudwick,
1973 : 271). Knowing that such help was essential and wishing to

minimize Guild influence in the Mississippi movement (Meier and Rudwick, 1973), Carl Rachlin, CORE's legal counsel, formed the Lawyers Constitutional Defense Committee (LCDC) in the spring of 1964 with the help of the ACLU, LDF, the American Jewish Congress, the American Jewish Committee, and the National Council of Churches. Despite the origins of LCDC in this interorganizational conflict, LCDC and the Guild were able to work effectively together in the 1964 Mississippi Summer Project.

Harassment of Civil Rights Attorneys

Attorneys who take on unpopular causes are particularly subject to legal harassment, physical threats, and social ostracism, as Harper Lee's *To Kill a Mockingbird* so eloquently illustrated. Many of the attorneys who defended communists in the Smith Act prosecutions, for example, were held in contempt or taken before disbarment proceedings (Auerbach, 1976). Southern attorneys, black or white, who worked on civil rights cases were also subjected to various forms of legal harassment (Pollitt, 1964). A 1963 study of the United States Civil Rights Commission indicated that Southern attorneys who defended civil rights clients were threatened with physical injury, a diminished practice, and social ostracism (Kunstler, 1966). The problems such attorneys faced limited the number of Southern lawyers willing to take on civil rights litigation and also tended to minimize the aggressiveness of the legal strategies they employed; in a 1959 case the Fifth Circuit Court of Appeals noted that local pressures deterred white attorneys from raising constitutional issues in cases involving blacks: "Lawyers residing in many Southern jurisdictions rarely, almost to the point of never, raise the issue of systematic exclusion of Negroes from juries. . . . [Those who do so run the] risk of personal sacrifice, which may extend to a loss of practice and social ostracism" (Meltsner, 1964 : 11). Similarly, Clifford Durr, a Montgomery lawyer and former member of the Federal Communications Commission, observed, "'Certainly in the present climate of opinion a white lawyer cannot handle cases of this kind without serious consequences to his law practice and, for that matter, his social position as well'" (in Kunstler and Kinoy, 1964 : 577).

Southern civil rights attorneys were harassed in several ways. Some were brought before disbarment hearings held by local and state bar associations (*New York Times*, 1963; Pollitt, 1964). Others faced contempt charges by trial judges. In Atlanta in the summer of 1963, for example, two local civil rights attorneys, both black, asked a municipal judge to disqualify himself in some sit-in trials because of bias. The judge had ordered a grand jury to indict the sit-in protesters even though the owners of the restaurants where the sit-ins took place did not want to press charges. In response to the attorneys' request to disqualify himself, the judge cited them for contempt of court (Galphin, 1964).

Southern legislatures also posed a threat. In 1961 in Norfolk, Virginia, a firm of three black attorneys had been involved in thirty-five cases challenging segregation; some had arisen out of criminal prosecutions, while others were law suits filed by the attorneys on behalf of civil rights plaintiffs. In autumn of that year, the Virginia General Assembly Committee on Offenses against the Administration of Justice obtained a writ from a state court demanding all the records of the law firm. The attorneys obtained a federal court order that prevented the firm's records from being confiscated by the committee (Scott, 1962). In another case, two of these same three attorneys were fined by a state judge for accusing him of bias in a contempt proceeding initiated by the judge against one of the two. The fines were reversed by the Supreme Court, which said in its opinion, "'Our conclusion is that these petitioners have been punished by Virginia for doing nothing more than exercising the constitutional right of an accused and his counsel in contempt cases such as this to defend against the charges made'" (in Kunstler, 1966:242).

Perhaps the most serious example of legal harassment occurred in October 1963 in Louisiana when Benjamin Smith and Bruce Waltzer, two white civil rights attorneys and members of the Guild, and James A. Dombrowski, executive director of the Southern Conference Educational Fund (SCEF), were arrested for allegedly violating the state's antisubversive law. A state legislator said later that the reason for their arrest was their "'racial agitation'" (in Kinoy, 1967: 8). At the time of the arrests, state and local police removed several files from the offices of the attorneys and of SCEF, and also raided the homes of the three men. Eventually the Supreme Court voided portions of the antisubversive law, with the Court's decision referring to the "chilling effect" of the law and the arrests on the exercise of constitutional rights (Kinoy, 1967).

Southern attorneys involved in civil rights litigation also risked serious physical injury. Beatings and death were constant threats for all civil rights protesters, and their attorneys, black or white, were not immune from such possibilities. In 1963 the only civil rights attorney in Albany, Georgia, C. B. King, went to see a client in jail. The sheriff refused to let him see the defendant and, when King insisted on his right to do so, hit the lawyer on his head with a heavy cane. The sheriff later said, " 'I'm a white man and he's a nigger. Yeh, I knocked hell out of him. I'd do it again' " (in Student Nonviolent Coordinating Committee, 1963). In another instance, King returned to his car after seeing another client in jail and found that his car seat had been eaten away by acid. In Jackson, Mississippi, in 1961, an attorney who had defended some Freedom Riders found the letters "KKK" smeared onto his car's windshield (Kunstler and Kinoy, 1964). In Birmingham, the home of Arthur Shores, a black civil rights attorney, was bombed three times. One of the bombings occurred the night after Shores had won a court order requiring the desegregation of Birmingham schools (Shores, 1977). The fear of arrests and beatings felt by lawyers and protesters alike is reflected in an observation recorded by a Northern law student who worked for C. B. King in Georgia, in the summers of 1963 and 1964 and part of 1965: "My whole outlook has changed down here. Things I never thought about, just ordinary actions such as walking down a street, take on a whole new perspective. I have to wonder if I'll be arrested for vagrancy or loitering. When I see whites on the streets, I wonder if I should cross to the other side, in case they recognize me. It is very hard to verbalize the feeling of never being sure that you are safe" (Roberts, 1965).

Finally, several civil rights lawyers in the South suffered a loss of clients and social ostracism because of their association with the movement. One Northern law student working in Alabama explained the reluctance of black attorneys in the state to take on civil rights cases, "They are this way because they uniformly came from families that did not even have a pot to piss in, and now that they have got that pot and a little more, they don't want to lose it" (Blicker, 1963). Despite the cynicism of the remark, the economic and social repercussions of civil rights practice were serious. One Tennessee lawyer who defended a group of civil rights protesters lost almost his entire practice as a result (Kunstler and Kinoy, 1964). A white Birmingham attorney, Charles Morgan, Jr., was forced by community pressure to leave Alabama because of his defense of movement protesters and especially because of his speech indicting Birmingham the day after the 1963 church bombing in the city that killed four black children (Morgan, 1964). Morgan later wrote of his experience, "It happens almost overnight. Old clients explain that they would like to remain with you but that they would be ruined if they did. More recent ones don't even bother to explain. They just never call you again" (Morgan, 1964). Another lawyer, William Higgs, was also harassed repeatedly in Mississippi. In June 1962 he was detained by police after attending a campaign meeting for a black man running for Congress. A local sheriff called him a traitor, and a deputy threatened to kill him. In January 1961 he began receiving harassing phone calls at night. In December 1961 his picture appeared in a Jackson newspaper beside that of James Meredith, whom Higgs was representing. Higgs was later told by a local citizens council member that the photograph "has been sent to every law enforcement officer throughout the state" (Carter, 1963:35).

The consequence of the legal and physical harassment and social ostracism facing civil rights attorneys was "timid lawyers and neglected clients" (Pollitt, 1964). Another consequence was that defense teams in civil rights trials did not mount political defenses of the kind discussed in chapter 2. Defense attorneys could not afford the luxury of trying in court to talk at length about the larger issues of racism and segregation. The mere representation of civil rights clients was risky enough; as noted earlier, a relatively mild request that a judge disqualify himself could bring on contempt. Thus civil rights attorneys typically limited themselves to technical rather than political arguments. Although the racial and political nature of the proceedings was apparent to all, race remained very much an unspoken issue, and political rhetoric by defense counsel was generally avoided (Ginger, 1979). In sit-in cases, for example, a typical defense was that the defendant's action of sitting quietly at a lunch counter did not disturb the peace. First and Fourteenth Amendment arguments were sometimes used as well during trials, but, as we have seen, raising such constitutional defenses risked legal and social retribution. The few lawyers who did try to discuss racism did so cautiously, and even here ran the risk of a more severe sentence for their clients.

Judges

If federal district judges tended to conform to community expectations, local judges did so to an even greater degree. This was true, of course, in normal criminal and civil cases, but in civil rights cases judges were even more biased. As one observer put it, the Southern local judge "knows the role he is supposed to play, and not only justice but his political future is weighed in the balance in the trial of a Negro" (Galphin, 1963:34). The result for civil rights forces was criminal proceedings that often lacked the standards of fairness and due process associated with the American legal system, with judges consistently ruling in favor of the prosecution and against the defense. In many cases they also required prohibitively high bail, despite the fact that most charges were for misdemeanor offenses and that the defendants could be expected not to flee the area (Lewis et al., 1966). Examples of the bias of Southern judges are legion, and several were given in the preceding section. Other judges also expressed hostility to civil rights efforts. One Montgomery judge told a civil rights attorney, "'The Fourteenth Amendment is a pariah and an outcast; it has no standing in this court'" (in Blicker, 1963). A judge in Gadsden, Alabama, usually refused to set any bail for local movement leaders who had been arrested (Blicker, 1963). Another judge held a black defendant in contempt in the summer of 1962 when she refused to answer the prosecutor's questions when he called her by her first name instead of using "Miss" or "Mrs.," courtesy titles typically extended to whites (Galphin, 1963). A judge in Albany, Georgia, overruled defense objections in a July 1963 trial when the prosecutor asked a civil rights defendant if he were a communist and had ever been to the Soviet Union (Roberts, 1965). In another Georgia case, the prosecutor was overheard telling the judge, "'This case won't hold up, but we got to convict these niggers for something'" (in Roberts, 1965:n.p.). And a Tallahassee, Florida, judge lectured eleven college students convicted for a lunch counter sit-in, "'Some of your professors have read so many books they're out of touch with reality. . . . Get off the trail of dreams and be practical. You must make a living sometime. You get a little education and feeling of importance by being in a publicity-happy group, but you ought to stop and think why you are in an unorthodox, dreamy, beatnik society instead of in that of ordinary people'" (*Southern Patriot*, 1960:3).

As a result of the conduct of judges at civil rights trials, the movement could not hope to win cases at the trial level. As one Northern law student working in Georgia observed, "I don't expect to even think of getting justice at the trial court level—when a Negro is involved with a white, or in a civil rights case, trial court is simply a place to build your record for the trip up the appellate route. You can only hope for justice once you get over into the Federal side" (Roberts, 1965:n.p.). The improbability of winning at the trial level was yet another factor that minimized attempts to politicize trial proceedings. As suggested in our earlier discussion of LDF, the primary emphasis in civil rights trials, including those handled by Guild attorneys (Ginger, 1979), was on building a proper record for appeal. Constitutional arguments in court might strengthen that record, but political and moral arguments, as legally extraneous issues, would not. Moreover, appeals of cases required trial transcripts to be typed by court reporters at movement expense. Thus the shorter the defense argument, the less costly the transcript, again helping to minimize politicization attempts (Ginger, 1979). Efforts to politicize the trial might also have undermined the nonviolent image that the movement sought to present to the public.

Juries

Southern juries also offered no hope for civil rights defendants. Blacks were systematically excluded from juries throughout the South, and the relatively few lawyers who challenged the racial composition of jury panels did so only for the record, not in hope of putting more blacks on the panel. Again reflecting the beliefs of the communities from which they were drawn, jurors almost always convicted civil rights defendants. Conversely, in prosecutions of whites accused of murdering, beating, or otherwise harassing civil rights activists, juries usually acquitted (Cumming, 1966; Meltsner,

1964). Thus when an all-white jury in a "strongly segregationist" section of southeast Alabama convicted members of the Ku Klux Klan (KKK) for the murder of civil rights worker Viola Liuzzo, many civil rights groups and other observers were "startled" (Reed, 1965). Ironically, the defense claimed that the United States "'was not trying the three men but the Ku Klux Klan.'" One member of the KKK said, "'Those people weren't on trial; it was the United Klans of America'" (in Reed, 1965).

Thus the hostility of juries to civil rights aims was yet another problem that confronted the civil rights movement in the Southern criminal courts. It was also one more factor that militated against attempts to politicize the proceedings. In chapter 2, I argued that the desire to win jury sympathy underlies many defense efforts to introduce political and moral arguments, and that where such sympathy seems unobtainable, politicization efforts are less likely to take place. With no real hope of gaining jury sympathy, defense teams in civil rights trials had one less reason to raise the larger political and social issues at stake.

Defendants

One additional category of trial participant is the defendant. In discussing defense attempts at politicization in the previous chapter, I emphasized the defendants' desires in the matter as a key determinant. Many arrested civil rights activists were not radicals. Though willing to undertake serious risks in challenging Southern segregation, they nonetheless remained "committed to the society and its middle class leaders" (Searles and Williams, 1962:219). Quite in contrast to their Vietnam-era counterparts, they did not feel it necessary to carry their radical protests into the courtroom. It was also not safe to do so. In one trial in Georgia, defendants who chose to ignore the segregated seating plan of the courtroom were hit by guards and carried roughly from the room. To have taken the further step in civil rights trials of insisting on discussing racial or other matters or actively disrupting the court would have risked contempt charges and physical injury, and would have undermined the nonviolent image the movement had adopted. Thus discussion of racial issues was kept to a minimum even in the well-publicized trials of Martin Luther King.

Police and Prisons

The criminal courts were not the only branch of criminal justice system that posed difficulties for the civil rights movement. Southern police and prisons also presented serious problems. Arrest was a daily threat, and the Southern jail an ugly institution. Southern police made arrests in almost every kind of sit-in, march, or demonstration, and also arrested known activists in the absence of actual protest activity. Most of these arrests were for actions that would have been legal outside the South (Lewis et al., 1966).

Southern jails also sapped the strength of the movement. Various members of CORE and SNCC advocated a "jail, no bail" policy as a way of demonstrating their sincerity and resolve, of winning publicity and sympathy in the North by so sacrificial an act, and of saving bail and fine money while imposing the financial costs of incarceration on Southern communities (Meier and Rudwick, 1973). In several communities protesters stayed in jail and achieved some of these goals. The first known "jail-in" occurred in Tallahassee, Florida, in February 1960, when five members of CORE chose to remain in jail for sixty days instead of paying fines. A jail-in a year later achieved national headlines when nine CORE and SNCC members arrested in a Rock Hill, South Carolina, sit-in chose thirty-one days at hard labor in lieu of $100 fines. One of the defendants said, " 'Surprise and shock filled the courtroom when it became known that we had chosen to be jailed-in. The only thing they had to beat us over the head with was a threat of sending us to jail. So we disarmed them by using the only weapon we had left—jail without bail . . . . It upset them considerably'" (in Meier and Rudwick, 1973:118).

But civil rights protesters soon found that jailhouse conditions were substandard for civil rights and conventional inmates alike. In one Georgia jail, 88 protesters were detained in one room with 20 steel cots and no mattresses. In another jail, a civil rights protester reported, " 'I was in the Leesburg stockade with 51 other women.

There was no place to sleep. The mattresses were wet and dirty. . . . They would put the food in a box, place it on the floor, and kick it into the cell'" (in Zinn, 1965:132).

Even worse, prison guards and white inmates were especially hostile toward civil rights defendants. One Mississippi Freedom Rider reported his experience at a penal farm in which he was detained: "'Soon they took us out to a room, boys on one side and girls on the other. One by one they took us into another room for questioning. . . . There were about eight guards with sticks in their hands in the second room, and the Freedom Rider being questioned was surrounded by these men. Outside we could hear the questions, and the thumps and whacks, and sometimes a quick groan or cry. . . . They beat several Riders who didn't say "Yes, sir"'" (in Zinn, 1965:52). In some jails, white activists were beaten by white inmates. One white SNCC worker in Georgia was beaten into unconsciousness by an inmate and suffered several broken ribs. The inmate said later that a deputy sheriff who put him in the cell with the SNCC worker had said, "'This is one of the those guys who came down here to straighten us out'" (in Zinn, 1965:62). Women protesters were subject to vaginal exams and ogling by male guards (Zinn, 1965).

Thus the rigors of Southern jails prevented the consistent use of the "jail, no bail" tactic (Meier and Rudwick, 1973), forcing local and national movement groups to spend large sums of money on bail bonds before trial, appeal bonds after convictions, fines, and the costs of legal defense. This was especially true of the spring 1961 Freedom Ride in Jackson, Mississippi. After conviction, most of the more than three hundred Riders chose to leave jail on appeal bond after thirty-nine days, the maximum time they could stay in jail and still retain their right to appeal their convictions. This forced CORE to spend over $130,000 by July 1961 on bail and legal fees. Then, in August, local officials began "what appeared to be a deliberate effort to drive CORE into bankruptcy" (Meier and Rudwick, 1973:142) when they ordered all 196 defendants already released on appeal bond to return to Jackson for arraignment within ten days, forcing the defendants and CORE to incur travel costs for their return. After officials announced that only one or two defendants would be tried each day, as discussed in the last chapter, CORE leader James Farmer said he would end his own appeal and serve the rest of his sentence, and he urged other Freedom Riders to do the same. But court officials said that the appeals for new trials in county court could not be withdrawn. Meanwhile, all of Mississippi's bondsmen refused to provide bail bond, forcing CORE to raise the full $372,000 required. In November LDF agreed to take on the cases and provided much of the bail money (Kunstler, 1976; Meier and Rudwick, 1973).

Which Kind of Civil Disobedience?

If we can distinguish American social movements where legal procedure provided an effective means of social control from those where it provided some hope of mobilization, then clearly the civil rights movement falls into the former category. At the criminal court level, justice had a "Southern accent" (Lusky, 1964), in normal and civil rights cases alike. The nature of civil rights protest in most cities exacerbated the problems facing civil rights forces. The protests were not discontinuous, but, rather, parts of ongoing campaigns. They lasted days, weeks, or months at a time; led to arrests of many dozens or hundreds of activists within a relatively short period; and as a result of the mass nature of the arrests, proved financially and legally burdensome to movement groups and the few attorneys willing to take on civil rights cases. A $500 fine or bail bond would not have been too high in and of itself, but when multiplied by 100 or 500 defendants, it became quite troublesome. This campaign mode of civil rights protest was quite different from that characterizing the contemporary antinuclear movement, to take one example (Barkan, 1979). In the latter movement, the typical protest tactic has been the one-shot occupation of a nuclear power plant, leading on the average to fewer arrests in a given period of time than was true in the South and thus minimizing the burdens posed by prosecution.

The campaign nature of civil rights protest and the legal difficulties the movement experienced as a result have been misinterpreted by many observers. Between the middle 1960s and early 1970s many legal scholars, political philosophers, and other writers debated the justifiability of civil disobedience in a democratic society. The spurt of writing on civil disobedience was obviously a result of its use in the South and then during the Vietnam War. Several of these authors (e.g., Cox, 1967; Fortas, 1968; Katzenbach, 1969; Marshall, 1969)

criticized the use of civil disobedience by Vietnam protesters and re-
ferred more favorably to the civil disobedience of the civil rights
movement. There, they said, activists committed civil disobedience
primarily to test in the courts the constitutionality of various laws
and policies upholding segregation, while others pleaded guilty out
of a principled belief in accepting punishment for breaking the law.
This latter type of illegal protest, these writers mentioned approv-
ingly, adhered to the philosophy of the classic act of civil disobedience, while the first type, entered under a claim of constitutionality, was also justifiable within the American legal context and, in
fact, did not truly constitute civil disobedience. In the view of these
observers, either kind of illegal protest was preferable to that employed by antiwar activists, whose acts were less often directed
against laws and policies claimed to be unconstitutional.

In thus commending the civil rights movement and criticizing
antiwar protests, these scholars misinterpreted the civil rights movement on two levels (see Zashin, 1970). First, the primary intent of
civil rights protesters and leaders who were arrested was not to
create test cases in the courts. Rather, their main goal was to dramatize their cause, achieve press publicity and Northern support, and
force concessions from city and business officials by causing economic and social disruption in Southern communities. Many of
their arrests did turn into cases that reached federal courts, but the
decision to appeal such cases was made after the fact by attorneys
who became involved only after arrests had occurred. As Casper
(1972:145) notes, "The lawyer entered the process at a later stage.
The basic strategy—direct-action protests and violation of discrimination laws—had been chosen by the leaders of civil rights groups or
simply by spontaneous action of black citizens. Such direct action
often led the protesters into court, and at this stage the lawyer became important. But the basic act had already taken place, and the
lawyer was confronted with a situation and had to deal with it."

Second, the pleas of guilty that were rendered in the South derived
not from principled belief in accepting punishment but, rather, from
a lack of hope in taking the case to trial, especially when defendants
could not obtain counsel. As in Jackson, Mississippi, after the Freedom Rides, guilty pleas sometimes occurred even when counsel was
present because of the financial and other burdens of representing
numbers of defendants. But the guilty pleas that did take place were

not nearly as numerous as popularly thought; instead they tended to be fairly infrequent (Ginger, 1979). Rosa Parks did not plead guilty. In his many arrests—and this will surprise many readers—Martin Luther King did not plead guilty (see for example, Lewis, 1970; Miller, 1968), despite his contention in his famous "Letter from the Birmingham Jail" that civil disobedients should "willingly accept the penalty" (King, 1969 : 78) which has been construed by many observers as equivalent to pleading guilty. As his own trials make clear, King evidently meant a willingness to wait to be arrested, or to go to jail upon conviction after a public trial, and not a willingness to plead guilty.

The distortion by the writers on civil disobedience of the true nature and intent of civil rights protest was perhaps unintentional and even understandable. But it still functioned, ideologically, to censure the antiwar civil disobedience, which suffered in comparison to its more favorably viewed civil rights counterpart. The style of civil rights and antiwar protesters did differ in many ways, but the goals and intent of their civil disobedience were far more similar than many scholars would have us believe.

Chapter Four

Legal Control of Civil Rights Protest Campaigns

The potential power of a social movement depends on at least two factors: the extent of its indigenous resources, such as money and preexisting organizational networks; and the disruptive potential of movement members, which derives from such factors as their numbers and structural importance to social institutions. These two factors vary from movement to movement, and those that score high on both variables are potentially more powerful than those that score low on both (Barkan, 1979; Jenkins, 1979).

However, scholars of social movements disagree over whether most movements are, in fact, potentially strong or weak in light of these variables. Several proponents of the resource mobilization perspective have argued, for example, that a movement's mass base commonly lacks the indigenous resources that are important for success and has little, if any, disruptive potential. In this view, then, most movements are potentially weak and can succeed, as discussed in chapter 2, only if they receive external support from sponsoring groups such as liberal organizations, labor unions, churches, and foundations (Jenkins and Perrow, 1977; Lipsky, 1968; McCarthy and Zald, 1973, 1977).* As Jenkins and Perrow (1977:251) argue, "for a successful outcome, movements by the 'powerless' require strong and sustained outside support."

In contrast, proponents of what may be called a "political process"

* The term *resource mobilization* actually refers to many different viewpoints that have been grouped under one rubric. The variant discussed here, as noted by McAdam (1982:262), is that which Perrow (1979) calls "RM II."

model have argued that the mass base of movements typically has many more resources, especially preexisting organizational networks, and much more disruptive potential than the resource mobilization perspective attributes to the base. As a result, most movements are potentially powerful and need not depend so much, if at all, on external support for success (McAdam, 1982; Morris, 1981; Piven and Cloward, 1977; Schwartz, 1976). As McAdam (1981:30–31), the clearest exponent of this model, puts it, "Except for the most deprived segments of society, aggrieved groups possess the ability to exert significant leverage on their own behalf and certain indigenous resources facilitative of organized protest. . . . In characterizing the majority of such groups as politically impotent, resource mobilization theorists are to be faulted for their failure to acknowledge the power inherent in disruptive tactics. Even the most deprived groups possess a greater potential for the successful exercise of political leverage than they have been given credit for in most versions of this perspective."

Much of the debate described here has centered on the civil rights movement. Expressing the resource mobilization perspective, for example, several writers (e.g., Marx and Useem, 1971; McCarthy and Zald, 1973) argue that the origins and successes of the movement depended heavily on the outside support of Northern liberals, church groups, mass media, and the federal government. In marked contrast, other writers using the political process model (McAdam, 1982; Morris, 1981; Piven and Cloward, 1977) trace the origins of the movement to its indigenous organizational network and resources, and emphasize the role played in its successes by its own capacity for disruption.

However, both sides to the debate on the movement's power have overlooked the kinds of obstacles, discussed in the last chapter, that the movement encountered in the criminal justice system. The movement, in fact, was too weak to bring about widespread desegregation and achieve other aims on its own. It is true that important civil rights victories were won because of white violence that attracted national media attention and Northern sympathy and the intervention of the federal government. But where Southern officials avoided such violence and instead used legal measures, civil rights forces suffered major setbacks, underscoring their weaknesses in the face of unyielding white resistance that relied on the legal process.

The four protest campaigns I shall examine took place in Albany, Georgia, 1961–63; Danville, Virginia, 1963; Birmingham, Alabama, 1963; and Selma, Alabama, 1965. I distinguish two models of official control of civil rights protest in these cities. The first approach, used in Albany and Danville, involved the frequent use of arrest, prosecution, and other forms of legal harassment to suppress dissent. Although the use of legal procedure instead of other, more brutal means of social control theoretically gave civil rights groups various procedural guarantees under the law, in both cities the use of the legal process by local officials eventually proved overwhelming. Moreover, the legitimacy conferred by the legal setting helped to minimize the criticism that would have arisen had other, extralegal methods of official control been employed (see Balbus, 1973). The second model, characterizing Birmingham and Selma, is distinguished from the first by the use of police violence that undermined attempts by officials to use legal means to control dissent. Publicized across the nation, the police violence negated the legitimacy surrounding the official use of legal procedure and helped pressure the federal government into taking action favorable to civil rights goals. Without the police violence, however, the legal control of civil rights protest in Birmingham and Selma might very well have succeeded.

Albany, Georgia

In Albany, Georgia, where blacks constituted 40 percent of the population, a concerted effort to desegregate bus and train terminals, lunch counters and restaurants, and other public facilities and accommodations began in November 1961 and lasted through the summer of 1962. In this period, well over one thousand people were arrested for sit-ins, marches, demonstrations, and the like. Despite the number of protests and arrests, little desegregation occurred, as civil rights forces encountered an intransigent local government and a legal system that provided an effective means of social control. Partly because of the involvement of Martin Luther King and his Southern Christian Leadership Conference (SCLC) in the protests, national attention was focused on Albany in the winter and spring of 1962, and the failure of civil rights activists to desegregate the city was thus emphasized as a telling blow for the movement.

Today it still remains an important example of how the entire legal machinery of a city was used to thwart civil rights goals.

Perhaps the most effective legal tactic employed by the city involved the use and behavior of local police. During and after the period in question, the police chief of Albany, Laurie Pritchett, was cited and, in many places, praised for his method of dealing with civil rights demonstrators. Following the example of the police in Jackson, Mississippi, during the Freedom Rides, Pritchett and his police arrested protesters in almost every demonstration and, most important, did so without violence. Pritchett's tactics presented the local movement with huge legal costs and other burdens, and effectively depicted a police force that quickly, efficiently, and impartially dealt with protesters breaking the laws. As a result, United States Attorney General Robert Kennedy sent Pritchett a telegram congratulating him for the peaceful arrests (Raines, 1977). Citing the praise of Pritchett, an Atlanta newspaper reported in 1963 that he was "widely known—not only in the South, but throughout the world— as a stalwart exponent of the nonviolent method of quelling integrationist uprising" (McLendon, 1963:14). And a remark by Pritchett evidenced the image of neutral law enforcement that his police force sought to project: "'It is our duty as police officers to enforce the laws and ordinances of our city for the safety and protection of all— regardless of race, color or creed. I . . . credit our success in handling racial disturbances to adherence to the nonviolent method of each member of the police force, as well as the citizens of Albany and the leaders who upheld our method, and cooperated—rather than interfered—with it'" (in McLendon, 1963:14).

Pritchett's "nonviolent method" was no accident. In the months before the Albany protests, the city police had been trained to handle civil rights arrests without violence and had seen films of demonstrations in other areas. The police had also made preparations to send demonstrators to jails up to 100 miles away in order to prevent them from filling the jails of Albany.

The Albany protests began 1 November 1961 when a group of black students sponsored by SNCC entered the white waiting room of the Trailways bus terminal in Albany. Their aim was to see whether the city would comply with the Interstate Commerce Commission's (ICC) desegregation order that went into effect that day. The city would not comply, and police ordered them to leave. On 17 November, the Albany movement, a coalition of SNCC, the NAACP, and local black ministers, was formed. Five days later, five local college students sat down in the bus terminal restaurant and were arrested. Arrests again occurred 10 December, when black and white SNCC members rode a train from Atlanta to Albany. When they entered the white waiting room at the Albany train terminal, Pritchett ordered them to leave; as they were entering cars to depart, they were arrested for obstructing traffic, disorderly conduct, and failure to obey an officer. The editor of a black weekly newspaper watched the arrests and later said, "'There was no traffic, no disturbance, no one moving. The students had made the trip to Albany [and] desegregated without incident. Things had gone so smoothly I think it infuriated the chief'" (in Zinn, 1962:4).

During the next week, the Albany movement held large meetings in the black churches and sponsored several downtown marches that ended in many arrests; one of the demonstrators said later, "'I didn't expect to go to jail for kneeling and praying at city hall'" (in Zinn, 1962:4). On the day of the trial of the 10 December protesters, 400 students were arrested as they marched downtown to demonstrate against the trial. On 16 December, Martin Luther King and Ralph Abernathy spoke at a black church and led another march downtown, where 200 more were arrested, including King. By now 737 had been taken to jail, and the protests and arrests had captured national attention. Negotiations began between city officials and movement leaders. The latter agreed to call off the demonstrations in return for desegregation of the terminals, release of those still in jail on property bonds, except for SNCC members arrested December 10, and the agreement of the city commission to discuss movement demands in January.

The agreement of movement leaders to stop demonstrations in return for these concessions caused considerable dissension among Albany activists. The promise of the city commission to discuss movement complaints was at best vague, these critics thought; the agreement of the city to desegregate the terminal facilities merely put it in compliance with the ICC order. One SNCC member said of the compromise, "'You curse first, then I will'" (in Zinn, 1965:131). To such critics the agreement "seemed a pitifully small payment for weeks of protest" (Zinn, 1965:131).

Martin Luther King's willingness to leave jail as part of the agreement also came under sharp attack. When arrested, King and others had refused bail, and King had called on clergy from across the country to come to Albany for a vigil. His subsequent decision to leave jail in the absence of significant concessions from city officials led to criticism by various civil rights activists and charges of the movement's defeat by the national press (Lewis, 1970). It also demoralized Albany blacks (Lomax, 1962). Thus the *New York Herald Tribune* called the compromise and King's agreement to leave jail " 'one of the most stunning defeats of his career'" (in Raines, 1977:402−403).

According to Lomax (1968), however, King had a good reason for leaving jail that became known only much later. One of the Albany movement leaders in jail with King had come to think of himself as Jesus, believing that with jailhouse bread he could feed thousands. King and other leaders in jail agreed that this man should be bailed out, lest a guard discover his delusions. The man refused to accept bail, however, unless King himself did the same, thus forcing King to agree to leave the jail so that he could take this leader with him.

Perhaps predictably, the city commission refused to take any action after hearing the demands of the Albany movement in a hearing on 23 January. A month later city officials began trials for the 737 protesters arrested in December. The first ones tried were King, Abernathy, and two Albany residents on charges of parading without a permit, obstructing the sidewalk, and disorderly conduct. With national attention focused on the trial, the defense claimed the arrests were intended to uphold segregation and violated the First and Fourteenth Amendments. In response, the prosecution maintained that the arrests were not racially motivated and instead were made solely for violation of an ordinance requiring parade permits (Zinn, 1962). A defense attorney asked Pritchett how a parade was defined; he answered that there was no definition of the term. When asked, " 'Then it's anything you want to make it?'" Pritchett replied that it was (in Zinn, 1962:7). Despite the important and complex issues at stake, the trial lasted only three hours. The judge delayed his verdict until July, when he found the defendants guilty and sentenced them to forty-five days in jail or a $178 fine.

In the intervening months the criminal justice system continued to affect the protest campaign. In March the trial of those arrested on

10 December in the train terminal began. When a black defendant sat down in a white section at the front of the courtroom, a policeman dragged him to the rear. Four white defendants who then sat down in the rear were dragged by deputies out of the courtroom. In April four movement leaders were tried and found guilty of disorderly conduct for picketing a downtown store that did not hire black workers. Thirty people were arrested in lunch counter sit-ins. In June nine more were arrested for picketing downtown stores. By the time the King and Abernathy verdict was announced in July, Albany had reached a point of high tension.

When their verdict was declared on 10 July, King and Abernathy decided to go to jail instead of paying the fine. With this dramatic act, "excitement rose to a high pitch not only in Albany but throughout the nation" (Zinn, 1962:9). More than thirty Albany blacks were arrested the next day after a protest march. The King and Abernathy convictions were denounced by Senator Joseph Clark of Pennsylvania. Robert Kennedy and Burke Marshall, head of the Civil Rights Division of the Justice Department, made several calls to Albany, including one to Coretta King. But with tensions and publicity mounting, King and Abernathy were released from jail the day after they were put in. Pritchett said at the time that an anonymous, well-dressed black man had paid their fines. At a mass meeting that night, Abernathy said, "'I've been thrown out of lots of places in my day, but never before have I been thrown out of jail'" (in Zinn, 1962:10). City officials said the man had been a member of SCLC; some of King's critics in the civil rights movement said he had again gone back on his word to stay in jail. Some journalists, knowing that the Kennedy administration disapproved of the Albany movement because of the disruptions it was causing, thought that the man might have been sent down from the Justice Department (Raines, 1977). But according to Pritchett some fifteen years later (Pritchett, 1977: 399–400), the man had been sent by "a coalition . . . between some blacks and some whites [in Albany] that felt that if he [King] was released from custody and left that the mass news media which was there would also leave and Albany would go back to their ways."

Despite the expectations of this coalition, mass meetings, sit-ins, and stand-ins continued in the few days after the release of King and Abernathy. A large prayer vigil was scheduled for the city hall on 21 July, but the city obtained a temporary injunction at midnight on the twentieth from federal district Judge J. Robert Elliott, a recent Kennedy appointee, prohibiting all marching, picketing, and congregating. Consequently, the planned vigil did not take place, as King, the featured speaker, refused to violate the order of a federal judge. That night, however, 160 blacks were arrested in a protest march for defying the injunction. Forty-seven more were arrested in marches two days later.

On 24 July a Fifth Circuit Court judge set aside the temporary injunction. That same day, Albany attorney C. B. King and four other lawyers, one from Atlanta and the others from out of state, filed two civil suits against the city to desegregate its public facilities and to enjoin the police from making arrests in peaceful demonstrations. A few days later Martin Luther King and Abernathy were again arrested when they and a few Albany movement leaders went to city hall to ask to talk with the city commission. On 28 July C. B. King was hit by a sheriff while trying to visit a client in prison, as mentioned in the last chapter.

By August more than twelve hundred had been arrested since the previous November. In the early part of the month, Justice Elliott heard arguments on a request by the city for a permanent injunction on demonstrations, though he was never to reach a decision. On 10 August, King, Abernathy, and the other defendants from the July city hall arrests were found guilty and given suspended sentences, perhaps to avoid the publicity that would have accompanied imprisonment. A Northern minister who attended the brief trial said, "'The trial was a farce. The judge had his opinion and judgement written out when he came into the court'" (in Miller, 1968:133). At the end of the month, seventy-five clergy came from Northern states and were arrested while praying in front of city hall. Most of them accepted bail after a few days and then returned to the North, but their stay in jail "greatly heartened" local blacks and helped mobilize support in the ministers' home communities (Miller, 1968:135).

But the mass protests and mass arrests of these ten months of the Albany struggle did not desegregate public facilities and accommodations. This was not to occur until after the Congress passed the 1964 Civil Rights Bill (Bleiweiss, 1969). An NAACP official put it well: "'Albany was successful only if the goal was to go to jail'" (in Miller, 1968:139), an assessment shared by much of the press and many people in the civil rights movement (e.g., Cleghorn, 1963;

Southern Patriot, 1962). Others have taken a more positive view, asserting that, at the very least, the Albany campaign focused attention on Southern racism (Walker, 1963) and showed that an entire black community could be mobilized to attack segregation (Miller, 1968; Piven and Cloward, 1977).

In the years since the Albany protests, at least two explanations of the Albany movement's failure to desegregate have been advanced (cf. Piven and Cloward, 1977). One line of analysis argues that leaders of the Albany movement should have concentrated on one or two examples of racial discrimination in the city instead of launching a general attack, which spread themselves too thinly (Lewis, 1970; Zinn, 1962). The second explanation attributes the movement's failure to desegregate to factionalism among its various groups, such as that between SCLC and SNCC members, which hampered the movement's operations (cf. Bleiweiss, 1969). The two explanations are not mutually exclusive, and some observers agree with both.

But if the organizational problems of the Albany movement finally proved fatal, the intransigence of city officials provided a decisive blow. In the officials' efforts at social control, the Albany criminal justice system provided a powerful weapon, a point overlooked by Piven and Cloward (1977). Most of the more than twelve hundred arrests that took place through the summer of 1962 were without legal merit. As Zinn (1962:21) points out, "There was no consideration of imminent disturbance, or impending violence, no concern with what is the prevailing judicial rule for the limits of free speech—the existence of a 'clear and present danger.'" Similarly, the head of the Southern Regional Council asserted, "'There are legitimate grounds for saying that in Albany sophisticated police work has done the traditional—almost legendary—job of the mob, i.e., the suppression of Negro dissent'" (in Zinn, 1962:vi).

The arrests, especially those of Martin Luther King, did help turn national attention to Albany, but they also presented the movement with serious legal problems. With cash bonds of $200 required for most of those arrested, the movement had to come up with some $200,000 in bail money; property bonds are often allowed, but Pritchett purposely refused them during the Albany protests to create financial problems for the movement (Pritchett, 1977). Moreover, the Albany movement was never able to overflow the local jails and force the city to spend large sums on incarceration, as had happened in

Mississippi during the Freedom Rides (Farmer, 1977). Long before King and SCLC came to Albany, Pritchett had read of King's admiration for Gandhi's method of filling the jails and determined that this would not happen in Albany. Arrangements were made to send anyone arrested to jails up to 100 miles from the city. Protesters were booked, fingerprinted, and photographed and taken immediately to buses to these jails. Pritchett said later of his tactics, "I think this is one thing that Dr. King was surprised at. This did away with his method of overextending the facilities" (1977:399). As Cleghorn notes (1963:16), the Albany city jail "proved a bottomless pit." The arrests also overwhelmed Albany's only civil rights attorney, C. B. King. Guilty verdicts were a foregone conclusion, and King's normal practice suffered because of the time required by his civil rights clients.

Just as important, arrests and prosecutions in the long run proved intimidating. In the late spring and summer of 1963, the Albany movement showed signs of rebirth, but it never achieved the numbers of participants of the previous year (cf. Sitton, 1963). By that time the prospect of arrest for any protest action aimed at the elusive goal of desegregation was uninviting. As a Northern law student working for C. B. King that summer observed, "The young people are not interested in peaceful demonstrations in the street. That only means arrest with no bail money. The people here have been going to jail for over two years now. They are tired of going to jail" (Roberts, 1965).

For those still willing to protest, jail was a certain fate. In June 1963, for instance, about one hundred people picketing and leafletting white businesses in support of a boycott were arrested for disturbing the peace, effectively "crippling the Negroes' efforts to boycott department stores" (Cleghorn, 1963:16). By late June, twenty out of twenty-six SNCC workers in Albany had been arrested, mostly for vagrancy. Thus by the middle of the summer a certain amount of despair had settled over Albany's black community. C. B. King remained busy; as his law student said, "There is no way to explain how overworked we are, how impossibly far behind, how many things have to be skipped, how much 'private' practice is lost, because we just don't have the time. We don't practice law here; we run around complying with all the irrelevancies" (Roberts, 1965). Noting the low attendance at protest meetings, King's law student also commented, "People are just physically exhausted and feel forgotten and hopeless" (Roberts, 1965).

The final legal blow to the Albany movement came in August 1963, and, ironically, it derived from a federal prosecution of movement activists that SNCC workers said was designed to appease Southern communities. At the beginning of the month, nine members of the movement and of SNCC were indicted by a federal grand jury for perjury and obstructing justice. The defendants had picketed and leafleted white-owned businesses, as mentioned above. One of the storeowners being picketed, Carl Smith, had been a juror in a federal suit filed by a black resident, Charles Ware, against a local sheriff for alleged brutality. The all-white jury ruled against Ware. On 1 August, a federal grand jury was convened in Macon, Georgia, and heard almost seventy witnesses, as more than thirty-five FBI agents conducted investigative work. Movement activists who testified before the grand jury had not been able to consult with C. B. King before doing so, since he was out of town on other cases. On 9 August, at the request of the United States district attorney, the grand jury returned indictments against the nine civil rights workers; the indictments were announced by the attorney general's office in Washington, D.C. Three defendants were indicted for interfering with a federal juror by boycotting Smith's store, and the remaining six were indicted for perjury in their testimony before the grand jury (Bay Area Friends of SNCC, 1963; *Nation*, 1964). All of the defendants were convicted.

After the indictments were announced, "people ran around all afternoon trying to convince the more affluent members of the Negro community to sign property bonds, which was like pulling teeth" (Roberts, 1965). Having regarded the federal government as an ally, blacks in Albany were "stunned" at the indictments (*Southern Patriot*, 1963:1). As one resident said, "Even the federal government's a white man" (Roberts, 1965). For the Albany movement, "the indictments were the last straw. Worn down by twenty months of protest with all their attendant economic and emotional consequences, the Negroes of Albany could not survive the shattering of their last great hope for deliverance. The impassioned voices that, one year earlier, had proclaimed that they weren't going 'to let Chief Pritchett turn us 'round,' were now silent. Laurie Pritchett was one foe; Bobby Kennedy was quite another" (Kunstler, 1966:130). The indictments also led to other problems. Some Albany blacks were now afraid to associate with members of the movement; one black businessman refused to allow activists to enter his restaurant, pool hall, or liquor store, and several other black-owned restaurants followed suit (Forman, 1973). Moreover, harassment of SNCC workers in Albany increased after the federal indictments as well. On 16 August one SNCC member who was taken from a porch to the police station for questioning was told by an officer, "Now that the federal government is going to put the Movement's ass in jail, we will put your ass, in too, if you don't stay off the street. The [federal] government will have Slater [King, one of those indicted] and all those niggers in jail in a month" (Roberts, 1965).

Thus it is evident that the legal system had a significant impact on the fortunes of the Albany movement; indeed, it is impossible to understand the movement's development and demise without taking into account the part played by the police, courts, and prisons. Arrests did result in sympathetic publicity in the North, an important aim of civil rights mobilization efforts, but in the long run the use of the criminal justice system by the city of Albany, and later by the federal government, encumbered the movement with burdens it could not escape. The use of the criminal justice system also affected civil rights efforts in Birmingham, Danville, and Selma, albeit in different ways. These campaigns are discussed below, though in somewhat less detail, to elucidate further the nature of political justice in the South.

Birmingham, Alabama

From his defeat in Albany, Martin Luther King went on to victory in Birmingham, thanks in large part to the violence of the white response. After the failure in Albany, King debated whether even to continue with his civil rights efforts (Young, 1977) but finally determined to stay in the movement. Thus when Birmingham civil rights leader Fred Shuttlesworth asked King and SCLC for help in May 1962, King quickly accepted. Birmingham had a reputation for its racism and seemed to offer a great opportunity to demonstrate the potential of nonviolence in the civil rights struggle. One Birmingham civil rights leader recalled later, "[the SCLC] had run into this slump in Albany. So coming to Birmingham gave them a shot in the arm. It was the very thing they needed, and it was the very thing we needed. They needed us and we needed them because King was a national symbol" (Gardner, 1977:153). Since Shuttlesworth had founded the Alabama Christian Movement for Human Rights (ACMHR) in 1956, a dozen black homes and churches had been bombed, fifty crosses burned on lawns, and several black women raped by white policemen. Police Commissioner Bull Connor was particularly hostile to civil rights efforts; in November 1961 he had arrested the manager of the city's bus terminal four times for complying with the ICC desegregation order. The stage was thus set for a protest campaign that offered good chances of success, as SCLC realized and even hoped that demonstrations would prompt "tough repressive measures" by the police (Cleghorn, 1970:114). Shuttlesworth said many years later, "Here, I thought, with 'Bull' Connor being the epitome of segregation and SCLC being organized by us to change it, the two forces should be met. . . . I think the idea of facing 'Bull' Connor was the thing. . . . We knew that we would have at least the spotlight, I think that" (Shuttlesworth, 1977:167–168).

In the middle of January 1963 King began a speaking tour where he mentioned the planned Birmingham campaign for the first time and obtained pledges of bail money for arrests in Birmingham; SCLC promised to bail out demonstrators after five days in jail. Sit-ins finally began 3 April, with 20 arrested at a local department store. Three days later a protest march led by Shuttlesworth ended in 42 arrests, and by the end of the first week of protests more than 150 had been arrested. Of these, 24 had been tried and found guilty of various offenses, fined $100 each, and sentenced to six months in jail. The city also obtained a local court injunction prohibiting civil rights demonstrations.

On Monday, 8 April, civil rights attorneys filed petitions under a Reconstruction statute to remove the cases of those who had been arrested but not yet tried into federal court; the statute had been passed to assure that blacks could avoid the prejudice of local Southern courts in the post–Civil War period. According to Kunstler (1966: 179), who was working with the Birmingham attorneys, "Although we were convinced that the cases would eventually be remanded to the state courts, we were also certain that the temporary halting of the prosecutions would give the movement a much needed respite."

The several dozen defendants covered by the removal petitions had been scheduled for trials that day but were allowed because of the petitions to be released on $200 bail each. "While we waited for the city's next legal move," Kunstler later wrote, "it was apparent that the transfer of the cases to the federal court had buoyed up the movement" (1966:180). Shuttlesworth remarked happily, "'We've taken them by surprise'" (in Kunstler, 1966:180).

On Good Friday, 12 April, King, Abernathy, and Shuttlesworth led some fifty marchers to the city hall, thus defying the city injunction; all the protesters were arrested. King's arrest again captured national attention. While in jail he wrote his famous "Letter from a Birmingham Jail." On Easter Sunday, about two thousand blacks gathered at the city jail to protest the arrests, and some people in the crowd threw rocks at the police. In return the police swung clubs and used police dogs.

The use of the clubs and dogs by the police marked a significant departure from the "nonviolent" tactics used by Albany police. While the latter had trained for mass protests, Birmingham's had not. One of Birmingham's police captains revealed later, "At that time . . . our management was really a crisis-type management. We waited until we had the situation to try to cope with it. . . . [Our police were] quite taken by surprise that this thing would happen, and they were not—well, they were not really prepared fully from a tactical point of view" (Evans, 1977:189).

On Saturday, 20 April, King and Abernathy agreed to $300 bail so that they could help plan strategy. Two days later they were found guilty and sentenced to five days in jail and a fifty dollar fine. The judge's "relatively mild sentences proved more a hindrance than a help to King's campaign. The demonstrations, which had begun to flag a week earlier, reached rock bottom" (Kunstler, 1966:189). At a church meeting a few nights later, only a dozen people volunteered to undertake a march that would end in arrest.

As a result, civil rights forces decided to employ schoolchildren in protests. On Thursday, 2 May, 38 children were arrested after a march; they were followed by several other groups ranging from 10 to 50. By the end of the day, 959 children and 9 adults had been arrested; more arrests would have taken place if the police had not run out of wagons. Five hundred more marched the next day, but were repelled by police using fire hoses and dogs. News photographs of the dogs "shocked the world" (Lewis et al., 1966:120). On Monday, 6 May, about one thousand more children were arrested for marching to city hall. All of the young girls jailed were given examinations for venereal disease, with the same rubber glove used on everyone. The number of arrests now exceeded two thousand. [11]

With no room left in the jails, 500 children who marched May 7 were not arrested, prompting SCLC leaders to send 3,000 more children downtown the same day. Dispersed by police, they went back to the church that had been their starting point and then returned to the downtown area. Police used fire hoses, and members of the crowd threw rocks in return; less than 50 were arrested. That night, 575 state troopers arrived in Birmingham at the request of Bull Connor. National attention centered on Birmingham, and United States Senators Morse and Cooper denounced the use by police of fire hoses and dogs.

Meanwhile, serious negotiations had begun between civil rights leaders, white and black clergy, and white merchants, and a three-day halt in the demonstrations began 7 May. The next day, however, King and Abernathy were unexpectedly put back in jail for the Good Friday arrests, and bail was now set at $2,500 each. Singer Harry Belafonte raised the $5,000 bail in New York, but in the meantime a wealthy black resident of Birmingham paid the fee. Leaders of SCLC "felt betrayed" (Miller, 1968:157) at the incarceration but decided not to hold a new protest march after talking to Robert Kennedy. By this time the movement had run up about $237,000 in bail costs, which were paid by Northern contributors, with the bulk coming from the United Auto Workers and National Maritime unions. On Friday, 10 May, the 790 protesters still in jail were released on bail, and that afternoon an agreement between the city and civil rights forces was announced; the federal government had threatened to send in troopers if a compromise were not reached. The agreement called for the desegregation of lunch counters, rest rooms, and the like in all downtown stores; the hiring of blacks in various jobs in the stores; and release of all those already convicted. Bull Connor criticized the agreement, but the head of the group of white merchants involved in the negotiations urged support of the settlement. But the next night two bombs destroyed part of the home of one of King's brothers outside Birmingham, while another damaged the motel where King had been staying. Blacks gathered at the motel and, angered, began fighting with police and set fire to three white-owned stores. State troopers arrived and made several arrests (Lewis, 1970).

In the next few weeks, white businessmen voted to support the settlement, and the charges against many of those arrested by the state troopers were dismissed by a judge for lack of evidence, "an unusual gesture in this city" (Miller, 1968:162). On Monday, 20 May, the Supreme Court ruled that Birmingham's ordinances upholding segregation were unconstitutional and overturned the convictions of all those arrested under the laws. Finally, on 23 May, the Alabama Supreme Court upheld the disputed mayoral election of Albert Boutwell, who had defeated Bull Connor, ending the era of the latter's influence (Miller, 1968).

The events in Birmingham "changed the thinking of the Kennedy administration," which had hitherto been opposed to new civil rights laws, "and of the country" (Lewis et al. 1966:121). Administration action was also precipitated by Governor George Wallace's standing in the doorway at the University of Alabama in symbolic defiance of an order that the school be integrated. Finally, on 19 June, Kennedy introduced in Congress the legislation that was to become the 1964 Civil Rights Act.

The protest campign in Birmingham was generally similar to that in Albany. Protest strategy in each city involved the use of sit-ins and especially mass marches. In each city, large numbers of arrests occurred as a result, although Birmingham had almost twice the number of Albany. Yet the campaign in Birmingham succeeded where, in many ways, it had failed in Albany. In addition to the better planning that marked the Birmingham effort, several factors seem to account for these different outcomes; the Albany civil rights forces faced difficulties that the Birmingham groups were able to avoid. First, in Albany the police sent demonstrators to jails outside the city, thus preventing the movement from overflowing the local jails, while in Birmingham, a much larger city, the jails did become full. Second, in Albany the movement had trouble raising bail money, while in Birmingham it was provided by two labor unions and Northern sympathizers. Third, and perhaps most important, the police in Albany arrested without violence, while those in Birmingham used fire hoses, dogs, and clubs and in so doing dismayed the North and forced federal officials to enter the struggle: "it was the confrontation between the people and the police that was [the Birmingham campaign's] distinguishing feature and the source of its influence on the national government" (Piven and Cloward, 1977:241). Fourth, in Albany the business community refused to negotiate a compromise, while in Birmingham it met with blacks, partly at the urging of the Justice Department, and partly because of the overreaction of the police, and forged a settlement. For all these reasons, the Birmingham campaign needed only six weeks to achieve its goals, while that in Albany encompassed some ten months with no success, allowing time for frustration to set in and spirits to lag.

In Birmingham, then, the law and the legal system again played an important part in the development and outcome of civil rights protest. As a model of legal control of civil rights dissent, Birmingham's effort is distinguished from Albany's by the violence of its police response. To succeed, Birmingham's protest campaign had to succeed quickly, lest it encounter the legal and financial problems that had beset the Albany movement. But its quick victory probably would not have been possible without the cooperation of Birmingham police, whose use of violence was exactly what SCLC and Birmingham leaders had hoped for and who had made no plans to send arrested demonstrators out of the city. Ironically, Birmingham's police chief had consulted with Laurie Pritchett, but his pleas for a nonviolent police response were vetoed by Bull Connor (Evans, 1977; Pritchett, 1977). Thus the Birmingham campaign might very well have failed if city officials had emulated the successful resistance of Albany whites, underscoring the profound difficulties that the use of the criminal justice system and other forms of white intransigence posed for the civil rights movement. The contrast between the two models is also pointed up in the Danville and Selma campaigns.

Danville, Virginia

The success at Birmingham inspired demonstrations in many other communities (Franklin, 1969). One of the most prolonged protest efforts in the aftermath of Birmingham occurred in Danville, Virginia, a city of about fifty thousand. There the local civil rights movement modeled its strategy on that used in Birmingham. However, the Danville protests largely failed to achieve their goals, and, as was true in Albany, the use of the legal system by white officials was a key factor in the movement's defeat, despite some imaginative legal maneuvering by the movement.

In 1960 sit-ins had helped desegregate lunch counters in downtown variety stores and a public park, but the intervening years little further progress had been made, and in 1963 hotels, motels, restaurants, theaters, and churches were still segregated. In August 1962, the Danville Christian Progressive Association (DCPA), the local civil rights organization, had filed an omnibus desegregation suit in federal court aimed at ending all forms of segregation in Danville. Shortly after it was filed, the city removed "white" and "colored" signs from bathrooms and drinking fountains. Meanwhile the suit wound its way through the usual many months of litigation.

Inspired by the Birmingham events, DCPA began marches on 31 May 1963, though without the organization and planning that had characterized the Birmingham protest effort. After several marches over the next few days, negotiations began between black and white leaders. On 5 June, however, two DCPA leaders were arrested for inciting to riot when they refused to leave city hall, where they had gone to try to talk to the mayor; their bail was set at $5,000 each. As a result of the arrests, the interracial negotiations ended. DCPA also asked SNCC, SCLC, and CORE for help; SNCC sent eighteen field secretaries soon afterwards. On 6 June, Judge A. M. Aiken, a city judge, issued an injunction prohibiting further civil rights demonstrations, but in the next few days 105 were arrested for violating the injunction. On 10 June, a march was undertaken to city hall to protest these arrests. Police and firemen used fire hoses on fifty protesters who were trapped in an alley and then beat them with nightsticks. Forty-seven of the 50 were later treated at a hospital for injuries they had suffered. Only 1 was arrested, ironically for resisting arrest when he crawled under a parked car to avoid being hit by the nightsticks.

Trials of the 105 who had been arrested for violating the injunction began the morning of 17 June. When the handful of civil rights attorneys walked into court, police took their pictures and searched the black attorneys in the group. As the proceedings began, the defense lawyers still did not know which defendant would be tried first. When attorney Len Holt was told in court that the first defendant would be one of his clients, a minor, he asked for a continuance so that he would have time to prepare the case. Judge Aiken denied his request and then refused Holt's defendant a jury trial. When Holt challenged the segregated seating plan in the courtroom, Aiken banned all spectators from the room, saying, "'Sure my courtroom is segregated, but not today, because nobody's allowed in'" (in Belfrage, 1963:11). He then turned down a defense motion to transfer the defendant's case to juvenile court and refused to allow discussion on the legality of the injunction. Finally, he refused to tell Holt which section of the injunction his client had allegedly violated. Holt then said he couldn't proceed with the case, since he had not had time to prepare it and didn't know which part of the injunction the defendant was accused of violating. The judge said, "'That's your problem'" and sentenced the defendant to ninety days in jail, with one-half the term suspended on condition of good behavior for two years, and a twenty-five dollar fine (Holt, 1965:153). As he announced his verdict, he read an opinion concerning the defendant's guilt that had been written before the trial had begun. He then refused to allow the defendant to stay out of jail while his case was being appealed, saying, "'That would result in an almost complete disruption of an effectiveness or any deterring effect of the injunction and render it almost meaningless'" (in Holt, 1965:153). It also meant that the defendant would have served his jail term long before his appeal had been decided. The next day Aiken sentenced a second defendant to sixty days in jail and later ordered the remaining defendants to be in court every day until all the individual trials had been completed.

On 22 June, a local grand jury indicted fourteen Danville civil rights leaders for inciting blacks "to acts of violence and war against the white population" under an antebellum state law that was passed in 1830 after Nat Turner's uprising and was used to hang John Brown. Thirteen of the fourteen were arrested and released on $5,000 bail each, which was raised by local blacks who pledged their homes as security, while the fourteenth person, SNCC leader James Forman, left the city in secret. The remaining thirteen were forced because of the indictments to limit their participation in civil rights demonstrations (Holt, 1965).

The next day Judge Thomas Michie, a federal judge, began hearing removal petitions filed by defense attorneys at the suggestion of William Kunstler to transfer the injunction cases of 17 June into Michie's court. Michie, as the result of a defense motion for *habeas corpus*, released the two defendants who had already been convicted for violating the injunction. His action "had a significant effect on movement morale. Not only did it end the threat of imprisonment without bail of hundreds of demonstrators, but it clearly marked the supremacy of federal law. From now on, Judge Aiken could no longer try cases that had been removed to Michie's court until they had been returned to him by federal order [of Michie]" (Kunstler, 1966: 223). Defense attorneys were also attempting to take the offensive in other ways; they filed suits in Michie's court against Aiken's injunction, against a city ordinance that had been passed to control the demonstrations, and against a decision by the Virginia Employment Commission to stop unemployment benefits of people who took part in the demonstrations. Interestingly, Jack Greenberg, head of LDF, had advised against filing the removal petitions in the first place, feeling they were a waste of time (Holt, 1965).

Then the Danvile movement scheduled a rally for Wednesday, 3 July, at which Martin Luther King would be the featured speaker. On 1 July, the city denied a permit for the rally. About this same time, the Danville police chief, wishing to avoid the error of Bull Connor, asked Laurie Pritchett in Albany for advice in dealing with the mass protests that seemed to be coming.

On the night before the rally, Judge Michie granted a city request for an injunction prohibiting all civil rights demonstrations. As a result, King decided not to participate in the rally and stayed in Atlanta, prompting the city to finally grant the permit. A hearing before Michie on the injunction was set for 9 July; hopeful that the injunction would be lifted, Danville civil rights forces scheduled a rally for 11 July, with King and Abernathy again set to take part. At the 9 July hearing Michie lifted his injunction, as two judges of the Fourth Circuit Court of Appeals had requested, but he also remanded the removed cases from Aiken's injunction back to Aiken's court. King arrived on 11 July, and sixty blacks who marched to city hall to mark his arrival were arrested, but the next day he flew to New York to help plan the March on Washington that was to become a high point of the civil rights movement. About the same time, the chief justice of the Fourth Circuit Court, Simon E. Sobeloff, held a hearing on the movement's request to end the city's antipicketing ordinance and to dissolve Aiken's injunction; six days later he said the full circuit court would hear the matter on 23 September, but that in the meantime the ordinance and injunction would stay in effect.

Sobeloff's decision to delay a ruling "was a serious legal blow for the Danville movement": "To say that we were profoundly depressed by the court's action would be the understatement of the summer. . . . If the federal courts would not help, where were they [Danville blacks] to go?" (Kunstler, 1966:228). City officials, on the other hand, greeted the news happily, one of them saying that he "'couldn't believe the good news at first'" (in Kunstler, 1966:229). The police chief announced that anyone violating Aiken's injunction would be arrested and that demonstrators from outside the city would be the first taken to jail (Kunstler, 1966). He also told local tobacco workers, the ones who had been denied unemployment benefits, that if they took part in demonstrations they would not be able to find work once the tobacco season began.

During the next two weeks, the Danville movement was fairly quiet. Then, on 28 July, eighty people were arrested for marching from a church to city hall. The next day Aiken made his injunction, which had been temporary, permanent: "With the exception of sporadic picketing, the permanent injunction completely paralyzed the protest movement. Because of the injunction's broad terms and the knowledge that Aiken would not grant bail in the contempt [that is, for violating the injunction] cases, persons sympathetic to the DCPA were inhibited from participating in any activity even remotely related to the protest movement" (Kunstler, 1966:230). In yet another legal tactic, on 6 August Aiken transferred forty-one of the injunction contempt cases from Danville to counties 80 to 250 miles away. His action intensified the legal intimidation of the city: "the prospect of having to travel hundreds of miles to be tried would keep most of Danville's Negro citizens from daring to violate the injunction or the ordinance" (Kunstler, 1966:231) and would cause further problems for the movement's attorneys, who would have to travel the same distance. However, a three-judge panel of the Fourth Circuit stopped all the cases until its hearing on 23 September. Sobeloff also suggested that the opposing parties try to reach a compromise.

But on the day after Sobeloff made his recommendation, six of the nine members of the Danville City Council said they would not take part in negotiations requested by three black ministers. The Danville movement had hoped and expected that King and SCLC would return to the city, but they never did so, as a result of obligations elsewhere. Despite the roughly two months of protests, "no dra-

matic gains resulted from Danville's hectic activities" (Miller, 1968:
185), though about eight hundred blacks did register to vote and the
city council passed a fair employment law, the first of its kind in the
South.

The Danville movement's failure can be traced to several factors.
In contrast to Birmingham, King and SCLC and the national press
came only for a few days to the city. Danville civil rights forces were
never able to mobilize the numbers that had marched and been arrested in Birmingham, or even in Albany. Except for the experience
of 10 June, police committed little or no violence. As a result, white
political and business leaders were able to continue their refusal to
negotiate. But, as in Albany, perhaps the primary factor that led to
the movement's defeat was the use of the legal system by the city of
Danville. Although civil rights forces did take the legal offensive at
times, improving morale and reducing intimidation, ultimately the
law, the courts, and their agents effectively stifled the movement's
aims. Thus in August 1963, a *New York Times* reporter wrote that
the "Danville method," one that followed the model of Albany, was
being studied by many Southern communities: "Officials of other
Virginia cities have traveled here to observe and learn in an unspoken compliment to a . . . strategy that is the most unyielding, in-
genious, and effective of any city in the South" (Franklin, 1963:71).

Selma, Alabama

Garrow (1978) has discussed the Selma campaign in
great detail, and thus only a brief summary is needed here. Before
1965, arrests by Selma police and state court injunctions had "greatly
hindered" (Miller, 1968:216) organizing efforts by SNCC in the city.
On 6 July 1964, for example, fifty blacks attempting to vote were arrested. Three days later, a local judge issued an injunction aimed at
civil rights activities that prohibited public gatherings of more than
three people; the injunction "halted" (Garrow, 1978:34) weekly mass
meetings that had been taking place.

Hoping for a violent white response, SCLC then decided to focus on
Selma to dramatize its call for congressional passage of voting rights

legislation, and it soon became clear that Selma law enforcement personnel had not learned the lessons of earlier protest campaigns (Garrow, 1978). As Laurie Pritchett later observed, "The people that were most responsible" for civil rights successes were Bull Connor and Jim Clark, sheriff of Selma. "Dr. King, when he left Albany, . . . was a defeated man. In my opinion, right or wrong, if Birmingham had reacted as Albany, Georgia did . . . they'd never got to Selma" (Pritchett, 1977:404).

In late January 1965, SCLC's campaign began. King and Abernathy led a march of 250 blacks and 15 whites to the Selma courthouse to protest the slow pace of registration of black voters. All 265 were arrested; most were released on bail, but King and Abernathy decided to stay in jail for five days. With King's arrest, national attention turned to the city. On 1 February, 550 more were arrested in a march, and by 5 February, 3,000 had been arrested.

The climactic events of Selma began Sunday, 7 March, when SCLC had scheduled a march from Selma to Montgomery. Governor George Wallace signed an order prohibiting the march and announced that state troopers with tear gas would try to stop the march if it took place. King decided to stay in Atlanta to help organize national support, expecting that the state troopers would avoid violence because of the presence of national press. As 525 people marched across a bridge on the way to Montgomery, they were ordered to turn back by a state trooper official. When they did not retreat, troopers used tear gas and beat the marchers with nightsticks as they tried to run away. Then Jim Clark ordered his police on horses to "'get those goddamn niggers—and get those goddamn white niggers'" (in Miller, 1968: 221); the horses plunged into the crowd. The police reaction was conveyed through the news media to the entire country, and several members of Congress came to Selma to investigate complaints by civil rights forces. As one SCLC member said, "'Jim Clark is another Bull Connor. We should put them on the staff'" (in Piven and Cloward, 1977:249).

In response to a call by King for sympathetic clergy and laity to come to Selma, hundreds began to arrive in the city on Monday 8 March. Meanwhile, a federal judge issued a temporary injunction against a march that King had announced for 9 March. With SNCC leaders charging that King had cowardly refused to take part in the

Sunday march and intending to take part themselves in the Tuesday one even if King did not, the SCLC leader decided to lead the latter demonstrations. The reservations King still had about violating federal court orders were allayed when a federal official induced Clark and the head of the state troopers to agree that the police would neither arrest nor use violence if the Tuesday marchers turned back when ordered; SCLC lawyers told King that if the marchers had turned back, no violation of the injunction would have occurred. Fifteen hundred, including 450 clergy, marched on Tuesday from Selma to Montgomery; they turned back, as had been arranged, when confronted by state troopers, although only leaders of the march had known this would happen. As a result, SNCC again criticized King and SCLC. The next day four members of the KKK beat to death a white minister.

The violence at Selma led to protests around the nation that demanded federal intervention in Alabama and passage of voting rights legislation (Garrow, 1978). Then, on 15 March, President Johnson announced on television that he would submit voting rights legislation to Congress. A few days later, 380 persons, most of them white ministers, were arrested in Selma for picketing and praying in front of the mayor's house. When the first 36 were booked and fingerprinted, they were released on their own recognizance; 21 of these refused to sign themselves out, but police refused in turn to jail them. Finally, on Sunday, 21 March, more than ten thousand people marched from Selma to Montgomery, after a federal judge had permitted the march to proceed. At the latter city they were joined by twenty-five thousand other protesters from many other states.

In Selma we again see the impact of the two models of official control that have been identified. The legalistic model of control used by officials in Albany and Danville had worked for Selma officials before SCLC began its campaign, when SNCC was trying to organize in the city. Legal means were also used in the early phases of the SCLC campaign. Eventually, however, the mode of control followed the Birmingham pattern of violence by law enforcement personnel. Coupled with the presence of Martin Luther King, the police overreaction in both cities helped lead to federal action. If the Selma police and Alabama state troopers had followed the legalistic model, they might very well have defeated SCLC's campaign.

How Powerful a Movement?

This analysis underscores the civil rights movement's weaknesses in the face of stubborn white resistance that resorted to legal repression and provides support for the resource mobilization argument in the debate discussed earlier. It is certainly true, as McAdam (1982) and Piven and Cloward (1977) emphasize, that protest may be very effective at times and was often effective in the South. There were many cities that did desegregate to some degree as a result of sit-ins and other demonstrations; the point is that the most intransigent cities were able to use legal means to defeat civil rights forces or could have successfully used legal means had not police and civilian brutality occurred. Yet in their treatment of the movement, Piven and Cloward (1977) gloss over the failure of the Albany movement when they stress its success in showing that blacks could be mobilized and do not discuss Danville at all. Though McAdam (1982) analyzes the failure in Albany, he also does not discuss Danville. Moreover, in emphasizing the role played by the white violence in Birmingham and Selma, all three analysts unwittingly undermine their own arguments on the disruptive potential of the civil rights movement. As Garrow (1978) has shown, Martin Luther King, Jr., and his aides realized after Albany that they needed the white violence, the Northern sympathy, and the federal intervention that sometimes resulted in order to win major victories. They realized, in other words, that disruption by civil rights forces was *not* enough, if white violence and ensuing Northern and federal "external" support did not also take place.

Yet, as Albany and Danville demonstrate, white violence was not inevitable, despite McAdam's (1982 : 174) assertion that "local white opposition could be counted on to provide the flagrant disruptions of public order that, when publicized, prompted federal intervention." And it is also true that, despite the "good" results of the white violence in Selma and Birmingham, such violence was not a sufficient condition elsewhere for civil rights success. In many Mississippi cities and other areas in the Deep South, white violence was common yet did not receive national press coverage and did not advance civil rights goals. In other areas, white violence did receive national media attention but did not prompt federal intervention. The 1964 SCLC campaign in St. Augustine, Florida, was one such example. Here white violence was so common that SCLC aid Andrew Young remarked, "'St. Augustine is really worse than Birmingham. It's the worst I've ever seen'" (in Goodwyn, 1965 : 78). The violence received national press attention (e.g., Bigart, 1964) but did not prompt federal intervention (Miller, 1968); SCLC's only victory in what has been called a virtual "second Albany" (Lewis, 1970 : 243) was the appointment of a biracial commission that accomplished nothing (Goodwyn, 1965).

Thus McAdam clearly overstates his case when he speaks of "the *typical* reactive patterns of [violent] white resistance and federal involvement" (1982 : 179; emphasis added) in the South. Instead, it may be more accurate to say that the examples of the Freedom Rides, Birmingham, and Selma upon which Piven and Cloward (1977) and McAdam (1981) base their arguments were in fact the exceptions in the South and not the rule.

Mississippi Summer Project, 1964

I would be remiss if I did not discuss the 1964 Mississippi Summer Project, where civil rights forces launched their most sophisticated legal attempt to defend arrested protesters and to file affirmative suits aimed at winning movement goals. As mentioned in chapter 2, COFO, a coalition of Mississippi groups dominated by SNCC, sought in the 1964 summer to register thousands of blacks to vote and to run "freedom schools" that would inform students of racism and political rights in addition to teaching them the basics of a good education. To aid in this effort, COFO imported some one thousand Northern white students not only for their skills but also for the attention they would win back home, in the press, and in Washington. The Mississippi Summer Project has often been recounted and analyzed (e.g., Belfrage, 1965; Forman, 1973; Raines, 1977; Welsh, n.d.); in this section I will thus briefly examine the project's creative use of the legal system to defend itself against white resistance.

Anticipating numerous arrests and other legal problems, and recognizing that only three black attorneys were in Mississippi, COFO requested the Northern attorneys spend time in the state that summer. Some of the rivalries and problems resulting from the request are discussed in chapter 2. During the Summer Project, the National Lawyers Guild sent down sixty-nine attorneys, twelve of whom were not members of the Guild, to the state; each stayed one or two weeks. Ninety other Guild members who remained in their home states assisted with briefs and other legal matters. The Guild's effort was coordinated by its Committee for Legal Assistance in the South (CLAS) office in Jackson. (CLAS was the new name for the earlier Committee to Assist Southern Lawyers [CASL].) According to the one report, the Guild attorneys "were generally acknowledged to be the most gutsy and the most creative in civil rights cases" (*Nation*, 1964). The Lawyers Constitutional Defense Committee (LCDC), which included the LDF and ACLU, sent down forty attorneys on a rotating basis and employed about twenty more in Memphis and New Orleans (Powledge, 1964). A law student organization, the Law Students Civil Rights Research Council (LSCRRC) sent down about fifteen students for two weeks or more each; they helped to prepare arrest data, collected affidavits, and lent other legal assistance. Both the guild and LCDC had bail funds, though each Northern student was told to have $500 ready for bail in case of arrest. More than one thousand COFO workers were arrested that summer, many on "harassing" charges and not for actual protests.

The legal strategy of COFO and its attorneys derived from their perception that the local and state courts in Mississippi were hostile to civil rights goals. The COFO legal guide for the project had cautioned the Northern student volunteers to "refuse to participate in any hearing without a lawyer" and to say nothing if the judge refused to allow them to obtain an attorney (Holt, 1966:272). At an orientation session for the volunteers, a COFO lawyer had recommended, " 'If you are riding somewhere and a cop stops you and starts to put you under arrest even though you haven't committed a crime—go on to jail. Mississippi is not the place to start conducting constitutional law classes for police'" (in Holt, 1966:49). Similarly, Northern attorneys heading to the state were told at a training session sponsored by LCDC, " 'You just can't win civil rights cases in the local and state courts in the South; your important job will be to help local counsel build a solid foundation for an eventual and successful appeal to the U.S. Supreme Court.'" They were also warned, " 'Please remember that you will be there strictly and solely as lawyers. Don't participate in any demonstrations. Don't go out of your way to be argumentative with the authorities; you will be there to get others out of jail, not get yourselves in'" (in Crowell, 1964:19).

Feeling they could not obtain just proceedings in the local and state courts, civil rights attorneys filed many civil suits and, drawing on the Danville experience, also removed virtually every arrest to the federal courts. The federal district judges in Mississippi ruled that out-of-state attorneys could neither file removal petitions nor initiate civil suits against segregation unless local attorneys were present in court. Since only three Mississippi attorneys were willing to handle civil rights cases, this requirement presented a serious obstacle to the COFO legal strategy. One federal judge also required that each removal petition apply to only one defendant and that each be accompanied by a $500 filing fee. During the summer, however, the Fifth Circuit Court ended all such requirements.

Though the many arrests of COFO did create the usual problems, the removal petitions and the civil suits helped keep these difficulties to a minimum. One of the Northern law students in the state claimed, "Our mere presence is a real deterrent. With the lawyers here, the chances of a person's being beaten are much less and the chances of getting a person released on his own recognizance instead of putting up a lot of bail are much better" (Welsh, n.d.:n.p.). Similarly, a Guild publication asserted that the filing of the removal petitions "'has had profound practical effects upon the civil rights struggle. It has slowed down the power structure in its attacks on the movement or forced new methods of attack outside the judicial system; it has boosted the morale of the movement and permitted civil rights workers to spend more time on constructive projects and less time in state jails and courtrooms'" (in Ginger, 1964:72a).

The Mississippi Summer Project registered relatively few blacks to vote, as white resistance and the intimidation of would-be voters proved too difficult to overcome. In other ways the project was successful, for it "had an effect impossible to calculate on young Negroes in the State" (Zinn, 1965:247). Thousands of Mississippi blacks wore SNCC buttons throughout the summer, and 200 attended more than thirty Freedom Schools. The project also led to the formation of the Mississippi Freedom Democratic Party, which selected its own delegates to the 1964 Democratic National Convention and tried, unsuccessfully, to have them seated in place of the official Mississippi delegation. Finally, the brutality and murder of civil rights workers by whites during the project increased Northern sympathy and intensified pressure on the federal government for new civil rights legislation.

The summer project represented the most extensive legal attempt by the civil rights movement to combat white intransigence during a protest campaign. But most of the Northern lawyers were gone by the end of the summer, and the Guild was forced to close down its CLAS office in Jackson in early 1965; LCDC continued its operations, though on a smaller scale.

The case studies and analysis in this chapter illustrate the many difficulties that legal procedure posed for civil rights forces. The nature of Southern resistance confronted the movement with a harsh dilemma. Its best hope lay in direct action, mass protests, and mass arrests. Though these tactics often succeeded, they did so at a terrible price, encumbering the movement with profound legal and other problems. And in some communities the tactics failed altogether, as white legal control stifled civil rights aims. The movement's successes were a result in large part of the excesses of white brutality and of its own conscious decision to be nonviolent. That this brutality was needed to overcome the problems the movement faced underlines the seriousness of the obstacles imposed by white legalism and other forms of social control.

Chapter Five

Criminal Prosecutions in the Vietnam Antiwar Movement

The American peace movement that protested the atomic bomb and civil defense drills in the 1950s and early 1960s did not try to turn the criminal courts into public forums that would attack nuclear weapons. Instead, pacifists arrested for such actions as refusing to find shelter during civil defense drills viewed their refusals as acts of moral witness and, consistent with this classical interpretation of civil disobedience, willingly accepted the legal penalty for conscientiously violating the law. Courtroom confrontations would have violated their pacifist belief in moral persuasion (Bannan and Bannan, 1974; Wittner, 1969).

As the Vietnam War escalated, the attitude of members of the peace movement toward protest and the courts changed dramatically. Many arrested antiwar protesters were reluctant to disassociate their criminal trials from the political origins of the prosecutions. The help that the civil rights movement had obtained from the Supreme Court and other federal courts in achieving its goals suggested that the Vietnam War could also be ended through legal intervention. Suits were filed in federal courts attacking the constitutionality of the war and the draft, while in criminal courts antiwar defendants and their lawyers tried to discuss the war in order to win acquittals, to convert jurors, to secure press publicity, and, more generally, to avoid proceedings that ignored the issues upon which they placed the greatest importance.

The appellate actions and criminal trials that resulted strained the legal system. The antiwar movement soon found that the courts were reluctant to deal with the war. It was far easier for the Supreme

Court and the federal appellate courts to rule against Southern segregation than to challenge the domestic and foreign policy of the executive and legislative branches of the government. In the criminal courts, judges usually invoked the neutral principles of trial procedure to limit or prevent discussion of the war that they held to be legally irrelevant.

Whereas the most important confrontations of the civil rights movement were held in the streets, some of the most significant battles of the antiwar movement took place in the courtroom. Thus the legal experience of the movement differed in several ways from that of the civil rights effort. For several reasons, the criminal courts during the Vietnam years presented far more opportunities for resource mobilization than was true in the South and fewer opportunities for social control by state officials. Yet the hope that the peace movement placed in the criminal courts made it that much more difficult to choose between a conventional or political defense. I shall examine the social, political, and legal context of the movement that affected the nature of its criminal proceedings, concentrating, as in chapter 3, on defense attorneys, judges, juries, and defendants. The strategic dilemmas that antiwar defendants and their attorneys encountered in the criminal courts will also be discussed.

Defense Attorneys

While the civil rights movement took place in the South, where legal proceedings were imbued with the racial hostility that characterized the region, the antiwar movement transcended geographical boundaries, leading to different legal responses and court experiences than those that typified the desegregation effort. Partly because the peace movement was more dispersed geographically, it did not suffer from the kind of siege mentality that gripped the civil rights movement. The type of ongoing, intensive protest campaign that led to mass arrests in the South did not generally take place during the antiwar movement; rather, protests that led to arrests were one-time or sporadic affairs. Thus the number of people arrested for civil disobedience or other reasons during the Vietnam War was usually not as great during a given period of time as that in the South, minimizing the legal costs and other problems that beset the civil rights effort. Partly because of this low density of arrests, the availability of defense attorneys during the war did not cause nearly the problem that it did in the South, and attorneys had more time to prepare their cases.

Moreover, many more lawyers were willing to defend antiwar clients than was true in the civil rights movement, and thus lawyers could be obtained even in the event of large numbers of arrests following mass demonstrations. The increased number of available attorneys during the Vietnam War can be attributed to at least two factors. First, lawyers were able to handle cases of antiwar clients with greater impunity than was true of their civil rights counterparts. Defense attorneys did face possible contempt charges or disbarment proceedings if they said too much in court about the war or other issues (Auerbach, 1976; Dorsen and Friedman, 1973; Lefcourt, 1971), but the threat of legal punishment was not nearly as great as it was for civil rights lawyers. Similarly, attorneys of antiwar clients did not have to fear losing their practice or being driven out of their communities, even at the height of the war's popularity. Many of their clients could also afford to pay them relatively large fees, which was not true in the South; some draft lawyers charged more than a thousand dollars for a case.

Second, by the Vietnam years an older generation of radical lawyers was ready to resume representation of political defendants, and a younger generation of radical attorneys was entering the field of law. In the McCarthy era, as mentioned in chapter 2, many lawyers were afraid to defend communists, and several who did take on their cases were disbarred or held in contempt. By the Vietnam War "McCarthyism" had abated, and defending an antiwar activist was less stigmatized than representing a communist had been.

These older attorneys were joined by younger ones who were in law school during the civil rights movement or the early years of the war. These younger attorneys were quite willing to defend antiwar clients, although most of their fellow law students continued to enter corporate and other kinds of legal practice. In several large cities radical law firms were formed (Douglas, 1971; James, 1973), with their members taking on many cases involving antiwar, black, and poor clients. Not surprisingly, the membership of the National Lawyers Guild, which had dwindled in the fifteen years after World War II, increased dramatically during the Vietnam war years (Auerbach, 1976).

Reflecting the growing number of radical attorneys, several books and articles in the period examined this new legal phenomenon (e.g., Black, 1971; Ginger, 1972; James, 1973; Lefcourt, 1971). These attorneys differed in their personal styles and political leanings, but, rejecting the traditional legal argument that courtroom actions affect only the individuals involved in the case, they generally believed that law and legal proceedings had consequences for groups and public policy outside the courtroom (Green, 1970). Thus the new public interest lawyers used the law and civil courts to advance the aims of consumer, environmental, and welfare groups (Handler, 1978; Riley, 1969; *Yale Law Journal*, 1970), while attorneys defending many stripes of clients in the criminal courts insisted that the trial courtroom was a proper place to discuss political matters they deemed relevant to the prosecution. They extended the concept of "political trial" to cover not only antiwar defendants but also black and other poor defendants arrested for so-called conventional actions that do not usually fall under the rubric of political protest (Burns, 1971; Burnstein, 1969; di Suvero, 1971). In criminal courts these attorneys thus were quite ready to argue political points vociferously on behalf of their clients. Their behavior was criticized by the ABA and other bar associations and was the subject of several law review articles and a New York bar commission investigation (Dorsen and Friedman, 1973; Lyman, 1973; Rockwell, 1970).

Defendants

If lawyers in antiwar protest trials tried to discuss the war, their clients often insisted even more vigorously that their antiwar beliefs deserved a hearing during their trials, and legal guides for the movement (e.g., Boudin et al., 1971) stressed the importance of trying to address the war and other issues in court. Some defendants sought to talk about their beliefs while on the witness stand; others, as chapter 6 will illustrate, acted as their own attorneys to increase their opportunities to talk about the war; and still others, though a small minority, disrupted the proceedings. In general their motives for such politicizing efforts were similar to those outlined in the theoretical discussion in chapter 2. Antiwar defendants felt conscientiously compelled to attempt to discuss the issues that led to their being in court; they wished to win jury sympathy by putting the war on trial; and they hoped that by discussing the war they would win favorable press coverage (cf., Bardacke, 1971; Boudin et al., 1971; *Law Commune*, 1971). Antiwar defendants were not the only ones in the late 1960s and early 1970s who sought to discuss legally extraneous issues or engaged in disruptive behavior; Black Panthers engaged in such tactics, as did other blacks and poor defendants (Dorsen and Friedman, 1973; Flaum and Thompson, 1970; *Georgetown Law Journal*, 1971).

In thus departing from the normal, passive role of conventional defendants, the behavior of antiwar protesters differed dramatically from that of civil rights activists. Although it is difficult to pinpoint the exact reasons for the different courtroom behavior of the two generations of defendants, several factors do seem relevant. First, in many ways antiwar protesters were more radical than their civil rights counterparts. They often did not accept the legitimacy of the federal government and federal courts, since the Vietnam War was a federal policy, and considered the war a symptom of a corrupt political and economic system (Lefcourt, 1971; Skolnick, 1969). Influenced by the reliance of the civil rights movement, in which many early antiwar activists had participated, on federal law, they thus thought the federal and state courts to be proper forums for the airing of their political grievances (Hayden, 1970).

Second, the antiwar movement placed much less stress than did the civil rights movement on nonviolence. Antiwar defendants therefore did not generally worry about the repercussions of politicization attempts, at least those short of outright disruption, for their public image. The country had changed somewhat during the first half of the 1960s, and attempts to discuss political and social issues in court that would have been severely criticized during the civil rights movement were more tolerated during the Vietnam period.

Third, antiwar defendants had less to fear legally and physically from politicization attempts than did civil rights workers. Although Vietnam protesters were unpopular, especially during the early years of the war, they did not suffer nearly the same hostility as that experienced by civil rights workers, black or white. As discussed in chapter 3, civil rights defendants who stepped out of line for such actions as violating the segregated seating plan of a courtroom were subject to legal and physical punishment. Antiwar defendants who tried to talk about the war generally did not have to fear contempt charges or other punishment, unless they persisted in their efforts, and even in these cases the threat was less than was true in the South. Defendants who actually disrupted the proceedings might be held in contempt but they did not have to worry about the murders and beatings at the hands of police and civilians that were a constant threat to civil rights workers. The racial factor cannot be ignored; as activists and as defendants civil rights workers were not just political protesters but also serious challengers to Southern segregation.

Thus several factors account for the desire of antiwar defendants to try to talk in court about the war and other issues. A later section in this chapter will explore the strategic dilemmas they experienced as a result of their efforts, and the following three chapters will examine the repercussions of their politicization attempts for the legal system and the antiwar movement.

Judges

State and federal judges in trials of antiwar defendants generally restricted or prohibited defense attempts to talk about the war, the draft, or other issues (Bannan and Bannan, 1974). Invoking various rules of trial procedure, especially the rules of evidence, judges repeatedly ruled that efforts by defendants and their lawyers to raise questions about the legality and morality of the war, draft, and American foreign policy were impermissible. Yet, as a whole, judges in antiwar cases were not nearly as hostile to the antiwar lawyers and clients before them and the cause they represented as they were toward civl rights workers. Relying on their legal discretion as referees to judicial proceedings, some sympathetic judges did give the defense latitude in discussing the war. The tension these judges felt between their role as arbiters and their views on the war is illustrated in the 1969 trial of the Milwaukee Twelve for burning draft files. As we shall see in chapter 7, the judge allowed the defendants a surprising amount of latitude in presenting critical arguments on the war and draft. After the defendants were found guilty, the judge wept softly as he sentenced one of them, a Benedictine monk, to jail. The judge in the Catonsville Nine trial, also a draft file burning case, indicated a similar conflict when he said at the end of the trial to the accused, "'You speak to me as a man and to me as a judge. To me as a man, I would be a very funny sort of man if I had not been moved by your sincerity on the stand and by your views. I have not attempted to cut off any of these reasons so that you can spread it to the people as a whole. I think many people will be inspired'" (in Bannan and Bannan, 1974 : 147). Other judges in antiwar cases allowed some discussion of the war and other issues to prevent greater courtroom disruption from occurring. Somewhat similarly, several observers of the Catonsville Nine case felt that the wide latitude the judge gave the defense was a result not only of his own views on the war but also of a desire to mollify the peace movement after the turmoil of the Chicago Democratic National Convention of the previous summer (Gray, 1970). Thus, partly because of the sheer numbers of defense politicization efforts, and partly because of the latitude judges sometimes gave, many defense teams did succeed in discussing political issues to at least some extent. The impact of the behavior and rulings of trial judges in Vietnam protest cases is explored in further detail in the next three chapters.

Juries

In chapter 2 I emphasized the influence of the jury on decisions by attorneys and their clients to conduct a conventional or political defense. One of the most important legal differences between the civil rights and antiwar movements lay in the attitudes of jurors toward the political defendants before them. As we have seen, jurors in civil rights trials simply promised no hope for acquittals, leading the civil rights movement to concentrate in its trials on preparing a proper record for appeal, and not on presenting racial and political arguments. Juries during the Vietnam War were not so hostile. Realizing that the American public was not of one mind on the war, many defense teams introduced political and moral issues to gain jury sympathy. Though most juries convicted, for reasons explored in chapter 8, some acquittals did result. Such verdicts were unlikely, but defense teams hoped to win over at least one juror, and this hope guided defense strategy. One antiwar lawyer said of the jury, "To the extent that it represents a cross-section of the community, it has on it people who are opposed to the war. . . . Secondly, I think the courtroom can be an educational forum. In trying a case to twelve jurors, you're educating them on . . . the attitude of these young people toward the draft, the reasons for their opposition to the war, and their hatred of war" (Brotsky, 1972 : 103–104). Thus, Vietnam protest juries paralleled those in the antebellum trials of abolitionists in the hope they promised political defendants, though the latter juries were more sympathetic.

During the Vietnam War, defense teams emphasized the *voir dire*, or questioning of prospective jurors, as a means of acquainting jurors with the defendants' political attitudes and of determining the jurors who would most likely respond favorably to defense efforts (Burnstein, 1969; Garry and Goldberg, 1977). In a few celebrated movement cases, social scientists helped develop profiles of ideal jurors that attorneys used when selecting people to serve on the jury (O'Rourke, 1972; Schulman, 1974). As chapter 8 will explore in some detail, debates took place inside and outside the courtroom over the issue of jury nullification, as opponents of the war argued that the jury should be informed of its historic power to acquit by nullifying facts and law relevant to the case that would otherwise dictate a conviction. Critics of nullification charged in return that it could lead to jury anarchy. In any event, judges typically refused to inform juries of their nullifying powers. But juries did sometimes acquit, most notably in most of the celebrated conspiracy cases of movement leaders.

Press Coverage of Antiwar Trials

Press coverage of the prosecutions that arose during the two movements illustrates the impact of the American press on whether political trials become vehicles for social control or occasions for effective dissent. In the antiwar movement, media coverage of prosecutions of movement leaders, and also of less well-known defendants, was often extensive and favorable to the defense. Many reporters sympathized with the aims of the movement and were critical of the attempts of the government to control it through the courts. Thus, defendants and their lawyers sought media publicity through moral and political arguments in courtrooms, and also sometimes through more disruptive tactics, as in the Chicago and Seattle conspiracy cases.

In this regard, the experience of the civil rights movement again stands in sharp contrast to that of its antiwar counterpart. As many observers have noted, the national press coverage of protests and police and civilian brutality in the South was crucial in securing Northern sympathy and in putting pressure on the president and Congress to pass legislation ending segregation. But coverage by the national press usually stopped at the courtroom door. The thousands of criminal proceedings that took place received little, if any, national publicity, though they succeeded in tying up the time, energy, and money of the movement. The local Southern press often ignored protests and trials altogether, or else depicted them unfavorably. Proceedings involving Martin Luther King did receive national publicity, but these were the exception. And even here, as seen in chapter 3, the defense emphasis was on a conventional defense designed to build a record for appeal. Thus the lack of any real prospect for favorable media publicity in most civil rights trials was yet another reason that civil rights defense teams shunned the kind of outright political defense that marked many more defense efforts in the antiwar movement and helped insure the success of the social control effort of the Southern court system.

The Dilemmas of Defense Strategy in Antiwar Trials

Ironically, the mobilization opportunities that the antiwar movement found in the criminal courts also led to difficulties in deciding on proper defense strategies. As discussed in chapter 2, conventional defenses may offer greater prospects for acquittal, depending on several circumstances, but they may also obscure the political issues surrounding the case. Conversely, political defenses may achieve publicity and satisfy the defendants' consciences, but they may also make convictions more likely. There were some antiwar trials where defense teams achieved acquittals with political defenses, but even here the amount of emphasis technical versus political arguments should receive remained a continuous problem. This section draws on several movement trials to examine the strategic dilemmas facing antiwar defense teams.

The strategic and tactical dilemmas facing antiwar defendants of all stripes were perhaps most critical in cases involving draft resisters. Before the Vietnam War, most draft resisters were Jehovah's Witnesses and other young men who had refused for religious reasons either to register for the draft or to be inducted into the army. When prosecuted, these men and their attorneys relied for the most part on First Amendment arguments concerning the freedom of religion. During the Vietnam War, however, the defense of most draft resisters changed dramatically. In place of First Amendment arguments their attorneys now sought acquittals on due process grounds, arguing that their clients had been served with induction orders by draft boards that had violated the many rules of procedure governing the issuance of such orders (Ginger, 1974). In developing such defenses, attorneys drew on the body of administrative law deriving from earlier deportation and Internal Revenue Service cases, which had held that federal administrative agencies are obligated to adhere to the rules guiding their operations.

During the Vietnam War, draft boards were notorious for violating their procedural guidelines; for example, they issued induction orders in the absence of a quorum of board members, ignored Selective Service regulations and Supreme Court guidelines in regard to conscientious objector applications, and illegally canceled the deferments of men who had protested the war and the draft. Because of such draft board errors, draft lawyers were able to convince prosecutors to dismiss charges in thousands of cases involving men who had refused induction orders (Baskir and Strauss, 1978). This process ferreted out the weakest cases from the prosecutor's standpoint, leaving the strongest ones to go on to trial. Acquittals still resulted in 30 percent of the cases that were tried, as defense attorneys usually used the procedural grounds discussed above (Baskir and Strauss, 1978; Howe, 1969). In many of these cases, the defense waived its right to jury trials, feeling that judges could best understand and decide the issues of administrative law that were in contention (Gutknecht et al., 1971; Tatum, 1972). Thus, "working alone or in small groups, one case at a time, lawyers developed an astonishing record of preventing the conviction of draft violators" as "Selective Service prosecutions became almost impossible" (Baskir and Strauss, 1978:68).

This particular legal strategy in Selective Service cases was the most promising if acquittal was the primary goal, but it obscured questions on the morality and legality of the war and the draft. For this reason, a number of draft resisters eschewed due process grounds in favor of arguments that hit more directly at the war and draft. They wanted to discuss their reasons for refusing induction and to try to convince juries to acquit out of sympathy with such reasons (Tatum, 1972; Useem, 1973). Although this approach was personally and politically satisfying to these defendants and their supporters, it was also far less likely to avoid convictions and, in some cases, led to more severe sentences. In San Francisco, for instance, federal judges typically sentenced draft offenders to two years probation but gave those raising political defenses jail terms (cf., Baskir and Strauss, 1978; Ferber and Lynd, 1971; Gutknecht et al., 1971; Tatum, 1972). The case of David Harris, a founder of the draft resistance movement, is perhaps the prototype. An eloquent defendant, he refused to let his attorney present technical arguments and instead testified about his reasons for opposing the war. Although a few jurors wept during his testimony, they nonetheless convicted, albeit after deliberating eight hours in an "open and shut" draft refusal case (Ferber and Lynd, 1971:215). In another case, a defendant fired his attorney, a well-known draft lawyer, who wanted to keep antiwar arguments to a minimum. Acting as his own attorney, the defendant rejected technical arguments and received a five-year prison term (Baskir and Strauss, 1978).

In the latter years of the war, judges in many parts of the country were more likely than previously to acquit draft resisters or to give them lighter sentences if convicted, reflecting the growing public distaste toward the war and their own annoyance at the procedural errors of draft boards (Baskir and Strauss, 1978; Hagan and Bernstein, 1979). The views of jurors in draft cases also changed. Before 1971, jurors convicted in such cases more often than did judges, perhaps because defendants requesting jury trials presented political defenses instead of technical arguments. But by the 1970s, "the growing public consensus against the war had reached the jury box" as well (Baskir and Strauss, 1978:82). In one draft resistance case, a juror who had voted to acquit said later that "'although we couldn't consider the war itself, we can't ignore it'" (in Baskir and Strauss, 1978:82).

Trials of Benjamin Spock (and others) and of
Daniel Ellsberg and Anthony Russo

In trials of antiwar civil disobedients who were not
draft resisters, decisions to disregard technical grounds were perhaps
not as difficult to make, since adequate grounds of this nature were
not as clearly present as in Selective Service cases. Thus where few
or no technical grounds were available, there was little hesitancy in
choosing a political defense. But in many trials during the movement the choice between a technical and a political defense often
proved critical. This was perhaps most vividly illustrated in the 1968
trial of Benjamin Spock and four other defendants for conspiracy to
aid and abet violations of the Selective Service law. As several observers have noted, the use of conspiracy charges in this and other
cases involving local and national antiwar leaders seemed designed
to expedite the government's aim of using the criminal courts as vehicles of legal harassment. The conspiracy charge has been called
"the prosecutor's darling" (Packer, 1970:176) because of the difficulties it creates for the defense (cf., Mitford, 1969; Packer, 1970). It
does not, for example, require evidence that a defendant actually did
anything illegal, but only that he or she intended to break the law.
Furthermore, the very definition of conspiracy, as a former Supreme
Court Justice Robert Jackson once wrote, "'is so vague that it almost
defies description'" (in Packer, 1970:170). In addition, each alleged
conspirator can be held responsible for statements and actions of his
or her co-defendants, even if she or he was not aware of their pro-
nouncements and behavior. Finally, the government can try a conspiracy case in any area where one or more of the overt acts alleged
in the conspiracy indictment were said to have occurred; thus it can
choose a location where the chances of conviction seem the greatest.

The difficulties that conspiracy charges thus present to defendants
and their lawyers have often led to their use in prosecutions of political activists. Clarence Darrow once observed of conspiracy, "'It is a
serious reflection on America that this worn-out piece of tyranny,
this dragnet for compassing the imprisonment and death of men
whom the ruling class does not like, should find a home in our country'" (in Mitford, 1969:61). Conspiracy charges were used in England
and the United States in the eighteenth and nineteenth centuries to
attack workers' attempts to form unions and increase wages; in the

United States in the twentieth century, conspiracy charges were again used against the labor movement, and after World War II they became central to prosecutions under the Smith Act.

Thus to many observers the use of conspiracy charges in the Spock case only accentuated the political motivation they saw at the base of the prosecution, especially since the charges raised serious questions regarding the defendants' rights to freedom of speech. One law professor wrote, "'It seems entirely possible that the government made a deliberate decision to increase the risks of ultimate reversal [by an appellate court, because of the free speech issue] in order to charge the kind of crime—a loosely knit, widespread and uncircumscribed conspiracy—that would have the greatest impact on discouraging organized opposition to the Vietnam War'" (in Mitford, 1969:5).

Owing to such speculation as well as to the celebrity of the Spock defendants, the press predicted a trial that would make history by challenging the morality and legality of the Vietnam War (Mitford, 1969). But after the judge in the case, Francis Ford, ruled in hearings on pretrial motions that evidence on these matters would not be permitted during the trial, the defendants' attorneys sought instead primarily to disprove the conspiracy charge. Their general aim was to depict the accused's ties as casual and their efforts as disorganized, and to prove that they did not actually counsel draft resistance. This strategy, however, made the defendants' antiwar efforts appear ineffective (Chomsky, Lauter, and Howe, 1970). It also avoided a dramatic confrontation and reduced the publicity the trial received (Elliff, 1971). As Mitford (1969:81) summed up the outcome, "Before and during the trial the exigencies of a conventional defense against their conspiracy charges often seemed on a direct collision with the needs of the antiwar movement." The defense strategy was indeed disappointing to the peace movement (Ferber and Lynd, 1971). As one antiwar leader maintained after the trial, "'It could have been a great trial. Instead it was pallid, dull, and carping. They should have admitted all the truthful facts proudly instead of trimming on the question of whom they sought to influence. They should have thunderously denounced the war and said it was their legal and moral obligation to urge all the kids to stay out'" (in Friedman, 1971:167). And Dr. Spock himself lamented, "'We sat like good little boys called into the principal's office. I'm afraid we didn't prove very much'" (in Lukas, 1970:11).

The politically disappointing outcome of the Spock case was a result largely of the behavior and desires of the defendants' attorneys. Each of the five defendants had retained his own lawyer or lawyers. Though involved in the same trial, the attorneys generally did not cooperate with each other. They did not consult about the testimony that each would have his client and his client's witnesses present; neither did they consult about the cross-examination of the prosecutor's witnesses. Although, as chapter 2 indicated, political defendants often find it advantageous to discuss their cases at public rallies and press conferences, attorneys for two of the Spock defendants thought the five men should say nothing about their case and about draft resistance. Similarly, when some of the defendants and their supporters wanted to form a defense committee that would raise funds, publicize the case, and organize demonstrations—again part of an overall political defense in some trials of protesters—only Spock's attorney, the most left-wing of all the counsel, approved the idea. Fearing that such a support committee would be evidence of a real conspiracy, the other attorneys opposed it (Mitford, 1969:82). As a third example, after the defendants were arraigned, four of them attended a church service where twenty-nine men handed in their draft cards. Again defense attorneys were opposed; as one of the defendants said later, "'But some of the lawyers objected to this sort of thing—the lawyers had a terrible effect on us. They began to separate us. The five of us never even saw each other until the pretrial hearings, when we just met in the courtroom. The lawyers prevented us from taking our case to the people, into the streets, holding demonstrations and picket lines, or from any sort of public collaboration with the Resist groups'" (in Mitford, 1969:82). Finally, one attorney in his closing argument to the jury carried the defense's conventional strategy to an extreme when he said, "'His Honor will tell you that [the war] is not what is being tried here. We are not trying the war. We are not even trying the constitutionality of the draft act'" (in Mitford, 1969:179). During this attorney's summation, groans were heard from the members of the resistance in the courtroom.

The Pentagon Papers trial of Daniel Ellsberg and Anthony Russo also advanced the antiwar movement's mobilization goals less than the movement had hoped, even though the judge dismissed the charges when he found that the government had broken into the office of Ellsberg's psychiatrist. Originally the defense had intended to turn the trial into a forum on the Vietnam War (Roberts, 1971). Yet Ellsberg's attorneys eventually decided to concentrate instead on narrow grounds relating to the charges. In one instance the defense sought to refute one of the charges by attempting to prove that the disclosure of the papers did not harm the national security. This argument, however, obscured the historic importance of the papers and diminished their education value. The resulting tediousness of the proceedings also made for a boring trial (*Newsweek*, 1973; Unger, 1973). The news media responded appropriately. "Disenchanted with the blandness and slow pace of the trial, the press had become increasingly perfunctory in its attention to Ellsberg" (Farrell, 1973 : 800).

Trials of the Oakland Seven and Chicago Eight

The Oakland Seven trial presents an illuminating contrast to the previous two. The defendants had been charged with conspiracy to commit misdemeanors at the Oakland induction center during "stop the draft week" in October 1967. During the planning of the protests, a split developed between two groups, one committed to a passive act of civil disobedience involving the blocking of the induction center's doors, and the other advocating the more active tactic of closing down the center. Seven members of the latter group were indicted and finally tried in early 1969. Despite the seriousness of the charges and the use of a conspiracy indictment, the defense team decided on a political defense that succeeded in discussing the war and the draft at length during the proceedings, and also won an acquittal (Bannan and Bannan, 1974; Bardacke, 1971; Garry and Goldberg, 1977; Langer, 1969; Rothschild, 1970). The defense team's effort was aided by the judge, who allowed a good deal of defense testimony about the war and draft, and then charged the jury that it could consider the defendants' motives in reaching its verdict. Although the defense denied any agreement to commit the misdemeanors alleged in the conspiracy indictment, its primary strategy aimed at informing the jury of the police brutality that led to violence at the induction center and of the accuseds' belief that their protests were justifed under the First Amendment and the Nuremberg Principles.

The final case to be considered is that of the Chicago Eight for conspiracy to cross state lines to incite a riot at the 1968 Democratic National Convention. This case has been examined in detail elsewhere (Danelski, 1971; Epstein, 1970; Lukas, 1970; Sternberg, 1972). As is well known, the defendants and their attorneys in this case engaged in many kinds of disruptive tactics. A few times they refused to stand up when the judge entered and left the courtroom; they served a birthday cake to a defendant marking his birthday; more seriously, they also attempted to read in court the names of American soldiers who had died in Vietnam (Dorsen and Friedman, 1973).

The defendants and their attorneys had several motives for their behavior. Determined at the outset to avoid in their own trial the politically disappointing outcome of the Spock case (Lukas, 1970), they decided to launch a continuous effort to indicate to the jury, the press, and the public the political circumstances surrounding the case. Yet it is also clear, as Dorsen and Friedman (1973) have pointed out, that many of their outbursts were instigated by the behavior of Judge Julius Hoffman, who conducted the trial in a prejudicial manner and argued constantly with attorneys and defendants.

The defense did succeed in keeping "the press interested with lots of flamboyant behavior" (Lukas, 1970:33), and, as one law professor observed, "no other strategy would have attracted the worldwide attention the case received" (Friedman, 1970:169). Yet these same defense tactics also increased the likelihood of the convictions that the jurors rendered, as the defense team earned the enmity of the jury by its behavior. One juror said afterwards that "'the defendants should be convicted because of their appearance, their language, and their life style'" (in Danelski, 1971:175). The jury foreman asserted,

> "I was a streetcar conductor. I've seen guys, real bums with no soul, just a body—but when they went in front of a judge, they had their hats off. These defendants wouldn't even stand up when the judge walked in. When there's no respect, we might as well give up the United States." (in Danelski, 1971:176)

Still a third juror said that the defendants

> "needed a good bath and to have their hair cut. . . . They had no respect for nobody, not even the marshals. When they told

them to get their feet off their chairs, they just put them right back up again. I don't think that's nice." (in Danelski, 1971:176)

Vietnam Protest Trials: Mobilization or Control?

The antiwar movement hoped that it could achieve its many goals of resource mobilization in the criminal courts. Though conviction was the most likely outcome in non-Selective Service cases, some acquittals and hung juries did result. Moreover, antiwar trials, including many not discussed here, also secured favorable national and local press coverage. Although it is difficult to assess precisely the consequences of the movement's attempts to use the criminal courts as public forums, it is safe to say that such efforts "did help to arouse the conscience of the nation" (Bannan and Bannan, 1974:212), and to galvanize the movement. Thousands marched in cities across the nation after the Chicago defendants were convicted; several thousand demonstrated in Harrisburg, Pennsylvania, when Philip Berrigan and six others were tried for conspiracy to kidnap Henry Kissinger and to blow up heating ducts in Washington, D.C.; several thousand demonstrated at the trial of the Catonsville Nine, to be discussed in chapter 7. Thus, although the criminal trials of antiwar activists did cost much time, energy, and money and often caused protesters much frustration, they did help advance the movement's aims. Contrary to the experience in the South, state officials could not be certain of the outcome of criminal prosecutions, and the antiwar movement did not experience the multitude of legal difficulties that hampered the civil rights efforts.

In Selma and other Southern communities, police sometimes declined to arrest demonstrators in order to limit the publicity they received. It is thus interesting to speculate whether the threat of attempts during the antiwar movement to discuss the war and other issues in the criminal courts prompted state and federal prosecutors to refrain from lodging criminal charges and sending a case to trial. If so, then the movement's defense strategy succeeded in these instances in preventing trials from even taking place. This strategy succeeded in the August 1972 trial in Hartford, Connecticut, of a group of defendants, including the author, who were charged with blocking the doors to the city's federal building in an antiwar protest. As will be discussed in the next chapter, the jury could not reach a verdict, and a mistrial was declared. The federal prosecutor decided not to retry the case, for reasons he explained in a document I obtained under the Freedom of Information Act:

> As much as it is disturbing to allow these four defendants to escape from the sentence that was imposed upon the other six defendants in the case, I feel that this is the only course at this time. To re-try would be costly and would occur just as school resumes, bringing on more demonstrations. The defendants remain ready to go to a new trial and have new courtroom disruptions planned.
>
> Also, a reading of the trial transcript indicates that at least two of these defendants told the jury that he had clearly broken the law and had blocked the doors. Apparently some members of the jury did not care to listen to the judge's charge. There is indication that any future jury will be more accommodating [to the defense]. Under the circumstances a dismissal appears to be the only answer. One only hopes that justice will be served by such a result. (Cohn, 1972)

Chapter Six

Pro Se Defense in Vietnam Protest Trials

During the civil rights movement, defendants who appeared in criminal courts without attorneys did not do so willingly. Rather, they defended themselves—acted *pro se*—simply because they had not been able to obtain the services of a lawyer (*Southern Patriot*, 1961). As discussed in chapter 3, few Southern lawyers were willing to defend civil rights clients; those that were willing found themselves extremely overworked, often having to travel from one community to another on the same day to handle different cases. Because of these factors, some civil rights defendants had to go without lawyers at arraignments and at trials, which usually occurred within a few days after arrest. Their decision to proceed *pro se* was not a political act; instead it was one born out of the shortage of civil rights attorneys.

In the Vietnam War years, a number of antiwar defendants also proceeded *pro se*, but for much different reasons.* These defendants

---

* The United States Supreme Court ruled in *Faretta v. California*, 422 US 806 (1975), that a defendant in a criminal trial has a constitutional right to refuse the services of an attorney and to act *pro se*. Before this decision, federal statute and over thirty state constitutions had given defendants this same right. But because the Supreme Court had not yet grounded the right in the Constitution, state and federal judges had severely restricted it in practice, refusing to allow self-representation when, in the judge's opinion, the defendant was neither intelligent nor competent enough to act as his or her own attorney, when the charges were too serious, or when an unnecessary delay of trial proceedings would result (Brick, 1971; Grano, 1970; *Journal of Criminal Law, Criminology, and Police Science*, 1973). Presently judges must permit self-representation as long as they are convinced that the defendant is intelligently and voluntarily deciding to act as his or her own counsel. Although the number of defen-

purposely turned down the services of competent attorneys so that, among other things, they could feel more involved in the proceedings and speak more directly to the jury about their views on the war, the draft, and other matters. Despite the old adage that someone acting as his or her own attorney has a fool for a client, these *pro se* defendants felt that agreeing to counsel would stifle the goals they had as antiwar protesters. Their trials placed unusual strain on a legal system accustomed to passive defendants represented by attorneys familiar with legal procedure. As one legal scholar put it, "Trying a case in criminal court with an unrepresented defendant is often like riding a tiger which one dares not to dismount, and many a trial judge supplements his crier's opening prayer with a muttered supplication of his own, '. . . and, please, God, let there be no unrepresented defendants in court today'" (Laub, 1964 : 245–246).

Reasons for *Pro Se* Defense

Whether political defendants choose a conventional or political defense, it is often to their advantage to obtain counsel. Attorneys, of course, possess legal knowledge and skills that can be invaluable for political and nonpolitical defendants alike. In political trials defense attorneys may make effective legal and political points through adept questioning of witnesses and in opening and closing statements to the jury, even if the judge restricts their freedom to do so. They are especially helpful in selecting jurors, in filing motions before and during the trial, and in requesting the judge include certain instructions in his charge to the jury (cf. Burnstein, 1969; Garry, 1971; Hakman, 1972). For political and other defendants facing serious charges, representation by counsel is crucial, as the Supreme Court recognized in extending the right to counsel to indigent defendants in the 1963 *Gideon* case.

Two Vietnam protest cases underline the help that attorneys may give political defendants. The accused in the Spock draft conspiracy case wanted to build a record for appeal and therefore decided not to act as their own counsel: "The chances are not good that a layman

---

dants representing themselves is still very small, there is evidence that it increased greatly after the Supreme Court decision in June 1975 (*New York Times*, 1975).

. . . could sufficiently master the ins and outs of legal procedures, particularly in the swampland of conspiracy, to build an adequate record for appeal" (Mitford, 1969:75). Similarly, David Miller, who burned his draft card in 1965, had first intended to proceed *pro se* since he had wanted "'only to bring up moral issues in my defense'" (in Bannan and Bannan, 1974:45). Deciding later, however, that by the process of judicial review he might overturn the law prohibiting the destruction of draft cards, Miller accepted the services of American Civil Liberties Union lawyers who could present the required legal arguments in court (Bannan and Bannan, 1974). The legal help that a lawyer may often give prompted a few Vietnam opponents to suggest that self-representation be employed only where the charges were minor (Boudin et al., 1971; di Suvero, 1971).

When defendants wish a political defense, however, the presence of an attorney may serve as a depoliticizing influence. As officers of the court, lawyers are expected to know and comply with institutional routines of the courtroom. As a result, the training, skills, and expertise that legitimate their position within the judicial system pressure them to conform to institutionally defined ways of conducting a defense. As we shall see, the attorney's power to deviate from this procedure is thereby more limited than that of a *pro se* defendant. One law professor, Richard Wasserstrom, says of the attorney's role, "There are all sorts of explicit and implicit constraints upon his thought and action. As a *lawyer*, there are some things he simply cannot do—without ceasing to play the role of a lawyer. The range of restrictions this basic fact imposes should never be underestimated. . . . The lawyer's entire cast of mind is one that seeks an acquittal, leading to a penchant for compromise, accord and accommodation" (1971:80; emphasis in original). Moreover, while a skillful radical lawyer, as we have seen, is often instrumental to a political defense, the threat of disbarment remains a potent, if subtle, restraint on his or her behavior (Axelrod, 1971:72).

Thus some political defendants acting *pro se* have felt that representation by even a radical attorney would confine them too strictly to legal procedure. As a 1971 manual for draft nonregistrants observed, "For a resister who wishes to make ethical and political, rather than factual and legal arguments, defending oneself may sometimes be the best course" (Gutknecht et al., 1971:47). Similarly, two *pro se* defendants in the 1973 White House Seven trial for breaking from a line of tourists and praying for peace on the White House lawn asserted, "We could not bring ourselves to be represented by counsel, feeling that to do so would be participating in a kind of cat-and-mouse game with the government. We felt that rather than seeking to support our legal innocence in court, it was our simple duty to speak the truth of how we were led to that place" (Martin, 1974: 489). And many decades earlier, anarchist Alexander Berkman, on trial in 1892 for attempting to assassinate the head of the Carnegie steel company, declined a legal defense and representation by counsel on the grounds that as an anarchist he did not believe in "man-made law." In a statement in court he said, "Secondly, an extraordinary phenomenon like an *Attentat* [political assassination] cannot be measured by the narrow standards of legality. It requires a view of the social background to be adequately understood. A lawyer would try to defend, or palliate, my act from the standpoint of the law. Yet the real question at issue is not a defense of myself, but rather the *explanation* of the deed. It is mistaken to believe *me* on trial" (Berkman, 1912:91; emphasis in original).

Other political defendants have represented themselves in the belief that they will be more able than even a radical attorney to understand and explain their beliefs and the political circumstances of the case to the jury, and therefore to conduct parts of the trial themselves. As Angela Davis argued in her behalf several years ago at her trial for allegedly helping to initiate a California courtroom shoot-out, "'I alone, I feel, can competently challenge witnesses and evidence pertaining to my political beliefs and actions, because no one is as intimately acquainted with my politics as I am'" (in Brick, 1971:1481).

Sometimes political defendants decide to proceed *pro se* out of outrage over government or judicial machinations. In Susan B. Anthony's 1873 trial for voting the previous November in violation of federal law, the prosecution read into the record a transcript of her testimony at a preliminary hearing instead of putting her on the witness stand; it wished to prevent Anthony from using the trial as a forum to espouse the right of women to vote. Anthony then tried to fire her lawyer and to act *pro se* in order to speak directly to the jury, but the judge did not allow her to do so (Friedman, 1971). In the 1971 Harrisburg Seven case, Father Philip Berrigan endeavored to fire his lawyers when the judge would not allow him to make an opening statement to the jury; again the judge refused (O'Rourke, 1972). The Milwaukee Twelve defendants, on trial for burning draft records, succeeded in dismissing their team of attorneys, including William Kunstler, when they were distressed by a state judge's legal maneuvering in pretrial stages (Gray, 1970). Similarly, when anarchists Berkman and Emma Goldman were denied a continuance in their 1917 trial for conspiracy to counsel draft evasion, they declared they would have nothing to do with the trial; when the judge said he would appoint an attorney to defend them anyway, they decided to act as their own counsel (Drinnon, 1961).

Another reason for self-representation derives from a defendant's mistrust of attorneys. Bobby Seale in the Chicago Eight trial declared himself his own attorney when the judge would not continue his case until Black Panther party lawyer Charles Garry recovered from an operation; Seale trusted no other attorney (Epstein, 1970). At the start of the Angela Davis trial, co-defendant Ruchell Magee sought to defend himself out of a similar lack of confidence in attorneys, charging that " 'every California lawyer that I have had has convicted me through fraud'" (in Brick, 1971:1500).

Still other *pro se* defendants have hoped to cut through the mystique of professionalism they see pervading the courtroom (cf. Schneir, 1971) and to avoid feeling removed from the proceedings. One writer's description of Daniel Ellsberg's reaction to his silent role at his trial indicates the alienation that political defendants wish to escape by defending themselves. The trial left Ellsberg "afflicted with the feeling of being invisible, insubstantial, 'as though my ectoplasm had faded'" (Farrell, 1973:88).

Self-Representation and Politicization

We have examined why self-represented political defendants may not prefer the services of a good, radical attorney—assuming one could be found—who would refuse to conform to the routine of the courtroom. Although, as we have seen, radical attorneys can be of enormous help in bringing political and moral issues to the forefront, *pro se* defendants' expectations regarding their own prowess at politicization do have some basis in actual courtroom practice. As their own attorneys, defendants have the right to give opening and closing statements to the jury, and to question witnesses as well. In all these matters judges may feel constrained to allow the accused latitude in what they say, precisely because the *pro se* is considered ignorant of traditional rules of evidence and proper courtroom procedure. As a result, the *pro se* defendant's very ineptitude can enable him or her to inject political or moral issues into the proceedings. As trial standards of the American Bar Association maintain, "'A layman representing himself cannot be held to the same standards of decorum or competence expected of a member of the bar'" (in Dorsen and Friedman, 1973:125).

The success with which self-represented defendants may introduce legally extraneous issues is apparent in an exchange from the Milwaukee Twelve trial, when one of the defendants was cross-examining a Selective Service official:

> ROBERT GRAF: Just a very simple question. Would you consider the value of property to be more important than the value of human life?
>
> MR. SAMSON [the prosecutor]: If it pleases the Court, I object to the question on the grounds that it is not material and it's not relevant and it's inflammatory.
>
> THE COURT: And it is inflammatory.
>
> MR. SAMSON: No question about it being inflammatory.
>
> MR. GRAF: I'm inflamed about the deaths.
>
> THE COURT: I just advise you, you must not ask a question that is intended to inflame the jury on an issue that is entirely apart from the subject matter the witness is testifying to.
>
> MR. GRAF: I think that's a point of view. To me the lives of my brothers in Vietnam is [sic] not apart from the Selective Service System.
>
> THE COURT: None of us like to see this happen. It is most sad and unfortunate. . . . But this is not the issue before the Court.
>
> MR. GRAF: It's my issue, and that's why I'm here in court. Those lives are my issue. (in Gray, 1970:138)

The relative patience a judge may have with the tactics available to "legally ignorant" *pro se* defendants is vividly illustrated in the following exchange from a 1972 trial, mentioned in the last chapter, where I was one of five co-defendants arrested in a protest at the

Hartford, Connecticut, federal building. I was on the witness stand, and a fellow co-defendant, David Batchelder, was questioning me,

MR. BATCHELDER: Are you familiar with this leaflet?

MR. BARKAN: May I look at it?

MR. BATCHELDER: May he?

THE COURT: Just ask him a question that might have some bearing on whether this comes in as an exhibit.

MR. BATCHELDER: Does this leaflet, which was passed out on May 16 at the time of the demonstration, reflect your views as to why you were at the Federal Building?

MR. BARKAN: Yes, very much so.

MR. BATCHELDER: May it be offered [as an exhibit]?

THE COURT: No, still excluded. He's not on trial for his views.

MR. BATCHELDER: It shows part of his intent, I believe, and he just said he went along with it.

THE COURT: What else do you have?

MR. BATCHELDER: May I show him this?

THE COURT: Are these pieces of paper that have to do with the war?

MR. BATCHELDER: Yes.

THE COURT: We already have enough of that.

MR. BATCHELDER: These are brand new.

THE COURT: We don't need any more.

MR. BATCHELDER: May I present it to him?

THE COURT: No.

MR. BATCHELDER: May I offer them as an exhibit?

THE COURT: No. The record is already replete on that.

MR. BATCHELDER: You're saying that these cannot be offered at all?

THE COURT: That's correct. Things have to come to an end. . . .

MR. BATCHELDER: I think the defendant has—

THE COURT: And I don't want any argument on it, Mr. Batchelder. Do you have anything else to ask of this witness by way of cross-examination?

MR. BATCHELDER: I did want to ask him if knowledge of these anti-personnel—

THE COURT: No, not about these pieces of paper because they have been excluded, so don't ask him about it.

MR. BATCHELDER: Okay, I'll put them down here so no one can see them. Does your knowledge of anti-personnel weapons and what they can do to people, did they have any—

THE COURT: Mr. Batchelder, this is the same line of questioning. I think you understand my ruling. We are not going to take further time on it. (*United States of America v. Steven E. Barkan et al.*, transcript of testimony of Steven E. Barkan, 1972:11–13)

These exchanges demonstrate the potential of the *pro se* political defense. In each case, the defendant was able to express his views on the war, even as the judge repeatedly advised him on proper rules of evidence and courtroom procedure. The *pro se* defendant violates formal rules of procedure as much by ignorance as by typical lawyerly cunning. Because such a defendant does lack knowledge of legal matters, the judge tries to be patient, allowing the accused to speak or act with considerable impunity in a judicially improper manner about political and moral issues. Here, then, we see a "social function of ignorance" not included in those treated by Moore and Tumin (1949). The "scenes" (Goffman, 1959) created by self-representation suggest that the normal rules of evidence and procedure, the courtroom emphasis on expeditious procedure, and the normal roles of defendant, attorney, and judge do not obtain when defendants represent themselves.

The two exchanges also suggest indirectly the depoliticizing consequences of allowing oneself to be represented by counsel. For were a lawyer to have followed such unacceptable lines of questioning, to have argued at length with the judge, or to have proceeded impetuously, it is fair to say that the judge would have rebuked and halted the attorney immediately.

Self-Representation and Jury Sympathy

Political defendants who engage in disrespectful ceremonial disruptions of courtroom etiquette and routine may be viewed by judge, prosecutor, jury, and public as the type of villain Klapp

(1954:60) calls the "mores-flouter, who seems to take a perverse pleasure in outraging decency and rebelling against order and authority." The jurors in the Chicago Eight trial were upset, as we have seen, that the defendants did not act with respect for the court; lawyers who overreach the restrictions of their status may meet with similar disapproval.

In contrast to the disapprobation that greets defendants and lawyers whose disruptive behavior is seen as mocking the dignity of the courtroom, *pro se* political defendants may disrupt and politicize the proceedings in a unique but respectful fashion that earns not the enmity but the tolerance and indulgence of judge, prosecutor, jury, and public. These parties expect such lay attorneys to act ineptly and thus do not take umbrage when their expectations are borne out.

Just as the judge may allow the *pro se* defendant considerable latitude, so may the prosecutor. To avoid arousing jury sympathy for a hapless *pro se* defendant, the prosecutor will often pursue his case with less energy than usual, as a survey of Illinois trial judges indicated (*Journal of Criminal Law, Criminology, and Police Science,* 1973:249). A prosecutor who objects to a *pro se* defendant's questions to a witness may appear symbolically to be a villain "exercising a blatant abuse of power" (Gray, 1970:146). As a district attorney in the Milwaukee Twelve *pro se* trial complained, "'I'm constantly having to argue admissibility of evidence in front of the jury, which makes me look as if I'm holding back all kinds of evidence which the jury is entitled to hear'" (in Gray, 1970:146). Similarly, the prosecutor in my own trial told me that he objected less often than he might have to our questioning of witnesses to avoid appearing as if he were, as he put it, "picking on" the defendants.

Self-representation may serve conversely to "de-villainize" the political defendant in the eyes of the jury and help win jury sympathy. To a much greater extent than is possible in a trial where the defendant sits passively at his or her lawyer's side, self-representation personalizes the proceedings by enabling defendants to present themselves directly to the jury as human beings with feelings, concerns, and even frailties. As a result, the defendant may convey to the jury "an impression of himself as a basically good person or as a blundering individual fighting along against the power of the state" (Brick, 1971:1404–1405): a David to the state's Goliath (O'Rourke, 1972:89).

In 1918 a lawyer for socialist leader Eugene V. Debs recommended that his client look like a man of decency; he urged that Debs's wife be present in court "so that the jurors would regard Debs as a normal citizen rather than as a monster" (Ginger, 1949:382). Angela Davis faced a similar danger many years later. Before her trial began, the jurors were afraid of her (Major, 1973). She was a communist; she was black, she represented unknown forces of evil. As the trial proceeded, however, "much of the feeling of dread was abated as the panel had an opportunity to see Angela Davis in action. . . . They were impressed by her opening statement, but more important, they observed her day after day, taking notes, conferring with her attorneys, and acting like any other defendant concerned with the problem of confronting a number of serious charges" (Major, 1973:300–301). Paradoxically, by deviating from the role of the normally passive defendant, Davis allowed the jury to see her for all intents and purposes as nothing more than a "regular" defendant.

Had Davis remained seated quietly at the defense table, the jurors' previous negative impression of her would have remained largely intact. She would have had little chance to demonstrate directly to the jury those favorable but subtle, intangible elements of personality that figure in many juries' deliberations (cf. Kalven and Zeisel, 1966). In the normal criminal trial, defense attorneys may emphasize their clients' "upright" character, but the most persuasive evidence of this can come only from the defendants themselves. Yet in the usual political or conventional trial, the only time the jury may be allowed to see the defendant "in action" (unless the defendant disrupts the proceedings and antagonizes the jury) is at the defense table, where woefully little defendant action takes place, or on the witness stand, where the defendant still has relatively little opportunity to demonstrate to the jury and public the many aspects of his or her character and beliefs: "The witness is not typically permitted to tell his story in his own way; he answers questions put to him, and if in the course of his answer to a question, he offers matter which is not strictly responsive to the question, or indulges in the expression of his opinion . . . he opens himself to a possible rebuke by counsel or perhaps an admonition by the Court" (Mayers, 1964:105).

Depending on the circumstances of the case, moreover, many defendants, political or conventional, may decide not to take the witness stand to avoid the rigors of cross-examination. The ability to avoid this risk while still testifying indirectly via opening and closing statements to the jury and the questioning of witnesses provides a tactical advantage of considerable proportion to *pro se* defendants—one reason that one of the defendants in the 1949 Smith Act case may have decided to act as his own attorney (Porter, 1949).

A word about the potential of a *pro se* political defendant's emotional appeal is in order. As many defendants will attest, trials can be intensely emotional experiences. But in a conventional trial the accused's emotions are not allowed full rein since the defendants are largely withdrawn from the proceedings. Only on the witness stand, if they take it, do the defendants become caught up in the minute-by-minute courtroom drama; only there, if at all, do they feel the full emotional weight of the trial, not to be equaled or surpassed until the verdict is announced.

But in a courtroom where political defendants are acting as their own attorneys, the trial is throughout a conscious reality for the accused, since they have become involved at every turn in helping to shape the outcome. Their involvement is, moreover, greater than that of political defendants who may help plan defense strategy but do not proceed *pro se*. Not only does the fate of self-represented defendants depend precisely on what they, and not their lawyers do; they also consider their politics and those of the state to be on trial. Throughout the proceedings, this combination can have quite an emotional impact on *pro se* defendants. They may respond in anger, as Robert Graf did in the Milwaukee Twelve case, demonstrating the intensity of their political and moral convictions while simultaneously making a political or moral point. Or they may respond by weeping at a particularly heartrending moment in the trial; if a lawyer's heartfelt or pretended tears can move a jury toward acquittal, then a defendant's own tears should be even more persuasive.

When I ended my summation to the jury in my own trial, I wept openly, as did several spectators. A few jurors stared at me as I then sat down at the defense table with my head in my arms. The public defender who had been advising the defendants and questioning some witnesses had planned to give a summation along legal and technical lines; instead, he passed a note to me saying, "Steven, I will not sum up. Anything I could say would be anti-climactic." Although the defendants had readily admitted blocking the doors to the federal building and had offered no legal defense, the jury deliberated some six hours and could not agree on a verdict. A few weeks later, as mentioned in the last chapter, the prosecutor dismissed the charges.

Other Tactical Advantages of the *Pro Se* Defense

Several other tactical advantages may derive from the latitude enjoyed by *pro se* defendants. When they are especially articulate, they will often be better able than an attorney to expound the political or moral considerations that led to their prosecution. Angela Davis is an example of one such defendant. At one point in the Milwaukee Twelve trial, moreover, Father Anthony Mullaney, a Benedictine monk with a Ph.D. in clinical psychology, set forth a scholarly, yet impassioned, three-hour account of his state of mind at the time he was helping to destroy the draft files. His testimony "was delivered in a luminous, booming voice into a suddenly still courtroom" (Gray, 1970:149–150).

The presence of a *pro se* defendant may also serve to turn the proceedings into extraordinary drama, especially when well-known defendants are on trial, increasing media publicity and capturing public attention. Mitford (1969:75) hypothesized about the spectacle of Benjamin Spock as a lay attorney: "The dramatic effect could have been dazzling: Spock in the dock quizzing the prosecution witnesses in his firm and fatherly way." When Eugene Debs, who was not defending himself, was nonetheless allowed to address the jury, "at once the atmosphere became concentrated in the courtroom. The badly diluted drama of the previous two days abruptly changed. A dull and ponderous proceeding acquired a tension that was immediately felt. An expectant air permeated the spectators, the prosecutor, and the judge" (Ginger, 1949:390). Finally, in the trial of the Gainesville Eight, a group of Vietnam veterans who had been accused of conspiring to disrupt the 1972 Republican National Convention, *pro se* defendant Scott Camil was questioning a prosecution witness who had once been a member of Vietnam Veterans against the War and Camil's best friend but turned out to be an FBI agent. As Camil asked him, " 'Would you say we were good friends?' ", the *New York Times* reported, "there was absolute silence in the courtroom" (in Kifner, 1973:11).

Still another tactical advantage of self-representation is that it may enable political defendants to make the best possible use of the energy and initiative they may bring into the fray. Of the *pro se* defendants in the 1973 Camden Twenty-eight draft file burning trial, political scientist Howard Zinn (1973:5) wrote, "They worked harder to prepare their case than even the most dedicated movement lawyers. In the courtroom they were a force, outnumbering, out-thinking, out-maneuvering the prosecution." Similarly, the judge in the Milwaukee Twelve trial said, "'Let the record show that while these defendants are in court without counsel, time and time again they have cited law which is very relevant, law which requires a learned legal mind to ferret out'" (in Gray, 1970:147). By the same token, however, self-representation also requires defendants to spend considerable time and energy preparing their defense, making it diffi-cult for them to lead their normal lives or to engage in demonstra-tions or other actions designed to publicize their case. This is one reason that the Chicago Eight defendants decided not to proceed *pro se*; instead they wished, as one of them put it, "'to roam throughout the country building up popular support and bringing the case to the people, which we considered the highest jury'" (in *Law Commune*, 1971:294).

Pro Se Defense and Resource Mobilization

Self-representation may aid in the mobilization of important movement resources, as we have seen exemplified in a number of trials. Although an attorney can be of great help, his or her presence may still limit the introduction of political and moral arguments. *Pro se* political defendants may win more latitude than that given to an attorney to discuss such issues, they may speak about them more articulately and more passionately, and they may win jury sympathy. In any particular case, the advantages and disad-vantages of *pro se* defense for a movement depend on a number of circumstances, among them the seriousness of the charges, the fac-tual and legal issues in question, the personality and speaking prow-ess of the defendants, and the attitude of the judges and prosecutors, some of whom will give more latitude than others.

Here again we can distinguish American social movements where *pro se* defense is of potential value, and those where it would be futile from the movement's perspective. The civil rights movement falls into the latter category. There the primary defense goal was to build a record for appeal, not to talk about political and social issues, and lawyers were better able than defendants to build such records. Moreover, judges would not have permitted defendants to talk about racial or other matters. In the antiwar movement, *pro se* defense did allow for some discussion of the war and related issues, though acquittals and hung juries were still difficult to achieve.

It is when political defendants depart from the accustomed mute role of the accused that political trials take on particularly dramatic qualities, illuminating the dependence of courtroom routine on defendant passivity. Yet *pro se* defense is still one that most political defendants are reluctant to undertake. Thus decisions to accept counsel or instead to proceed *pro se* will continue to pose dilemmas for social movement activists.

Chapter Seven

Radical Catholics and the Destruction of Draft Files

Several important criminal prosecutions that arose during the Vietnam peace movement involved radical Catholic clergy and laity who waited to be arrested after defacing or destroying Selective Service records. Their dramatic acts of civil disobedience received considerable press attention and aroused a good deal of controversy within the peace movement and the Catholic church as well. In their trials these defendants challenged the criminal courts to allow them to discuss their religious and moral beliefs against the war and the draft. Outside the courts, the defendants and their supporters urged the church to take a bold stance in opposition to American involvement in Vietnam.

The Crisis of the Catholic Church

The accommodation of churches to the demands of secular society is a recurring theme in the sociology of religion. Faced with a conflict between religious ethics and worldly pressures, churches are likely to conform in large measure to the latter (O'Dea, 1966; Troeltsch, 1931). Perhaps nowhere is the tension between religion and society so great, and the urgency to compromise so pressing, as in time of war. As Yinger (1946) noted long ago, churches commonly shift from antebellum pacifist stances to enthusiastic support of military action once war has broken out, sharply illustrating the political and economic stakes that organized religion has in society.

The accommodation of American churches to the Vietnam War contributed to the more general controversy that beset the churches in the 1960s and early 1970s over their proper role in American society. The social upheaval caused by the Southern civil rights movement, the Vietnam War, and growing concern over poverty and discrimination in Northern cities had affected religious bodies as well. Serious debate ensued over whether organized religion should adhere to its traditional, priestly aim of personal salvation or instead act prophetically to improve social conditions. The proper stance of churches over the Vietnam War was a topic of especially heated controversy. Many observers argued that churches had nothing relevant to say about the war, while other critics urged churches to speak out against the Vietnamese conflict (cf. Brown, 1967; Kucheman, 1970; *Newsweek*, 1967).

These debates were intensified by the activism of many clergy in the major issues of the time. Clerics in many churches became involved in the Southern civil rights movement or worked to end segregation, discrimination, and poverty in Northern communities (Cogley, 1965; Ryan, 1966). Still others protested the Vietnam War (Tygart, 1973). Clerical activism in all these areas often prompted serious rebukes by church officials and congregations. Several activist clergy were transferred from their posts, while others suffered lay disapproval as their congregations responded with letters of protest and reduced financial contributions (cf. Nelsen, Yokley, and Madron, 1973; Winter, 1977).

Controversy over the involvement of churches, clergy, and laity in social and political issues was especially great in the Catholic church. For several historical and theological reasons, the church had long been regarded as a conservative element in American life (Gray, 1971). Catholic officials, clerics, and laity were considered to be particularly loyal and patriotic citizens (Yinger, 1946). Inevitably, the participation of priests, nuns, and laity in the antiwar and civil rights movements and in other social and political efforts aroused considerable antagonism within the church. Several Catholic members of the "new breed" of clergy (Cox, 1967) suffered official or congregational punishment.

The debate within the church over the war and other issues intensified the more general crisis of authority that beset the church during those years. The declarations of Pope John XXIII and the Second

Vatican Council, along with other various changes of the decade, had led to considerable upheaval within the church over such issues as birth control, clerical celibacy, and liturgical procedure (Cogley, 1970; O'Dea, 1966). Several critics attacked the lack of freedom of thought and expression that they saw characterizing the church (Blanshard, 1966; Kahn, 1966). Many priests and nuns left the church in protest and frustration (Sheerin, 1970).

The clerical and lay critics of the church over these "internal" religious matters also became severe critics of the church's reluctance to involve itself in the social and political issues of the day. The refusal of the Catholic hierarchy to comment on the Vietnam War before late 1966 came in for special attack, and the November 1966 statement of the National Conference of Catholic Bishops in support of the American effort in Indochina only served to arouse more criticism by liberal Catholic journals and various clergy and laity opposed to the war (Sheerin, 1966; Zahn, 1966). Attacks on the bishops continued even after they called for an end to the fighting in November 1971 (Berrigan, 1972).

Catholic Antiwar Protest

The clerical and lay critics of the church's refusal to oppose the war took their protest beyond the pages of progressive Catholic journals. In one instance in the early 1970s, a group of nuns lay down in an aisle of St. Patrick's Cathedral in New York City, while in another protest, several priests and nuns lay across the street in front of the cathedral (*Commonweal*, 1972). Many clergy and laity also took part in various protest actions designed to impress the general public and elected officials with what they believed was the immoral nature of the Vietnam War. One vehicle for their protest efforts was Clergy Concerned about Vietnam, founded in 1965 and composed of members from the three major American faiths, albeit with far fewer Catholics than many of the church's Vietnam critics wished (Gray, 1970).

Two of the most controversial and celebrated priests in the church were Daniel and Philip Berrigan. Both had long been betes noires to Catholic officials. Daniel Berrigan had taken part in civil rights protests and was a founder of Clergy Concerned about Vietnam. Banished to Latin America in late 1965 for these and other activities, Berrigan returned to the United States in March 1966 after fifty Fordham University students had picketed the residence of Cardinal Spellman of New York and more than ten thousand members of the church had taken out a full-page ad in the *New York Times* calling for his return. Philip Berrigan had been no less controversial, having been reprimanded by church officials in 1965 for signing a "declaration of conscience" against the war.

The Berrigans were involved in the first two draft board raids of the Catholic "ultra-resistance" (Gray, 1970). In October 1967, Philip Berrigan and three other members of the church poured blood on some six hundred files at a Baltimore draft board. A statement they gave to news reporters who had been summoned to the scene said in part that they invoked the " 'nation's Judeo-Christian tradition, against the horror in Vietnam and the impending threat of nuclear destruction'" (in Gray, 1971 : 120). The four men waited to be arrested, as one handed out copies of the New Testament to building guards and draft board clerks.

The next draft board raid, and the one that became the most celebrated, was that of the Catonsville Nine in May 1968, in a suburb of Baltimore. In addition to Daniel and Philip Berrigan, seven other people, including two lay Catholics, a Christian brother, a former Catholic missionary, and a former priest, former nun, and former brother of the Maryknoll order, removed 378 files from the Catonsville draft board and burned them with homemade napalm. As they did so they recited the Lord's Prayer and awaited arrest, all in front of several reporters and television cameras. One protester said, "Our Church has been silent. We speak out in the name of Catholicism and Christianity," while a statement handed to the press declared in part, " 'We confront the Catholic Church, other Christian bodies, and the synagogues of America with their silence and cowardice in the face of our country's crime. We are convinced that the religious bureaucracy in this country is racist, is an accomplice in war and is hostile to the poor'" (in Gray, 1971 : 46).

The action of the Baltimore Four, as Philip Berrigan and the other three men were called, and especially that of the Catonsville Nine inspired many other protesters around the country to commit similar acts of civil disobedience. In June 1968 two people in Boston poured black paint on several hundred draft files, while in September of that year fourteen persons in Milwaukee burned about ten thousand draft records with napalm. According to various estimates (e.g., Bannan and Bannan, 1974; Rowley, 1969), about thirty draft board raids were committed from 1967 to 1971, in cities such as Philadelphia, Rochester, New York, Pasadena, Indianapolis, Minneapolis, and Chicago, in addition to the ones already mentioned. These actions involved more than one hundred and fifty people, a majority of them priests, nuns, or lay Catholics, resulted in the destruction of about four hundred thousand draft files, and led to at least fifty-five convictions in the criminal courts. The early raids followed the Baltimore and Catonsville models; participants in these protests tended to be Catholic clergy or laity in their late twenties or older, and they waited for arrest (Gray, 1970). Many of these protesters had been strongly influenced by membership in or association with the Catholic Worker movement headed by Dorothy Day (Palms, 1966). Participants in the later raids were younger and more secular, and several did not wait for arrest (Riley, 1969).

These draft board raids marked a new kind of antiwar protest that aroused a good deal of debate in the peace movement over the destruction of property that was involved (cf. Gray, 1970; Zahn, 1970). The raids had several aims, depending on the particular background of the participants (Gray, 1970; Riley, 1969). First, the raids were meant as acts of communication and witness by which the local and national public would learn of the protesters' grievances against the war, the draft, and other domestic and foreign policies, as well as the silence of religious bodies on all these matters. This goal was especially important for the radical Catholics who took part, since they hoped this sacrifice of their freedom would transform their "sabotage into a religious and instructive act" (Gray, 1970:127). Second, the draft board actions were intended to shame and spur other opponents of the war into new forms of nonviolent antiwar resistance involving similar personal risk. After the Catonsville raid, for example, the Berrigans were critical of their friends who were reluctant to undertake similar acts of civil disobedience (Forest, 1969).

A third goal was to impede the Selective Service system. Though the Catonsville Nine's burning of 378 files was seen as primarily symbolic, other actions that destroyed as many as seventy-five thousand files imposed a more serious burden on draft officials to replace the files. As several observers pointed out, however, draft boards that were not raided increased their inductions to compensdate for boards that were affected (Riley, 1969). Finally, these members of the "ultra-resistance" intended their draft board raids to lead to criminal trials that would challenge the morality and legality of the Vietnam War and the draft. Next, I will examine some of these trials and discuss the success and failure of the Catholic left's attempts to turn the criminal courts into political forums.

The Baltimore Four

The Baltimore Four defendants wanted their trial in April 1968 to be "as dramatic as the action that brought it about, and as well publicized" (Deedy, 1968a: 426). The drama and publicity of the trial, they felt, would arise from their efforts to speak in court about their religious and political motivation for destroying the draft records. However, the trial failed to serve as a public forum for their antiwar views. The judge prohibited testimony and witnesses not directly related to the actual defacing of the draft files. Moreover, press and public attention was diverted from the trial by the assassination of Martin Luther King, urban riots in Baltimore, and the Wisconsin presidential primary (Deedy, 1968b). The defendants received six-year prison sentences, which several observers considered overly harsh punishment that was politically motivated. The *Boston Globe*, for example, commented editorially that "'convicted thugs and murderers have been treated more gently'" (in Deedy, 1968c: 394).

The Catonsville Nine

Quite in contrast, the four-day trial of the Catonsville Nine in October 1968 in Baltimore proved to be perhaps the high point of all the trials of radical Catholics who destroyed draft files. More than two thousand people, including several hundred priests, nuns, seminarians, and lay Catholics, came to Baltimore from across the nation to take part in vigils, demonstrations, and public meetings and teach-ins. As several observers have noted (e.g., Kroll, 1971), the civil disobedience of the Catonsville Nine, Baltimore Four, and other such protesters was theatrical in form and structure; their acts of protest put as much emphasis on their dramatic features as on their political aspects. The trials of the Catonsville Nine and the other groups were no different, as Gray (1970) recognized, calling them "morality plays."

The Catonsville defendants wanted a trial that would achieve drama and publicity by raising political, moral, and religious arguments inside the courtroom and provoking demonstrations outside. They wished to avoid the disappointing outcome of the Spock trial that had taken place earlier in the year and thought that a jury acquittal based on the arguments it intended to offer would be a sign that the larger public was opposed to the war. They would freely admit that they had burned the draft files but would argue that they did so without criminal intent, since they were trying to save lives by destroying property. The defense did not participate in the selection of the jury, feeling that one jury would be as good as another and wishing to expedite the proceedings (Bannan and Bannan, 1974).

A bit surprisingly, the judge allowed the accused to discuss in considerable detail their work in Northern ghettos, Latin America, and elsewhere, and their views regarding the war and the draft. Ironically, the prosecutor objected often to the latitude given to defense testimony. As mentioned in chapter 5, the latitude the judge allowed may have been a result of a desire to placate the peace movement in the wake of deepening frustration over the war and the violence that had occurred during the Chicago Democratic National Convention a few months earlier. "Judge Thomsen's desire to mollify the peace movement led him to permit a startlingly wide airing of antiwar views. [He] was intent on restoring faith in American institutions to the angry mobs of protesters, bandaged in mourning for the Vietnamese dead, who milled around his courthouse. He was said to be painfully aware of them" (Gray, 1970: 176). The defendants also gained some latitude in the testimony the judges allowed by their appearance and demeanor, as they "exploited respectability to the hilt" (Gray, 1970: 177). They dressed neatly, some in clerical attire, and presented their views in a quiet but determined, articulate manner, contributing to the kind of witness they wished to present. As one federal marshal in the courtroom for security reasons said to a colleague, " 'Reading the papers, you'd have thought they were a bunch of kooks. But they're not, they're a great bunch of guys' " (in Gray, 1970: 184).

On the witness stand, the defendants readily conceded that they had defaced draft records but argued that their actions lacked criminal intent: "'If I see a person being asphyxiated inside of a burning car and break the window to save his life, I am not committing a crime by breaking the window'" (in Gray, 1970:169). In other testimony they connected their work in Latin America and United States slums with their decision to burn the draft records. One defendant who had taught in a St. Louis ghetto said, "'I was appalled that our country could be spending eighty billion dollars a year . . . raining destruction on hundreds of thousands of innocents when it couldn't even bother to feed its own children'" (in Gray, 1970:178). The defendants also discussed in some detail their religious motives for their act of civil disobedience and their concern over the church's silence on the war. One of the accused said,

> "When you look around and see the imperatives placed on you by the amount of lives lost openly in Vietnam . . . then it is time that you stand up. This is what it means to be a Christian . . . to not only talk about things, but to do something about it." (in Gray, 1970:189)

Another defendant stated,

> "The nonviolent tradition of our religion has always drawn the line between people and things. . . . Jesus Christ beat the moneychangers and threw over their tables because these were properties which were desecrating a more sacred property—life. Was Jesus Christ guilty of assault and battery?" (in Gray, 1970:179)

When asked whether his participation in the Catonsville protest was motivated by Jesuit philosophy, Daniel Berrigan replied, "'May I say that if that is not accepted as a substantial part of my action, then the action is eviscerated of all meaning'" (in Gray, 1970:202).

After the prosecution and judge had delivered their summations, the judge charged the jury to ignore most of the testimony it had heard. In typical instructions, he told the jury, "'The law does not recognize political, religious, moral convictions, or some higher law, as justification for the commission of a crime, no matter how good the motive may be. . . . The protester . . . may, indeed, be right in the eyes of history, or morality, or philosophy. These are not controlling in the case which is before you for decision'" (in Gray, 1970:214).

Later, while the jury was deliberating, the defendants recited the Lord's Prayer in court, with the judge's permission. The jury found them guilty after deliberating for only an hour, and the defendants later received prison terms ranging from two to three and half years. Despite the verdict, the peace movement considered the trial a victory of sorts, owing to the publicity it won and the defendants' success in discussing the war, draft, and other issues.

The Milwaukee Twelve

I have discussed the Catonsville trial in some detail to indicate the essentially religious nature of the defendants' testimony, the reasons they were able to discuss the war and other matters to a great extent, and the ways in which it achieved various antiwar goals. The jury's quickly reached conviction can be attributed to the property destruction involved and to the judge's charge that ruled out motive as proper defense. These elements were also present in the Milwaukee Twelve case, to which I now turn.

As mentioned earlier, in September 1968 fourteen men, including five Catholic priests and one Protestant minister, used napalm to burn ten thousand draft files taken from a Milwaukee draft board. Acting as their own attorneys, twelve defendants were tried together in May 1969. Admitting the facts in the case, they intended to base their innocence on Wisconsin's "privileged statute," which provides that an apparent crime may be considered privileged, and not punishable, if it is undertaken with the reasonable belief that bodily harm may be prevented to other people. The judge repeatedly warned the defendants not to discuss the war and to limit their comments to their state of mind at the time they destroyed the draft records. He also curtailed or prohibited testimony from expert witnesses the defense had wanted to speak about Vietnam War civil disobedience, and the Nuremberg Principles. In addition, the two prosecuting attorneys repeatedly objected to attempts by the accused to talk about these issues as well as Christian beliefs in the legitimacy of resisting illegitimate power (Gray, 1970).

Despite the insistence of the judge and prosecution that these issues were not relevant matters, the defendants were still able to say a good deal about the war, the draft, and their motives for protesting the two by burning draft files. In large part the latitude they enjoyed derived from their status as *pro se* defendants. The accused made clear their religious motivation for burning the files, though not to the extent they wished. One defendant attempted to introduce the New Testament as a defense exhibit, but the judge did not allow him to do so (Gray, 1970). A second defendant, a priest, attempted to quote from Pope John's *Pacem in Terris* encyclical regarding the duty to disobey law contrary to the will of God, but this was not permitted either. However, as mentioned in the previous chapter, another defendant who was a Benedictine monk was allowed to talk several hours on his state of mind as he burned the files, referring often to the Benedictine tradition of peace.

After the defendants summed up for the jury, the judge instructed the jury to ignore the accused's religious, moral, or political motives as it debated its verdict. The jury found the accused guilty after deliberating an hour. However, the defendants and their supporters took some satisfaction from their success in talking about the war and other issues, and from the reactions of the judge and prosecuting attorneys during and after the trial. Toward the end of the case, one of the prosecutors, Harold Jackson, Jr., requested the jury to be dismissed for a moment and said, "'The state is very much opposed to the position it finds itself in, because both counsels for the state do not think that the war in Vietnam is irrelevant in and of itself. We find it to be irrelevant in terms of the act for which we are prosecuting. . . . It is impossible for the state represented by human beings to sit here any longer having it said that they believe in and of themselves that poverty and war are irrelevant. I just can't take it'" (in Gray, 1970:152). Earlier Jackson had said to a reporter, "'I'm more torn by this case than at the beginning. I see nothing but honesty and intelligence here, depth of perception and integrity, an atmosphere that I can only describe as very loving'" (in Gray, 1970:151). After the case ended, Jackson resigned his position to work on civil rights cases, commenting, "'That trial tore me up. I'm still not sure what they accomplished politically. But whatever religion is, they're where it's at'" (in Gray, 1970:152). The judge had also been moved by the proceedings. As mentioned in chapter 5, he wept for a few seconds as he sentenced the Benedictine monk a few weeks after the trial had ended.

The "Ultra-Resistance" and Resource Mobilization

The civil disobedience and criminal trials of the "ultra-resistance" received considerable press publicity and helped galvanize antiwar protest. Many of the prosecutions of draft file burners attracted " 'fesivals' of support which drew admirers and well-wishers from all over the country as the various cases came to trial'" (Zahn, 1970:126). The Catholic left and other participants in the draft board raids were thus able to use their prosecutions to mobilize support: "It is a conservative estimate to say that tens of thousands were reached by the action and many of these were undoubtedly moved to more direct opposition to the war" (Zahn, 1970:126). The destruction of draft files also impeded draft board operations. However, war opponents became frustrated with the trials' failure to end the war. As Gray (1970:157) noted, "The trials seem like chamber music played to the intimate audience of the peace community."

The Catholic draft board raids and resulting trials also helped mobilize the religious community against the war and draft. They aroused a good deal of controversy among clergy and laity. Many liberals and radicals in the Catholic church and other religious bodies were profoundly affected by the witness offered by the "ultra-resistance" (cf. Duff, 1971). The Berrigans and others involved in the draft board raids had hoped to move the Catholic bishops and other church officials to oppose the war. The draft board raids and resulting trials did indeed deepen opposition to the war among the Catholic left to an extent that the bishops were not able to ignore, helping to lead to their November 1971 statement calling for an end to the fighting.

Courts As Secular Institutions

Much of the tension arising in the trials of the Catholic left and other antiwar protesters derived from the attempts of these groups to discuss issues considered legally irrelevant. The rules of evidence are meant to provide for judgments based solely on the law and the facts in the case; juries are not allowed to be swayed by any emotions they may have for or against the defendants as particular human beings or political activists.

The trials of the Catholic "ultra-resistance" seem to have had a special impact on courtroom participants and the outside public, owing in large part to the religious backgrounds and rectitude of the defendants. From a defense standpoint, these trials were religious events that in varying degrees excluded religion from the proceedings and particularly from jury deliberation (cf. Gannon, 1968). Thus the trials of the "ultra-resistance" throw into sharp relief the secular nature of criminal courts, and remind us that criminal trials and other courtroom events are secular rituals (cf. Moore and Myerhoff, 1977) as much as they are legal encounters. As such, they have a cognitive dimension that specifies proper forms of social relationships and political behavior (cf. Arnold, 1935; Lukes, 1975), and, especially in cases involving religious and political protesters, acts as a shield for established political and social institutions. At the same time, however, protesters want to avail themselves of the legal trappings surrounding the proceedings and the public forum they provide. The drama of the trials of the Catholic left and other antiwar protesters "was courtroom drama. The courts did not supply only the stage setting, they also provided the structure of the action. The clash of articulate positions and personalities in an encounter where the stakes involve both future victims of a future war and the future freedom of the just men and women accused, the shaping of the whole event toward a climax of guilty or not guilty, it is to this that the sensitive respond. That drama has always belonged to the doing of justice in court" (Bannan and Bannan, 1974:212).

There is a need for research on other social movements where protesters acted for religious as well as political motives, and where the churches and courts posed serious obstacles to their efforts to change existing conditions. One such movement was the abolitionist movement that preceded the Civil War. Antislavery advocates called on their churches to work for an end to slavery, and many abolitionists left their churches because of the continuing silence of religious bodies (Mabee, 1969). The courts also acted as supporters of slavery, as the *Dred Scott* Supreme Court decision illustrates. As we will see in the following chapter, Northern juries promised some hope for abolitionists, since they often voted to acquit defendants charged with aiding fugitive slaves. Such research on the involvement of churches and courts in social movement protest would increase our understanding of the tension between religious ethos and secular demands, and would contribute in many ways to the study of social movements and to the sociologies of religion and of law.

Chapter Eight

Jury Nullification in
Vietnam Protest Trials

We have seen that in stark contrast to Southern juries in the early 1960s, Vietnam-era juries promised some hope, however slim, for antiwar defendants. Defense strategy in Vietnam protest trials often centered on the winning of jury sympathy through attempts to introduce arguments on the morality and legality of the war, the draft, and other concerns. In this tactic usually lay the only hope of acquittal for those defendants who had deliberately broken the law for reasons of conscience. Some defense teams in trials resulting from trumped-up charges also appealed to the jury to acquit in light of the repressive origins of the proceedings.

But defense efforts in both kinds of trials typically ran into the roadblock of formal justice. Various procedures and principles governing the conduct of criminal trials, such as the rules of evidence, hampered defense attempts to politicize the trials. Though the rules of trial procedure are neutral on the surface and, in theory, designed to protect the defendant and to ensure that the rule of law, not of emotion, will prevail, in cases involving Vietnam protesters they served to prevent juries from hearing antiwar arguments to the extent desired by defense teams. In several trials they also helped ensure that even sympathetic jurors would vote to convict, lest they violate their oaths as jurors to follow the law as set forth by the judge.

This last concern is the subject of this chapter. A fascinating paradox of the American legal system is that jurors are not allowed to be told of their power to refuse with impunity to convict a defendant whose guilt is otherwise clearly established by the facts and law in the case. The nation's leading digest of federal and state case law, for example, advises that the "jury should not be told that they may disregard law and decide according to their prejudices and consciences" (*American Digest System*, 1976: Criminal Law 768 (10)). Maryland and Indiana are the only states where judges instruct juries in criminal cases that they may judge law as well as fact, although the jurors are also urged not to make arbitrary decisions (Aaronson, 1975:3). Throughout the United States, then, jurors have the *power* to disregard the law in reaching their verdict, since they cannot be punished for doing this, yet outside of Maryland and Indiana jurors do not, according to prevailing judicial opinion, have the *right* to do so. An English judge, Edward Willes, put the distinction well: "I admit the jury have the power of finding a verdict against the law, and so they have of finding a verdict against evidence, but I deny they have the right to do so" (*Rex v. Shipley*, 4 Doug. 171, 178, 1784).

Judges, lawyers, and legal scholars have long debated the merits of the jury's power to "nullify" the law, and many (e.g., Frank, 1949) have condemned the irrationality of the jury system that arises from the jury's freedom to acquit, while others have contended that such "jury lawlessness is the great correction of law in its actual administration" (Pound, 1910:12) and an example of "justified" discretion in the legal process (Kadish and Kadish, 1973; Moran, 1981). The debate over jury nullification intensified during the Vietnam War (Allen, 1971; Sax, 1968; Scheflin, 1972; Simson, 1976; Van Dyke, 1970). Several defense teams in trials of United States antiwar protesters argued that they should be allowed to tell jurors that they had the power to nullify, and that judges should include this same information in their instructions. Trial judges and appellate courts rejected these arguments, asserting that such instructions would undermine the rule of law.* The refusal of these courts to inform juries of their power to nullify helped minimize the number of acquittals or hung juries that might otherwise have occurred, thus impeding antiwar goals.

This conclusion complements recent works on ideological aspects of the American legal system. The sociological study of ideology as a set of beliefs that maintains and justifies the status quo stems in

---

* See Scheflin (1972) and Simson (1976) for lists and discussions of several appellate decisions that rejected defense appeals based on the refusal of trial judges to inform jurors of their power to nullify.

large part from the work of Marx and Mannheim. Marx's famous dictum that in every era the ruling ideas are those of the ruling class (Marx and Engels, 1846/1947:39) was an important part of his social theory. Mannheim (1936) extended the concept as part of his treatment of the sociology of knowledge by noting the social origins of ideological beliefs, in addition to the economic basis favored by Marx (cf. Merton, 1968; Zeitlin, 1968). The concept has since been the subject of several works, including Mills's (1943) classic critique of the ideology of social pathologists, Form and Rytina's (1969) study of the ideological beliefs of American stratification, and Ryan's (1976) examination of the "blaming the victim" perspective that he saw underlying studies and policies regarding various aspects of poverty and race.

Law and the criminal justice system also have ideological functions (Sumner, 1979). Arnold (1935) noted several decades ago the symbolic importance of American law and criminal trials as dramatic representatives of democratic ideals; indeed, the rule of law is generally considered the cornerstone for legitimacy in the democratic state (Selznick, 1969). But Arnold also contended that law is "the greatest instrument of social stability" since the rule of law "ordinarily operates to induce acceptance of things as they are" (1935: 35, 34) by comforting the powerless with the belief that the law makes no distinctions between the rich and the poor or the strong and the weak. In the last decade "new" criminologists and other radical critics have adopted this thesis of the establishment law professor and set forth several ideological functions of the American criminal justice system. Blumberg (1974) and Reiman (1979), for example, assert that the focus of the system on poor criminals diverts attention from crimes by the powerful and from injustices of the social order. Balbus (1973) argues that applying a criminal label to political rebels stigmatizes the latter's demands and helps convince them that their illegal actions are examples of common criminality and not of political protest. Krisberg (1975) takes up Balbus's theme, maintaining that the criminal justice system affects the consciousness of the "everyday" criminal in the same manner.

The arguments in the Vietnam era against the jury's right to be told of its power to nullify also had ideological functions, even as the critics of nullification stressed their worthy aim of upholding the rule of law. These functions can be appreciated only in the context of the historical development of the jury's nullifying power and its use in celebrated political trials.

The Development and Use of Nullification

The jury has long been regarded as a "bulwark against grave official tyranny" (Kalven and Zeisel, 1966 : 296). It was honored in England in the seventeenth and eighteenth centuries for the protection it afforded from judges who served the desires of the Crown (Thayer, 1898). In America, colonial judges before 1776 provided the same protection from royal judges, leading the new nation to write the right to jury trial into federal and state constitutions (Hyman and Tarrant, 1975).

But the right to trial by jury means little if the jury can be punished for returning an acquittal, and thus one of the most important developments in the common law history of the jury was the 1670 Bushell's case in England. Significantly, this case resulted from the trial of William Penn and William Mead for preaching about Quakerism to an unlawful assembly. During the previous six years, juries had often acquitted Quakers of various charges but were fined for refusing to convict, and the result in the Penn and Mead trial was no different. Although the defendants had clearly committed the acts for which they were being prosecuted, four of the twelve jurors voted to acquit them. They continued to acquit even after they were imprisoned and starved for three days by the judge, fined some forty marks each, and imprisoned until they paid the fines. Litigation arising from a writ of *habeas corpus* by one of the jurors, Edward Bushell, established the principle, now so fundamental in common law, that jurors may not be punished for their verdict (Forsyth, 1898/ 1971; Moore, 1973). But this principle also meant that jurors would have the power to disregard with impunity the judge's instructions on the law and acquit in the face of all evidence and law to the contrary.

Jurors exercised their new power in eighteenth-century England in trials of defendants charged with seditious libel against government and Crown. In these cases judges instructed juries that their only question to decide was whether the defendant had in fact published material that was said to be seditious; if so, the jury was to find the defendant guilty. Jurors were not, charged the judges, to decide whether such publication was in fact seditious and hence criminal. Objecting to these instructions, defense attorneys sought to tell juries that they were not obliged to accept the law as laid down by the judge. Several juries did nullify the law and acquit in such cases (Moore, 1973). Finally, in a landmark of common law, Parliament passed Fox's Libel Law in 1792, officially allowing juries to consider the seditious nature of the publication. Several members of Parliament who debated the bill stressed that juries had not only the right but also the power to nullify laws that violated their consciences (Sax, 1968).

In the next century, the refusal of juries to convict despite law and evidence to the contrary again affected English law and politics. In the early 1800s, England had some two hundred and thirty capital offenses, many of them political in nature (Hay, 1975). Thinking the death penalty for these crimes was too severe, juries often acquitted defendants charged with capital offenses. As a result, the English jury "played a major role in the gradual abolition of the death penalty in England" (Kalven and Zeisel, 1966:49). In 1819, for example, British bankers were forced to ask Parliament to make forgery a noncapital offense, since it had become almost impossible to obtain jury convictions in such cases (Kalven and Zeisel, 1966).

The history of American law and political protest is likewise marked by celebrated instances where jurors exercised their power to acquit in the face of the law and facts. Perhaps the most famous case was that of John Peter Zenger in 1735 (Levy, 1960). Zenger's newspaper had published material critical of the New York royal governor, and he was prosecuted for seditious libel. The colonial law, similar to that in England at the time, made it a crime to publish any statement, true or false, that criticized the conduct of public officials, laws, or government and tended to bring them into disrepute. Thus, juries in colonial trials for seditious libel were to decide only whether the defendant had published the material in question; judges were to decide whether the material had the required criminal tendency. Zenger's attorney conceded that his client had indeed published the material and asked the jury to acquit in light of the truth of the material: "'And this I hope is sufficient to prove that jurymen are to see with their own eyes, to hear with their own ears, and to make use of their own consciences'" (in Goodell, 1973:23). Though the judges in the case ruled that truth was no defense, the jury acquitted, and the verdict helped reduce prosecutions in colonial America for seditious libel (Finkelman, 1981). Ironically, although the Zenger trial involved a striking example of jury nullification, criticized so roundly during the Vietnam War as undermining the rule of law, the case is celebrated in history textbooks (e.g., Morrison and Commager, 1962) for helping to establish the freedom of the press in the United States.

The refusal of colonial juries to convict Americans accused of violating British mercantile laws is likewise heralded. For example, colonial juries consistently refused to enforce the Navigation Acts that were designed to channel colonial trade through England; the acquittals released ships that had been held for violating the acts. As a result, the British were forced to establish courts of vice admiralty that tried navigation cases without juries. These courts deepened the colonists' antipathy for England and were included as one of the grievances mentioned in the Declaration of Independence (Scheflin, 1972).

After the break with England, it is thus not surprising that the American jury was considered the judge of both law and fact, and that the right to trial by jury was written into the Constitution (Howe, 1939). John Adams had said of the juror in 1771 that "it is not only his right, but his duty . . . to find the verdict according to his own best understanding, judgment, and conscience, though in direct opposition to the direction of the court" (*Yale Law Journal*, 1964: 173), and this view prevailed in the early decades of the new republic. Underlying this view was a faith in the judgment of common people and a belief in natural law (*Yale Law Journal*, 1964). Thus Alexander Hamilton said in 1804 that the jury was obliged to disobey the instructions of the judge and acquit "if exercising their judgment with discretion and honesty they have a clear conviction that the charge of the court is wrong" (Sax, 1968:487). In the first half of the nineteenth century, federal and state judges often instructed juries that they were free to disregard the judge's view of the law (Howe, 1939). In typical instructions, John Jay, chief justice of the Supreme Court, told the jurors in a trial before the Court that they had a right to "determine the law as well as the fact in controversy" (*Yale Law Journal*, 1964:178).

In trials of abolitionists who had violated the Fugitive Slave Law, Northern jurors adopted this widespread view of their role in yet another striking use of nullification in protest cases. The law required citizens to help capture and return runaway slaves, and prohibited interfering with such return and capture. Some sixty thousand slaves tried to escape in the thirty years preceding the Civil War. Abolitionists were imprisoned in the South for helping them escape and in the North for obstructing their capture. But in the North juries often acquitted abolitionists who had violated the law. In 1851, for example, twenty-four people were indicted for helping a fugitive slave to break out of a Syracuse jail. A federal judge in Buffalo called the defendants "'disorderly and turbulent men, the common disturbers of society'" (in Younger, 1963 : 99). The first four trials of the group resulted in three acquittals, forcing the government to drop the rest of the charges. In the same year, a crowd broke into a Boston courtroom and rescued a slave. President Fillmore called for the prosecutions of those involved, and the judge who requested indictments from a grand jury termed the abolitionists "'beyond the scope of human reason and fit subjects either of consecration or of a madhouse'" (in Friedman, 1971 : 38). The grand jury indicted three people involved in the rescue, but after an acquittal and several hung juries, the government dropped the charges. Again it is worth noting that although the acquittals and mistrials of this period resulted from the nullification by jurors of clear violations of the Fugitive Slave Law, modern treatments of abolitionism (e.g., Campbell, 1970) praise the verdicts for helping the antislavery cause instead of condemning them for undermining the rule of law and the consistency of adjudication.

In the last half of the nineteenth century, federal and state judges attacked the principle of jury nullification, and judicial decisions and new state laws ruled that juries were to decide only the facts. Finally, in 1895, the Supreme Court ruled in *Sparf v. The United States of America*, 156 US 51, that defense teams had no right to inform jurors that they could judge law as well as fact, and that judges were not obliged to tell jurors of their power to do so.

These attacks on nullification reflected increasing criticism of the jury at the end of the century. Citing the admonition of the editor of the *American Law Review* that jurors had "'developed agrarian tendencies of an alarming character,'" one author (in *Yale Law Journal*, 1964 : 191–192) contends that the attacks on the jury, especially on its nullification powers, derived from the number of jury verdicts against corporations in damage suits and labor disputes, and fears of influential members of the American Bar Association that jurors were becoming too hostile to their clients and too sympathetic to the poor. Chambliss and Seidman (1971) likewise argue that the increasing criticism of juries in this period reflected the new legal emphasis on the protection of property that developed after the Civil War.

Thus we see that the history of the jury has been intimately connected with struggles for political, economic, and social power. Sax (1968 : 488) says that "it is no accident" that the development and use of jury nullification arose in cases of political dissent since in such cases there is a particular danger of "political craft and oppression . . . perverting justice," as one member of Parliament termed it during the debate on Fox's Libel Law. The American colonial, abolitionist, and postbellum periods were three eras where juries were reluctant to convict political defendants. The Vietnam years were possibly a fourth. Had jurors in this period been informed of their historic power to nullify, it is very possible that even more acquittals might have resulted, profoundly advancing the aims of the antiwar movement. In the following section I draw on several Vietnam protest cases to argue this point and to illustrate the ideological functions of instructions to juries to follow the law laid down by the judge.

Jury Nullification in Vietnam Protest Trials

In criminal trials judges give juries standard instructions regarding the function of the jury. Those used in every criminal case in California are typical: " 'It becomes my duty as judge to instruct you concerning the law applicable to this case, and it is your duty as jurors to follow the law as I shall state it to you. . . . You are to be governed solely by the evidence introduced in this trial and the law as stated to you by me. The law forbids you to be governed by mere sentiment, conjecture, sympathy, passion, public opinion, or public feeling'" (in Van Dyke, 1970: 17–18). Most judges in trials of Vietnam War protesters gave similar instructions. Thus Judge Ford in the Spock case charged the jury, " 'You must apply the law that I lay down. If I fall into error in laying down the principles of law, my error or errors can be reviewed in a higher court. If you apply your own law and make an error, it cannot be reviewed and corrected. Your domain is the determination of the facts'" (in Mitford, 1969 : 198–199). Similarly, in the beginning of the Chicago Eight trial, Judge Hoffman told the jurors they must always follow his instructions in regard to law. Defense attorney Leonard Weinglass objected, "'The defense will contend that the jury is a representative of the moral conscience of the community. If there is a conflict between the judge's instructions and that of conscience, it should obey the latter'" (in Van Dyke, 1970 : 17). Not surprisingly, the judge overruled the objection.

In the Catonsville Nine trial, the issue of jury nullification became a point of particular tension. In his opening statement to the jury, defense attorney Kunstler said, "'We have in this courtroom . . . what the defendants consider an historic moment: a moment when a jury may, as the law empowers it, decide the case on the principal issues involved'" (in Bannan and Bannan, 1974 : 129). The judge interrupted Kunstler and asserted, "'The Court will instruct the jury, Mr. Kunstler, to decide the case on the facts as they appear from the evidence and upon the law as it may be given to them by the Court'" (in Bannan and Bannan, 1974 : 129). In his closing argument to the jury, Kunstler quoted the statement by John Peter Zenger's attorney cited earlier in this chapter. The judge again interrupted Kunstler and said emphatically that it is the jury's obligation "'to follow the instructions of the Court as to the law, as we do, and should do in each and every case if our system is to survive'" (in Bannan and Bannan, 1974 : 137). In his charge to the jury the judge asserted, "'It is your duty to accept without question for the purpose of the case the statements which I make to you about the law. . . . If I make a mistake in what I tell you, it will be reversed by a higher court that sets the matter straight. That is the rule of law in this country'" (in Bannan and Bannan, 1974 : 193).

The impact on jurors of these and similar instructions in antiwar trials was ideological. Evidence from simulated jury research on the impact of the instructions is admittedly inconclusive (Erlanger, 1970; Gerbasi, Zuckerman and Reis, 1977; Kessler, 1975): some researchers have found that jurors do obey the judge's instructions (Reed, 1980; Simon, 1967, 1980) while others have concluded that jurors often ignore them (Sue, Smith, and Caldwell, 1973; Thompson, Feng, and

Rosenhan, 1981). But Kalven and Zeisel (1966) found in their sample of real criminal cases from 1954 to 1958 that the incidence of jury nullification was only 8.8 percent,* leading them to conclude that "the jury, despite its autonomy, spins so close to the legal baseline." They further suggest that "one reason why the jury exercises its very real power [to nullify] so sparingly is because it is officially told it has none" (1966:498).

In antiwar trials, defense and prosecution teams that clashed over the issue of informing the jury of its power to nullify clearly felt that the judge's instructions might affect the jury's verdict. Appellate courts that later rejected defense appeals of denials of nullification instructions held the same view. As one federal court put it, "The jury should [not] be encouraged in their lawlessness . . . [By] clearly stating to the jury that they may disregard the law . . . we would indeed be negating the rule of law in favor of the rule of lawlessness" (*U.S. v. Moylan*, 1969:1006).

Interviews with jurors after several important antiwar trials confirm the impact of judicial instructions on the jury's likelihood of disregarding the law. One member of the jury that convicted Benjamin Spock and three of his co-defendants said:

> "I had great difficulty sleeping that night after the summing-up arguments. I sympathized very strongly with the defendants—I detest the Vietnam war. Also to some extent I think there is unfairness in the draft law. But it was put so clearly by the judge. It was a law violation. . . . The jury can't say, 'Was he justified in violating the law?' If the judge had said, 'If you find they were justified, find them not guilty,' it would have been beautiful." (in Mitford, 1969:224)

Another juror commented,

> "I'm in agreement with what they're trying to accomplish— my friends were amazed I found them guilty; but they did break the law. . . . I think it's a senseless war. But my personal

---

* Kalven and Zeisel (1966) found that juries disagreed with the hypothetical verdict of the judge in 22 percent of the criminal trials they examined. Of these disagreements, 40 percent (a weighted figure, adjusting for the multiplicity of reasons) arose from jury sympathy for the defendant or from implied jury criticism of either the law or legal result. Multiplying these two figures together (.22 × .40) yields my calculated 8.8 percent figure of jury nullification.

views don't count. I'm convinced the Vietnam war is no good. But we've got a Constitution to uphold. If we allow people to break the law, we're akin to anarchy. . . . If the defendants had been found not guilty—we'd have chaos. . . . Technically speaking, they were guilty according to the judge's charge. If there had been a different charge, we could have voted differently—if he had said, 'Let's face it, they're entitled to their opinions.'" (in Mitford, 1969 : 227–228)

Still a third Spock juror said,

"Of course you wonder if you made the right decision; but the way the judge charged us, there was no choice. People I've talked with since the verdict are sympathetic to the actions of Spock and Coffin—they seem to think the jury should have been there to decide if the law is right or wrong, but we weren't there to decide that. You can't have juries deciding whether laws are right." (in Mitford, 1969 : 234–235)

Here Van Dyke's (1977 : 236) comment is apt: "Not everyone impanelled as a juror remembers the lessons of their history courses when they learned about John Peter Zenger."

The Chicago Eight trial also demonstrates the impact of the judge's charge to follow the law. Initially four jurors were for acquittal on all counts. Then a juror proposed a compromise where five defendants would be found guilty of the charge of crossing state lines with intent to riot, and two defendants would be acquitted altogether.

Three of the jurors who had stood firm for complete acquittal for three days could not at first accept the compromise. They said the anti-riot law was unconstitutional. But that was not, Miss Richards [the juror proposing the compromise] explained, for them to determine; they had only to decide if the defendants had violated the law. That was the turning point; on the fourth day of deliberation, all the jurors had agreed to the compromise. (Danelski, 1971 : 176)

In at least a few Vietnam protest trials, juries acquitted after the judge's instructions gave them some latitude in reaching a verdict. In the Oakland Seven trial discussed in chapter 6, one juror was asked what would have happened if the judge in the case had not instructed the jury that the First Amendment and the accused's honest belief that their actions were protected by it were proper defenses. The juror replied, " 'They would have been guilty. That's it' " (in Bannan and Bannan, 1974 : 123). The 1973 trial of the Camden Twenty-eight for destroying draft files was another example of a jury acquitting after the judge's instructions allowed it to do so. Testimony revealed that an FBI informant had supplied the defendants with the tools and knowledge they needed to destroy the files. At one point in the trial the judge told the jury it had no power to nullify, but he later declared that his earlier comment had been incorrect and charged the jurors that " 'if you find that the overreaching participation by government agents or informers in the activities as you have heard them here was so fundamentally unfair to be offensive to the basic standards of decency, and shocking to the universal sense of justice, you may acquit the defendant to whom this defense applies' " (in Van Dyke, 1977 : 241). The judge also permitted a defense attorney to talk in his closing statement about the jury's power to nullify. The attorney said in part, " 'This power that jurors have is the reason why we have you jurors sitting here instead of computers. Because you are supposed to be the conscience of the community. You are supposed to decide if the law, as the Judge explains it to you, should be applied or if it should not' " (in Van Dyke, 1977 : 242). The jury acquitted on all counts.

In a third case, a jury acquittd ten Seattle protesters who had tried to block a munitions train carrying bombs. The judge had allowed the defense in its closing argument to ask the jurors to object to the war by acquitting. During the trial, one juror said, " 'They were all guilty of violating the law. But, you know, this war is a nasty situation. If it weren't so nasty, we probably wouldn't have made the decision we did' " (in Engstrom, n.d. : n.p.). The judge also commented, " 'I've never had a case quite like this where the young people came in and said, 'Yes, we did it,' and then were acquitted. And they may feel it's [the acquittal] a kind of signal to them' " (in Engstrom, n.d. : n.p.). And a second juror added, " 'I think all of us [on the jury] felt much the same about the bombing going on over there. It's a strange war. Here Congress is trying to stop it and Nixon keeps on with it. Technically they were guilty, we knew that. But we felt they had a good point and we may have done the same as they did. I'm not anti-government or anti-anything but in my own mind I was protesting as much as they were' " (in Engstrom, n.d. : n.p.).

Especially in the context of the history of jury nullification, instructions to Vietnam-era jurors to follow the law as laid down by the judge were ideological because they ultimately served to shield the government from the challenge of jury acquittals. The same ideological component was present in the refusal of trial judges to allow defense attorneys to inform jurors of their power to nullify. If, as Stanley Milgram's famous experiments (1975) indicate, Americans may obey authority that demands unjust actions, they should be even more likely to want to follow the instructions of a judge. Before they enter court, most jurors have at most a vague understanding of the philosophical, political, legal, and sociological sources and implications of the rule of law. At most they perceive it as forming the foundation of our democratic system of government, thus being worthy of their support. Their convictions are reinforced by the statements and instructions of trial judges, who, as I've argued, hold a good deal of sway over jurors. As Kalven and Zeisel (1966:498) put it, the "jury is not simply a corner gang picked from the street; it has been invested with a public task, brought under the influence of a judge, and put to work in solemn surroundings." Thus most jurors think that they are morally and perhaps even legally bound to follow the judge's instructions, lest they violate a principle dear to democracy. According to Bannan and Bannan (1974:198), "The ultimate resource of jury power is supposed to remain unknown to the jurors. The defense attorneys . . . can only hope that the realization will dawn on jurors as they deliberate." *

One final question arises. During the Vietnam War, why did most judges and legal scholars argue against the jury's right to be told of its power to nullify? Did they do so as a deliberate means of social control of the antiwar movement, or was their purpose and concern the more neutral one of maintaining the rule of law? Former Supreme Court Justice Abe Fortas was typical in denouncing one proposal to inform juries of their nullifying powers, " '[It is] an attack

---

* I once gave a lecture to an undergraduate class on political trials and presented the arguments for and against informing juries of their power to nullify. One student asked, "How can juries just ignore the law like that?" I responded by asking what her verdict would have been had she been a juror in the Zenger or abolitionist cases. The student answered that she saw my point and couldn't really say how she would have voted. But the argument and analogies she heard were not the kind of discussion that judges in antiwar trials usually permitted.

upon law itself. . . . This goes to the heart of our society because it says that this shall not be a society in which there are general rules of law and conduct which apply to everybody and to which everybody is held accountable'" (in Van Dyke, 1977:277). Another judge said that such a proposal would create "'a law-less society, a society without law, without regulations. That is a monstrosity.'" He added, somewhat ahistorically, "'No such society has ever existed or ever will exist'" (in Van Dyke, 1977:278). Still a third judge maintained, again ahistorically, "'I don't think that is what our form of government was ever intended to set up, that there should be—whenever there is a jury trial—that the question of the morality of law would come into play'" (in Bannan and Bannan, 1974:194).

The real reasons underlying such statements are impossible to discern; judges will not readily admit to deliberate attempts at social control. But it is not inconceivable that these statements did derive in large part from the lack of sympathy of judges for the antiwar movement. We have seen that in colonial times the British ended jury trials for those accused of violating the Navigation Acts and that the attacks on the jury in the last few decades of the nineteenth century may have been prompted by the threat jurors posed to corporate interests. At the very least, Vietnam-era judges must have realized that refusing to have jurors informed of their nullifying powers would help ensure convictions, even if their own purpose in preventing jurors from being so informed lay in the value they placed on the rule of law. One judge recognized both these reasons when he said, "'The question becomes . . . has the defendant violated the law, or hasn't he, by his conduct. And this, of course, by its very process avoids a great many of the arguments the defendants attempt to raise which go to the legality of the Vietnam war. . . . I think it misplaces the jury's functions to attempt to have the jury pass upon that morality'" (in Bannan and Bannan, 1974:194).

Yet, in a sense the question of the real aims of these judges is moot, for the social control that their arguments and the instructions of trial judges led to was the same nonetheless. Mannheim (1936) stressed the unwitting, unintentional nature of ideological statements; in light of his remarks, the arguments and instructions of Vietnam-era judges against nullification look to be ideological even if it can be shown that their intent was to uphold the rule of law and not to effect social control. As Merton (1968) pointed out, the consequences of human behavior are often unintended, and in the study of such consequences lie "the distinctive intellectual contributions of the sociologist" (Merton, 1968 : 120).

Theoretical and Research Implications

Although I have focused on Vietnam protest trials, my arguments apply equally to conservative movements, whose members' activities may also lead to criminal prosecution (Moran, 1981). My discussion also applies to trials of persons accused of committing crimes *against* members of reform movements. As we have seen, for example, prosecutions of defendants in the 1960s for murdering and beating civil rights activists in the South often ended in acquittals (Cumming, 1966; Meltsner, 1964), because white jurors were so opposed to civil rights goals that they nullified law and evidence without being told in court of their power to do so. Nullification can also work the other way: juries may *convict* political defendants who represent a movement they oppose, as happened repeatedly during World War I (Chafee, 1941; Peterson and Fite, 1957). The jury's power to nullify is thus a double-edged sword, and arguments to inform juries of their power can both advance and impede social change efforts. There remains the larger issue of what would happen to the legal system in the United States and its rule of law if juries in all criminal cases were informed of their power to nullify. Acquittals would probably increase, though it is difficult to predict by how much; convictions might increase as well. This issue has been treated extensively in law review articles and other sources (Moran, 1981; Sax, 1968; Scheflin, 1972) and is beyond the scope of this chapter, which has concentrated on the ramifications for political trials and social movements.*

Several theoretical and research implications arise from this chapter. Legal doctrines and various rules of judicial procedure may have

---

* It is interesting here to speculate on the effects of public campaigns by social movements to inform citizens of the jury's historic power to nullify. Thus an attorney writing in the newsletter of the Central Committee for Conscientious Objectors (ccco), a national antidraft group based in Philadelphia, urged the peace movement to undertake such campaigns in light of the renewal of draft registration in July 1980.

a subtle, yet important, ideological basis that needs to be elucidated by sociologists, other social scientists and legal scholars. Such elucidation requires understanding the historical roots of various ideological doctrines and rules, for they do not arise in a social and political vacuum. This chapter has treated the principle of jury nullification from such a sociology of knowledge perspective, and the same could be done for the rules of evidence, the political question doctrine, the legal distinction between motive and intent, and other doctrines and rules that affect adjudication of political and nonpolitical matters. The extent to which Americans have internalized the various ideological tenets of the legal order likewise needs to be explored empirically.

Further research is also needed on the history, ideology, and operation of the jury. The debate over the jury's irrationality cannot be fully appreciated in the absence of an understanding of its use in political trials. Simon (1975) observes that the increased attention paid by social scientists to the jury in the late 1960s and early 1970s was due in large part to the celebrated political cases of the period. The history of the jury in Great Britain and the United States is strongly tied to various political and religious struggles, but this relation between legal and political change has not received sufficient sociological attention.

The proponents and opponents of the "new" criminology also need to look more closely at the jury. Chambliss and Seidman (1971), for example, are two of the few members of the debate over the "new criminology" who do discuss the jury. Contending that the very possibility of a trial by jury legitimates a criminal justice system that they themselves criticize, they echo Arnold's (1935) earlier, more dispassionate observation. One aim of this book has been to illustrate that the right to trial by jury in American democracy is not so easily adapted to the arguments of either side in the debate prompted by the "new" criminology.

George Bernard Shaw once commented, "'The power of the jury on occasion to deliver an accused person from both the police and the letter of the law is the sole reason for its existence as an institution'" (in Mitford, 1969 : 211). In this observation lies the fascination of the jury; though used in only a small proportion of all criminal cases, it continues to capture the imagination of Americans as one of the most important symbols of our liberty. The legitimacy it thus lends to our legal and political systems is praised by some and scored by others, and thus its consequences for social movement protest as well as for conventional criminal activity need further exploration by social scientists and legal scholars.

Chapter Nine

Conclusion: Social Movements and Political Justice

I n American democracy the outcome of political justice is by no means certain. Rights to due process, jury trials, and press coverage of trial proceedings may limit government efforts to use the criminal courts as vehicles of repression, and, conversely, sometimes make it possible for social movements to use the courts to mobilize important resources. The potential of political justice for either side depends on a number of conditions that have been examined in the preceding chapters. Among the most important is the political climate—public opinions toward protesters and their goals.

There are several correlates of such opinions. As representatives of the public, juries reflect the political climate, and their readiness to convict or acquit political defendants is a variable of profound importance for the dynamics and outcome of political trials. The political climate is also reflected in the attitude of the press toward protest goals, and the likelihood of press coverage favorable to the defense is yet another important variable for the study of social movement litigation. Finally, the political climate is manifested to some degree in the attitudes and behavior of judges and prosecutors. In some eras they may be more sympathetic, or at least less hostile, to the aims of social movements than in other eras. Here the discretion of trial judges in conducting the procedings assumes considerable importance. They may conduct trials in a manner prejudicial to the defense; they may guide trials in a neutral manner; they may allow the defense a good deal of latitude in presenting political and moral issues. The social movement trials I have examined illustrate the impact of judges' rulings on the success with which defense teams may politicize their trials, and the influence of judges' instructions on the willingness of jurors to nullify the law.

Political climate affects the fortunes of social movements in the criminal courts in other ways as well. The availability of attorneys and the degree of legal, physical, and social harassment they encounter depend in part on the political climate and constitute another crucial variable that shapes the dynamics and outcome of political justice. The willingness of defense attorneys and political defendants to attempt to politicize their trials also varies, for reasons I have mentioned earlier. These trial participants are less likely to launch such efforts if they think that juries and the press will be unresponsive, and if they fear legal and other forms of punishment.

Since political climate and its many social, legal, and political correlates vary over time and space, it is possible to place social movements along a spectrum of political justice ranging from complete social control on the part of the government and other antagonists to complete mobilization on the part of the movement. The colonial, abolitionist, and Vietnam War periods were three eras where the criminal courts offered striking possibilities of mobilization for social movements, while the federalist struggles in the late 1700s, the years during and immediately after World War I, and the civil rights movement in the South were three periods where the criminal courts served as effective means of legal harassment and control. Hagan and Bernstein (1979:109) note that "surprisingly little attention has been given to the actual empirical connections that have existed in our recent history between social and political movements and patterns of criminal sanctioning." These connections become apparent when we examine the use of the criminal courts during the Southern civil rights and Vietnam antiwar movements; in the preceding chapters I have elaborated on a number of factors that affected defense strategies in the two movements and determined the degree of mobilization and social control that the courts offered to social movements and their opponents.

Criminal prosecutions of civil rights and antiwar protesters were not just legal events restricted to the immediate parties to the proceedings. They were also political activities that originated in the efforts of two social movements to change the status quo and that affected the success of their insurgency. It is thus impossible to understand the origins, dynamics, and outcomes of prosecutions in the two movements from the standpoint of traditional legal theory. But neither is it possible to understand the prosecutions unless we keep in mind their legal context as well. Even in the South, where legality made only a token appearance at the trial level, legal forms were still followed. Although outright, brutal repression was far from rare, the South used legal procedure and legal agents as a primary means of social control. In Vietnam protest trials, the neutral rules of legal procedure profoundly affected the nature and outcome of the political conflict that took place in the courts. That in general judges and prosecutors conformed to due process made for fair trials, but these same rules of legal procedure limited the extent to which the antiwar movement could turn its trials into forums for the expression of its grievances.

Thus the two movements present vivid contrasts in political justice. In the South, the criminal courts were effective vehicles of social control. Few attorneys were willing to defend civil rights defendants. The political prosecutions that arose were largely devoid of the procedural guarantees associated with the American legal system. For many historical and political reasons, legal authorities felt little need to invoke "formal legal rationality," and juries expedited the use of the courts for purposes of social control. The risk of political justice was all on the side of the civil rights movement, and the "rewards" accrued to local and state officials. In the criminal courts, civil rights defense teams employed technical arguments, feeling that political lines of argument would be futile and lead to several difficulties. Although numerous convictions were later overturned on appeal, in many ways that can be of small comfort to the defendants who spent many days in Southern jails and to the movement itself, which lost valuable time, money, and energy. The prosecutions of movement protesters were just one facet of the total effort of the South to defeat the movement.

In the antiwar movement, a different view of political justice emerges, as the use of the criminal courts brought both risks and rewards to both sides to the proceedings. Thousands of antiwar protesters were arrested and convicted. The government indicted several movement leaders in celebrated conspiracy cases, but it often failed to obtain convictions in these cases and ultimately embarrassed itself in the view of many observers. In these and other trials, defendants and their lawyers were much more willing than their civil rights counterparts to use the courts as forums for political and moral arguments. Trials usually followed due process standards, though judges and prosecutors limited the degree to which the defense could talk about the war and other issues. Juries acquitted at times and at least offered defense teams some hope of favorable verdicts, prompting defense efforts at politicization. These efforts also won press attention, helping to publicize movement goals.

To return to a question raised in the first chapter: what conclusions can be drawn from the contrasting pictures of political justice in the civil rights and antiwar movements for theories of law, power, and American society? Before suggesting some answers to this question, it will be helpful to review briefly the major theories. Pluralist theory, as developed by Dahl (1956, 1967) and others (Auerbach, 1959; Pound, 1943; Rose, 1967; Truman, 1951), assumes that society is composed of various interest groups that often compete for power and influence. Individual groups sometimes win, but other times they fail, with no single group able to achieve its goals consistently over the long run. In this view, the state and its legal order (which, following traditional legal theory, is considered independent from the state) act as neutral referees or umpires over the interest group conflict.

In contrast, Marxist and conflict theories argue that law and the state act on behalf of powerful groups in society and against the interests of the powerless (see Bernard, 1981, for differences between conflict and Marxist theories of crime and law). It is true, as several observers have pointed out (Cain and Hunt, 1979; Collins, 1982; Jessop, 1977), that Marx and Engels did not develop a complete, coherent theory of the state or of law. In recent years, however, Marxist thinkers in Europe and the United States have attempted to develop such a theory. Although all agree that the state and its legal order broadly serve the interests of the capitalist ruling class, at least three competing Marxist views on the nature of this relationship have emerged. (For fuller discussions and critiques see Balbus, 1982; Beirne and Quinney, 1982; Block, 1977; Gold, Clarence, and Wright, 1975a, 1975b; Gordon, 1982; Greenberg, 1981; Greenberg and Anderson, 1981; Hepburn, 1977; Inciardi, 1980; Jessop, 1977; Wolfe, 1974.)

The instrumentalist view sees law and the state as tools that can be directly manipulated by the ruling class to dominate subordinate groups and to protect and advance its own interests (Kolko, 1962; Lefcourt, 1971; Michalowski and Bohlander, 1976; Miliband, 1969; Quinney, 1974, 1977). As Quinney (1977:45) puts it, "The state exists as a device for controlling the exploited class, the class that labors, for the benefit of the ruling class. . . . Contrary to conventional wisdom, law instead of representing community custom is an instrument of the state that serves the interests of the developing capitalist ruling class." Marxist and non-Marxist critics of this perspective counter that it is too simplistic (Balbus, 1982; Chambliss and Seidman, 1982; Gold, Clarence, and Wright, 1975a; Greenberg, 1976; Mankoff, 1978). It can be readily shown, they argue, that ruling-class members often suffer political and legal losses, and, further, are divided among themselves over important issues.

The Marxist structuralist view attempts to avoid those problems. As developed by French thinkers Poulantzas (1973) and Althusser (1970, 1971), this view admits that ruling-class members disagree over important issues and compete among themselves for power and influence. Such competition may lead to short-term victories that benefit a particular ruling-class group but threaten the long-term interest of all ruling-class members in preserving the existing capitalist order. The state (and its legal order) thus exist to prevent threatening short-term victories by a particular ruling-class group. For such a strategy to succeed, however, the state and legal order must be "relatively autonomous" from the ruling class (Beirne, 1979). Such relative autonomy not only guarantees the state the power to act in the long-term interests of the capitalist class but also helps legitimate the existing order in the eyes of the public. Chambliss and Seidman (1982:308) summarize this view: "The state and the legal order best fulfill their function as legitimizers when they appear to function as value neutral organs fairly and impartially representing the interests of everyone." But such fairness and relative autonomy inevitably make possible short-term legal and political victories by subordinate groups. According to structuralists, these victories are sham ones, since they ironically, and ideologically, serve to legitimate the state and existing order while still preserving the long-term interests of the capitalist class (Poulantzas, 1973). Echoing Pashukanis's earlier view (1929/1978), attempts by subordinate groups to use legal means are consequently seen as inherently self-defeating (Bankowski and Mungham, 1976; Collins, 1982; Mathiesen, 1980).

Marxist critics of this view reply that it is tautological and non-falsifiable since it does not admit the possibility of any real victories by subordinate groups (Balbus, 1982; Chambliss and Seidman, 1982; Jacobs, 1980). As Chambliss and Seidman (1982:314–315) argue, "One cannot disprove so tautological a theory. If the state acts in defense of capitalist interests, it acts because of capitalist control of the state. If it acts against capitalist interests, despite appearances, the state still acts in capital interests. A theory that data cannot conceivably contradict—that is, a nonfalsifiable theory—tells us very little."

As an alternative view, some Marxist thinkers have developed what may be called a "class struggle" (Chambliss, 1979; Skocpol, 1980; Wright, 1978) or "dialectical" (Chambliss and Seidman, 1982) view of law and the state (see also Grau, 1982; Trubek, 1977). In this view, legal and political relations are the result of an ongoing struggle between ruling and subordinate classes. While acknowledging the ideological functions of law, class struggle theorists feel that efforts by subordinate groups in the legal and political arenas can lead to real, not just sham, victories. They emphasize, moreover, that while law is often used by ruling-class members as an effective weapon, law simultaneously restricts their capacity to suppress the powerless. Civil liberties and the rule of law are thus seen as real, important benefits for the powerless groups, and not just shams that legitimate an oppressive system (Gabel and Harris, 1982–1983; Gordon, 1982; Rabinowitz, 1982). E. P. Thompson (1975:263–264) articulates this perspective in his famous and, in Marxist circles, controversial (see Redhead, 1982) conclusion to his study of crime in eighteenth-century England: "We reach, then, not a simple conclusion (law = class power) but a complex and contradictory one. On the one hand, it is true that the law did mediate existent class relations to the advantage of the rulers. . . . On the other hand, the law mediated these class relations through legal forms, which imposed, again and again, inhibitions upon the actions of the rulers. For there is a very large difference, which twentieth-century experience ought to have made clear even to the most exalted thinker, between arbitrary extra-legal power and the rule of law."

How well, then, do the pluralist and competing Marxist theories fit the legal experiences of the civil rights and antiwar movements? The answer depends largely on the degree of autonomy from the state experienced by the legal order in each movement (see Balbus, 1977 : xxi). In the civil rights movement, there can be little question that the Southern legal system served, with few exceptions, as an instrument for white officials to suppress black protest and goals. If this is true, then the instrumentalist Marxist theory, despite its simplicity when applied to other settings, best fits the civil rights experience. This conclusion, however, would not trouble most pluralist defenders of the American legal and political systems. Although the example of the civil rights movement does not support their argument, they would counter that the movement took place in a segregated, undemocratic region and thus is an exceptional case that is irrelevant to their pluralist thesis. For this reason, Marxist or other conflict-oriented critics would be remiss in pointing to the civil rights movement to support their perspectives. Thus it is to the antiwar movement that we must turn for more compelling evidence to support either camp.

Here the conclusion is by no means simple, as should be clear from this work, since outcomes of antiwar trials were not at all certain. The courts served as both mechanisms of social control and of mobilization. Pluralists would be quick to point out (as structuralists nod knowingly) that trials of antiwar protesters generally followed standards of due process, with some defendants even avoiding convictions, and to argue further that the courts thus functioned as a neutral setting for the conflict between the antiwar movement and the state. The fact that the war lasted some ten years and remained impervious to legal challenge should suggest, however, that the legal setting was stacked against the movement (cf. Handler, 1978). Further, even with the protection of due process, the jury, and the press that are hallmarks of American democracy, it is still important to ask, as Mitford (1969 : 238) does in regard to the Spock case, "When applied to a [political] case, does not the cherished concept of due process of law . . . become an elaborate sham to mask what is in reality a convenient device to silence opponents of governmental policies?" Moreover, certain aspects of the criminal trial process, such as the rules of evidence, were used repeatedly to shield the war and the draft from defense scrutiny. The refusals of trial judges to notify juries of their powers of nullification may have been, in a legal sense, well motivated, but once again served an ideological function, namely, to protect the government from the impact of jury acquittals or deadlocked verdicts.

The acquittals that were won, the due process that was followed, and the views against the war that were aired in trials seem to dispute an instrumentalist argument, often heard at the time (see Lefcourt, 1971), that the legal system served merely as a tool to repress the movement. But structuralists would add that the acquittals, due process, and defense comments on the war were at best minor victories which did not come close to threatening the war's conduct and which served ideologically to confirm to editorial writers and the public the fairness and impartiality of the "system." They would add, further, that although the courts afforded the antiwar movement protection from brutal repression and the opportunity to mobilize some resources, the cost was high. Countless hours and hundreds of thousands of dollars were spent in the defense of antiwar activists, whether they were in court as civil disobedients or as defendants in state-initiated prosecutions; countless lives were disrupted for days or months at a time. And still the war went on.

Class struggle theorists would agree with much of the structuralist argument but claim that the acquittals and defense discussions of the war were real, important victories that helped further antiwar goals. Further, they would add, legal challenges to the draft succeeded, while the legality and due process enjoyed by antiwar defendants protected them from brutal repression or summary punishment, especially when compared to the experience of protesters in the World War I era or in undemocratic nations.

The picture of the legal experience of the antiwar movement developed in this book fits most closely to the class struggle perspective, especially as articulated by E. P. Thompson. It is true that prosecutions of antiwar activists cost the movement large amounts of time, money, and energy. It is also true that the legal victories of the movement did not stop the war and were readily interpreted by conservatives and liberals alike as confirmations of the fairness of the American system. But they were victories nonetheless that helped the movement in important ways. Moreover, although the legality and due process enjoyed by the movement should not lead to unreserved praise for the American legal system, these legal protections nonetheless prevented the kind of legal repression facing civil rights activists in the South or labor radicals and socialists in the World War I era. As Thompson (1975:266) reminds us, "It is true that in history the law can be seen to mediate and to legitimate existent class relations. Its forms and procedure may crystalize those relations and mask ulterior injustice. But this mediation, though the forms of law, is something quite different from the exercise of unmediated force. The forms and rhetoric of law acquire a distinct identity which may, on occasion, inhibit power and afford some protection to the powerless."

This conclusion will seem unradical and certainly unMarxist to some; indeed, Thompson's own views have been criticized by several Marxist thinkers as blindly extolling law and ignoring its inherently oppressive character (e.g. Redhead, 1982). I have certainly not meant to celebrate the American legal and political systems; nor, however, have I meant categorically to condemn them. The fact remains that political justice in American democracy is indeed fraught with risks and rewards for government and social movement alike. Formal legal norms and rules of procedure may constrain public officials while simultaneously stifling the attempts of radical activists to effect social and political change through legal means. At the same time, whether movements stand to gain or lose in the legal arena depends on the particular historical circumstances in which every movement finds itself. The help that the jury and the press may give political defendants changes from one era to another. The willingness of officials to conform to formal norms of the legal system to preserve legitimacy is likewise historically specific, contrary to what Balbus (1973, 1977) and other structuralists imply in their critique of instrumentalist Marxism. Here we need only recall the use of law during World War I to suppress dissent. What is needed then, is a theory of the conditions under which officials resort, or do not resort, to legal repression aided by an obliging legal system. My emphasis on political climate represents a start at exploring one such condition, but only a start.

Political trials are not just settings for the struggle between protesters and state officials. They also reflect a larger conflict between formal (or procedural) and substantive (related to the justness of outcomes) that Weber (1922/1967) long ago saw as inevitable and viewed as the frame of reference for understanding the struggle for power in the modern state (see Bendix, 1962). He considered a balance—however strained—between the two kinds of justice as characterizing modern systems of legal domination. Formal justice, he thought, worked both for and against the dominant interests in society; while it impeded the efforts of the powerless to advance their interests, it also circumscribed attempts by the powerful to strengthen their own (Weber, 1922/1967:228–229).

If history is any guide to the future, political trials and other legal actions involving social movements will always be with us. Criminal courts will continue to be especially dramatic settings for the conflict between protesters and the state. These trials allow us to assess the role of law in American society and the validity of various conceptions of law and the state. Despite their internal disagreements, Marxist and other radical critics have made a valuable contribution by emphasizing the ideological functions of law in capitalist society. Although some of these critics believe that victories by social movements and other interest groups may ultimately "produce only limited infringements upon the prerogatives of the ruling class" (Michalowski and Bohlander, 1976:100; see also Bankowski and Mungham, 1976; Mathiesen, 1980) and lull the powerless into complacency, others feel that law provides the opportunity for real, effective change and, at the very least, protects against the use of arbitrary power.

Such is the blessing and curse of the American legal system. Its complexity defies easy understanding and interpretation, yet remains ever open to analysis from competing perspectives. If we are to fully understand the impact of law in American society and the factors that influence the outcome of the conflict between social movements and their opponents, then the operation and influence of the legal system in times of social unrest should occupy a central place in future research on law, protest, and society.

Bibliography

Aaronson, David E., ed.
1975   *Maryland criminal jury instructions and commentary.*
                Charlottesville, Va.: Michie.

Alexander, Milnor
1962   The right to counsel for the politically unpopular. *Law in
                Transition* 22 (Spring): 19–45.

Allen, Francis
1967   Civil disobedience and the legal order. *University of Cin-
                cinnati Law Review* 36: 175.
1974   *The crimes of politics: Political dimensions of criminal
                justice.* Cambridge, Mass.: Harvard University Press.

Althusser, Louis
1970   *Reading capital.* London: New Left Books.
1971   Ideology and ideological state apparatuses. In *Lenin and
                philosophy and other essays,* pp. 121–173. London: New
                Left Books.

American Digest System
1976   Eighth decennial: Criminal law 768 (10). St. Paul, Minn.:
                West.

Antonio, R. J.
1972   The processual dimension of degradation ceremonies:
                The Chicago conspiracy trial: Success or failure? *British
                Journal of Sociology* 23 (September): 287–297.

Arnold, Thurman
1935   *The symbols of government.* New Haven: Yale University
                Press.

Auerbach, Carl
1959   Law and social change in the United States. *UCLA Law
                Review* 6: 516.

Auerbach, Jerold S.
1976   *Unequal justice: Lawyers and social change in modern
                America.* New York: Oxford University Press.

Axelrod, Beverly
1971   The radical lawyer. In *Radical lawyers: Their role in the movement and in the courts,* ed. Jonathan Black, pp. 69–74. New York: Avon.

Bailey, Harry A., Jr.
1969   Negro interest group strategies. *Urban Affairs Quarterly* 4 (September): 26–38.

Balbus, Isaac
1973   *The dialectics of legal repression.* New York: Russell Sage.
1977   *The dialectics of legal repression.* Paper ed. New York: Transaction Books.
1982   *Marxism and domination.* Princeton: Princeton University Press.

Ball, Harry V., and Lawrence M. Friedman
1965   The use of criminal sanctions in the enforcement of economic legislation: A sociological view. *Stanford Law Review* 17: 197–223.

Bankowski, Zenon, and Geoff Mungham

1976   *Images of law.* London: Routledge and Kegan Paul.

Bannan, John R., and Rosemary S. Bannan
1974   *Law, morality, and Vietnam: The peace militants and the courts.* Bloomington: Indiana University Press.

Bardacke, Frank
1971   The Oakland 7. In *Radical lawyers: Their role in the movement and in the courts,* ed. Jonathan Black, pp. 176–191. New York: Avon.

Bardolph, Richard, ed.
1970   *The civil rights record: Black Americans and the law, 1849–1970.* New York: Thomas Y. Crowell.

Barkan, Steven E.
1979   Strategic, tactical and organizational dilemmas of the protest movement against nuclear power. *Social Problems* 27 (October): 19–37.

Baskir, Lawrence M., and William A. Strauss
1978   *Chance and circumstance: The draft, the war, and the Vietnam generation.* New York: Vintage.

Bay Area Friends of SNCC
1963   Leaflet, no date. In files of Meiklejohn Civil Liberties Institute, Berkeley, California.

Becker, Theodore L., ed.
1971   *Political trials*. Indianapolis: Bobbs-Merrill.

Beirne, Piers
1979   Empiricism and the critique of Marxism on law and
               crime. *Social Problems* 26 (April): 373–385.

Beirne, Piers, and Richard Quinney, eds.
1982   *Marxism and law*. New York: Wiley.

Belfrage, Sally
1963   Danville on trial. *New Republic* (2 November): 11–12.
1965   *Freedom summer*. Greenwich, Conn.: Fawcett.

Belknap, Michal R.
1978   *Cold War political justice: The Smith Act, the CIA, and
               American civil liberties*. New York: Greenwood.
1981   Introduction: Political trials in the American past. In
               American political trials, ed. Michal Belknap, pp. 3–20.
               Westport, Conn.: Greenwood.

Bell, Derrick, A., Jr.
1973   Race, racism, and American law. Boston: Little, Brown.

Bendix, Reinhard
1962   *Max Weber: An intellectual portrait*. New York: Anchor.

Bennett, Lerone, Jr.
1970   When the man and the hour are met. In *Martin Luther
               King, Jr.: A profile*, ed. C. Eric Lincoln, pp. 7–39. New
               York: Hill and Wang.

Berkman, Alexander
1912   *Prison memoirs of an anarchist*. New York: Mother
               Earth Publishing Association.

Bernard, Thomas
1981   The distinction between conflict and radical criminol-
               ogy. *Journal of Criminal Law and Criminology* 72(1):
               362–379.

Berrigan, Philip
1972   An open letter to a bishop. *Commonweal* (26 May):
               282–285.

Bickel, Alexander
1962   *The least dangerous branch: The Supreme Court at the
               bar of politics*. Indianapolis: Bobbs-Merrill.

Bigart, Homer
1964   St. Augustine mob attacks Negroes. *New York Times* (26
               June): 1+.

Black, Donald
1973   The mobilization of law. *Journal of Legal Studies* 2:125.

Black, Jonathan, ed.
1971   *Radical lawyers: Their role in the movement and in the
               courts.* New York: Avon.

Blankenburg, Erhard
1975   Studying federal civil litigation in Germany. *Law and So-
               ciety Review* 9:307–320.

Blanshard, Paul
1966   Liberty within the Catholic church. *Catholic World* (Sep-
               tember): 335–340.

Bleiweiss, Robert M., ed.
1969   *Marching to freedom: The life of Martin Luther King, Jr.*
               New York: New American Library.

Blicker, David
1963   Letter to Ann Fagan Ginger, 29 June. In files of Meiklejohn
               Civil Liberties Institute, Berkeley, California.

Block, Fred
1977   The ruling class does not rule. *Socialist Review* 7 (May–
               June): 6–28.

Blumberg, Abraham S.
1967   *Criminal justice.* Chicago: Quadrangle.
1974   Crime and the social order. In *Current perspectives on
               criminal behavior,* ed. Abraham S. Blumberg, pp. 3–24.
               New York: Knopf.

Boudin, Kathy, Brian Glick, Eleanor Raskin, and Gūstin Reichback
1971   From the bust book. In *Radical lawyers: Their role in
               the movement and in the courts,* ed. Jonathan Black,
               pp. 99–107. New York: Avon.

Boynton v. Virginia, 364 US 454 (1960).

Brick, Steven A.
1971   Self-representation in criminal trials: The dilemma of the
               pro se defendant. *California Law Review* 59 (November):
               1479–1513.

Brown, Robert McAfee
1967   The church and Vietnam. *Commonweal* (13 October):
               52–55.

Brown v. Louisiana, 383 U.S. 131 (1966).

Burns, Haywood
1971   Racism and American law. In *Law against the people: Es-
               says to demystify law, order, and the courts*, ed. Robert
               Lefcourt, pp. 38–54. New York: Vintage.

Burnstein, Malcolm
1969   Trying a political case. *Guild Practitioner* 28 (Spring):
               33–40.

Cain, Maureen, and Alan Hunt, eds.
1979   *Marx and Engels on law*. London: Academic Press.

Campbell, Stanley W.
1970   *The slave catchers: Enforcement of the Fugitive Slave
               Law, 1850–1860*. Chapel Hill: University of North Caro-
               lina Press.

Carter, Barbara
1963   A lawyer leaves the South. *Reporter* (9 May): 33–35.

Casper, Jonathan D.
1972   *Lawyers before the Warren Court: Civil liberties and
               civil rights, 1957–1966*. Urbana: University of Illinois
               Press.

Central Committee for Conscientious Objectors (ccco)
1980   Legal refusal to participate in government programs de-
               signed to kill people. *Counter Pentagon* 7 (April): 3–4.

Chafee, Zechariah, Jr.
1941   *Free speech in the United States*. Cambridge, Mass.: Har-
               vard University Press.

Chambliss, William J.
1974   The state and criminal law. In *Whose law? What order?
               A conflict approach to criminology*, ed., William J.
               Chambliss and Milton Mankoff, pp. 66–107. New York:
               Wiley.
1979   Constraints and conflicts in law creation. In *Research in
               Law and Sociology*, ed. Steven Spitzer, pp. 3–27. Vol. 2.
               Greenwich, Conn.: JAI Press.

Chambliss, William J., and Robert B. Seidman
1971   *Law, order and power*. Reading, Mass.: Addison-Wesley.

1982   *Law, order and power.* 2d ed. Reading, Mass.: Addison-
              Wesley.

Chiricos, Theodore, and Gordon Waldo
1975   Socioeconomic status and criminal sentencing: An em-
              pirical assessment of a conflict proposition. *American
              Sociological Review* 40:753–772.

Chomsky, Noam, Paul Lauter, and Florence Howe
1979   Reflections on a political trial. In *Trials of the resistance,*
              pp. 74–105. New York: New York Review.

Clark, Kenneth B.
1969   The social scientists, the Brown decision, and contempo-
              rary confusion. In *Argument: The oral argument before
              the Supreme Court in Brown v. Board of Education in
              Topeka, 1952–1955,* ed. Leon Friedman, pp. xxx–l. New
              York: Chelsea.

Cleghorn, Reese
1963   Epilogue in Albany: Were the mass marches worthwhile?
              New Republic (20 July): 15–18.
1970   Crowned with crises. In *Martin Luther King, Jr.: A pro-
              file,* ed. C. Eric Loncoln, pp. 113–127. New York: Hill and
              Wang.

Clinard, Marshall B., and Richard Quinney
1973   *Criminal behavior systems: A typology.* 2d ed. New
              York: Holt, Rinehart, and Winston.

Cogley, John
1965   The clergy heeds a new call. *New York Times Magazine*
              (2 May): 42–43.
1970   A church torn between dogma and dissent. *Life* (20
              March): 22–31.

Cohen, Carl
1971   *Civil disobedience: Conscience, tactics, and the law.*
              New York: Columbia University Press.

Cohn, Henry S.
1972   Request and Authorization to dismiss criminal case.
              Document in FBI file of Steven E. Barkan, obtained under
              Freedom of Information Act.

Collins, Hugh
1982   *Marxism and law.* Oxford: Clarendon.

Commonweal
1972   The real America. (26 May): 275–276.

Cortner, R. C.
1968   Strategies and tactics of litigants in constitutional cases. *Journal of Public Law* 17 : 287–307.

Cox, Archibald
1967   Direct action, civil disobedience, and the Constitution. In *Civil rights, the Constitution, and the courts*, ed. Archibald Cox, Mark DeWolfe Howe, and J. R. Wiggins. Cambridge, Mass.: Harvard University Press.

Cox, Harvey
1967   The "new breed" in American churches: Sources of social activism in American religion. *Daedalus* 96 (Winter): 133–150.

Crow, Ginny, and Sue Davidson
1978   Bringing your action to court. *WIN Magazine* (20 January): 4–6.

Cumming, Joseph B., Jr.
1966   Morgan's crusade for Negro jurors. *Reporter* (10 February): 39.

Dahl, Robert A.
1956   *A preface to democratic theory.* Chicago: University of Chicago Press.

1967   *Pluralist democracy in the United States: Conflict and consent.* Chicago: Rand McNally.

Danelski, David J.
1971   "The Chicago Conspiracy Trial." In *Political trials*, ed. Theodore L. Becker, pp. 134–180. Indianapolis: Bobbs-Merrill.

Deedy, John
1968a   News and views. *Commonweal* (12 January): 426.
1968b   News and views. *Commonweal* (10 May): 220.
1968c   News and views. *Commonweal* (21 June): 394.

di Suvero, Henry
1971   The movement and the legal system. In *Radical lawyers: Their role in the movement and in the courts*, ed. Jonathan Black, pp. 51–69. New York: Avon.

Dorsen, Norman, and Leon Friedman
1973   *Disorder in the courts.* New York: Pantheon.

Douglas, James
1971   Organization, ego, and the practice of alternative law. *Yale Review of Law and Social Action* 2 (Fall): 88–92.

Drinnon, Richard
1961   *Rebel in paradise: A biography of Emma Goldman.*
               Boston: Beacon.

Drysdale, Scott
1978   Personal interview with the author by member of Abalone
               Alliance. Palo Alto, California, June 8.

Duff, Edward
1971   The burden of the Berrigans. *Holy Cross Quarterly* 4
               (January): 4–12.

Eisenstein, James, and Herbert Jacob
1977   *Felony justice.* Boston: Little, Brown.

Elliff, John T.
1971   *Crime, dissent, and the attorney general: The Justice De-
               partment in the 1960's.* Beverly Hills, Calif.: Sage.

Engstrom, Karen
n.d.   Jury frees activists as war protest. *Guardian.* Clipping in
               files of Meiklejohn Civil Liberties Institute, Berkeley,
               California.

Epstein, Jason
1970   *The great conspiracy trial.* New York: Vintage.

Erlanger, Howard S.
1970   Jury research in America: Its past and future. *Law and
               Society Review* 4 (February): 345–370.

Evan, William M.
1965   Law as an instrument of social change. In *Applied so-
               ciology,* ed. Alvin Gouldner and S. M. Miller. New York:
               Free Press.

Evans, Glenn V.
1977   Interview with Glenn V. Evans. In *My soul is rested,* ed.
               Howell Raines, pp. 187–196. New York: Bantam.

Farmer, James
1977   Interview with James Farmer. In *My soul is rested,* ed.
               Howell Raines, pp. 128–138. New York: Bantam.

Farrell, Barry
1973   The Ellsberg mask. Harper's (October): 79+.

Felstiner, W. E.
1974   Influences of social organization on dispute processing.
               Law and Society Review 9:63–94.

Ferber, Michael, and Staughton Lynd
1971   *The resistance.* Boston: Beacon Press.

Fingerhood, Shirley
1965   The Fifth Circuit of Appeals. In *Southern justice,* ed.
               Leon Friedman, pp. 214–227. New York: Pantheon.

Finkelman, Paul
1981   The Zenger case: Prototype of a political trial. In *American political trials,* ed. Michal Belknap, pp. 21–42. Westport, Conn.: Greenwood.

Flaum, Joel M., and James R. Thompson
1970   The case of the disruptive defendant: *Allen v. Illinois. Journal of Criminal Law* 61:327.

Forest, Linda
1969   Moses and the Milwaukee 14. *Commonweal* (27 June): 410–413.

Form, William H., and Joan Rytina.
1969   Ideological beliefs on the distribution of power in the United States. *American Journal of Sociology* 34:19–31.

Forman, James
1973   *The making of black revolutionaries.* New York: Macmillan.

Forsyth, William
1971   *History of trial by jury.* 2d ed. Prepared by James A.
[1898]   Morgan. New York: B. Franklin.

Fortas, Abe
1968   *Concerning dissent and civil disobedience.* New York: Signet.

Frank, Jerome
1949   *Courts on trial.* Princeton: Princeton University Press.

Frankfurter, Felix
1971   *Law and politics: Occasional papers of Felix Frankfurter.* Edited by Archibald MacLeish and E. F. Prichard, Jr. Gloucester, Mass.: Peter Smith.

Frankfurter, Felix, and Nathan Greene
1930   *The labor injunction.* New York: Macmillan.

Franklin, Ben A.
1963   Danville method studied in South. *New York Times* (11 August): 71.

Franklin, John Hope
1969   *From slavery to freedom: A history of Negro Americans.*
                3d ed. New York: Vintage.

Friedman, Lawrence M.
1973   *A history of American law.* New York: Simon and
                Schuster.
1975   *The legal system: A social science perspective.* New
                York: Russell Sage.

Friedman, Leon, ed.
1965   *Southern justice.* New York: Pantheon.
1969   *Argument: The oral argument before the Supreme Court
                in Brown v. Board of Education of Topeka, 1952–1955.*
                New York: Chelsea.
1970   Political power and legal legitimacy: A short history of
                political trials. *Antioch Review* 30:157–170.
1971   *The wise minority.* New York: Dial.

Gabel, Peter, and Paul Harris
1982–1983   Building power and breaking images: Critical legal theory
                and the practice of law. *NYU Review of Law and Social
                Change* 11:369–411.

Galanter, Marc
1974   Why the "haves" come out ahead: Speculations on the
                limits of legal change. *Law and Society Review* 9:95–160.

Galphin, Bruce
1963   When a Negro is on trial in the South. *New York Times
                Magazine* (15 December): 17+.
1964   Judge Pye and the hundred sit-ins. *New Republic* (30
                May): 8–9.

Gamson, William
1975   *The strategy of social protest.* Homewood, Ill.: Dorsey.

Gannon, Thomas M.
1968   Trial of the Catonsville 9. *America* (26 October):
                377–379.

Gardner, Ed
1977   Interview with Ed Gardner. In *My soul is rested*, ed.
                Howell Raines, pp. 149–157. New York: Bantam.

Garner v. Louisiana, 368 US 157 (1961).

Garrow, David J.
1978   *Protest at Selma: Martin Luther King, Jr., and the Voting
                Rights Act of 1965.* New Haven: Yale University Press.

Garry, Charles
1971   Political lawyers and their clients. In *The relevant lawyers*, ed. Ann Fagan Ginger, pp. 68–97. New York: Simon and Schuster.

Garry, Charles, and Art Goldberg
1977   *Streetfighter in the courtroom: The people's advocate.* New York: E. P. Dutton.

Georgetown Law Journal
1971   Judicial response to the disruptive defendant. 60:281.

Gerbasi, Kathleen C., Mirion Zuckerman, and Harry T. Reis
1977   Justice needs a new blindfold: A review of mock jury research. *Psychological Bulletin* 84 (March): 323–345.

Ginger, Ann Fagan
1963   Litigation as a form of political action. *Wayne State University Law Review* 9:458–483.
1964   *Civil liberties handbook.* Berkeley, Calif.: National Lawyers Guild.
1972   *What's new in the law?* 2 (October): 5.
1974   Due process in practice or whatever's fair. *Hastings Law Journal* 25 (March): 897–961.
1979   Interview with the author at Meiklejohn Civil Liberties Institute, Berkeley, California, May 21.

Ginger, Ray
1949   *Eugene V. Debs: A biography.* New York: Collier.

Goffman, Erving
1959   *The presentation of self in everyday life.* New York: Doubleday.

Gold, David A., Clarence Y. H. Lo, and Erik Olin Wright
1975a   Recent developments in Marxist theories of the capitalist state. *Monthly Review* 27 (October): 29–43.
1975b   Recent developments in Marxist theories of the capitalist state, Part II. *Monthly Review* 27 (November): 36–51.

Goodell, Charles
1973   *Political prisoners in America.* New York: Random House.

Goodwyn, Larry
1965   Anarchy in St. Augustine. *Harper's* (January): 74–81.

Gordon, Robert W.
1982   New developments in legal theory. In *The politics of law*, ed. David Kairys, pp. 281–293. New York: Pantheon.

Grano, Joseph D.
1970   The right to counsel: Collateral issues affecting due process. *Minnesota Law Review* 54:1175–1208.

Grau, Charles W.
1982   Whatever happened to politics? A critique of structuralist Marxist accounts of state and law. In *Marxism and law*, ed. Piers Beirne and Richard Quinney, pp. 196–209. New York: Wiley.

Gray, Francine du Plessix
1970   The ultra-resistance. In *Trials of the resistance*, pp. 125–161. New York: New York Review.
1971   *Divine disobedience: Profiles in Catholic radicalism.* New York: Knopf.

Green, Mark
1970   Law graduates: The new breed. *Nation* (1 June): 660.

Greenberg, David F.
1976   On one-dimensional Marxist criminology. *Theory and Society* 3:610–621.
1981   ed., *Crime and capitalism: Readings in Marxist criminology.* Palo Alto, Calif.: Mayfield.

Greenberg, David F., and Nancy Anderson
1981   Recent Marxisant Books in Law: A Review Essay. *Contemporary Crises* 5:293–322.

Greenberg, Jack
1959   *Race relations and American law.* New York: Columbia University Press.
1968   The Supreme Court, civil rights, and civil dissonance. *Yale Law Journal* 77:1520.

Greer, Scott, and Peter Orleans
1964   Political sociology. In *Handbook of modern sociology*, ed. Robert E. L. Faris. Chicago: Rand McNally.

Grossman, Joel B., and Austin Sarat
1975   Litigation in the federal courts: A comparative perspective. *Law and Society Review* 9:321–346.

Gurr, Ted
1970   *Why men rebel.* Princeton: Princeton University Press.

Gusfield, Joseph
1968   The study of social movements. In *International encyclopedia of the social sciences*, ed. David Sills. Vol. 14. New York: Macmillan.

Gutknecht, Dave, Peggy Naas, Scott Sandvik, and Dave Wood
1971　　　　　*Check out the odds*. Minneapolis: Twin Cities
　　　　　　　Resistance.

Gyrogy, Ann and friends (eleven authors)
1979　　　　　*No Nukes*. Boston: South End Press.

Hagan, John
1974　　　　　Extra-legal attributes and criminal sentencing: An assess-
　　　　　　　ment of a sociological viewpoint. *Law and Society Re-
　　　　　　　view* 8:357–383.

Hagan, John, and Ilene N. Bernstein
1979　　　　　Conflict in context: The sanctioning of draft resisters,
　　　　　　　1963–1976. *Social Problems* 27 (October): 109–122.

Hagan, John, and Jeffrey Leon
1977　　　　　Rediscovering delinquency: Social history, political ide-
　　　　　　　ology, and the sociology of law. *American Sociological
　　　　　　　Review* 42:487–498.

Hahn, Jeanne
1973　　　　　The NAACP Legal Defense and Educational Fund: Its ju-
　　　　　　　dicial strategy and tactics. In *American government and
　　　　　　　politics*, ed. Stephen L. Wasby, pp. 387–400. New York:
　　　　　　　Charles Scribner's Sons.

Hakman, Nathan
1972　　　　　Political trials in the legal order: A political scientist's
　　　　　　　perspective. *Journal of Public Law* 21:73–126.

Hall, Robert T.
1971　　　　　*The morality of civil disobedience*. New York: Harper
　　　　　　　and Row.

Handler, Joel
1978　　　　　*Social movements and the legal system*. New York: Aca-
　　　　　　　demic Press.

Hay, Douglas
1975　　　　　Property, authority, and criminal law. In *Albion's fatal
　　　　　　　tree: Crime and society in eighteenth-century England*,
　　　　　　　ed. Douglas Hay, Peter Linebaught, John G. Rule, E. P.
　　　　　　　Thompson, and Cal Winslow, pp. 17–63. New York:
　　　　　　　Pantheon.

Hayden, Tom
1970　　　　　*Trial*. New York: Holt, Rinehart and Winston.

Hepburn, John R.
1977   Social control and the legal order: Legitimated repression in a capitalist state. *Contemporary Crises* 1:77–90.

Holms v. Atlanta, 357 US 879 (1955).

Holt, Len
1965   *An act of conscience.* Boston: Beacon Press.
1966   *The summer that would not end.* New York: William Morrow.

Hopkins, Andrew
1975   On the sociology of criminal law. *Social Problems* 22 (June): 608–619.

Howe, Charles
1969   Draft resisters multiply—so do "new lawyers." *San Francisco Chronicle*, n.d., n.p. Clipping in files of Meiklejohn Civil Liberties Institute, Berkeley, California.

Howe, Mark DeWolfe
1939   Juries as judges of criminal law. *Harvard Law Review* 52:582–616.

Hyman, Harold M., and Catherine M. Tarrant
1975   Aspects of American trial jury history. In *The jury system in America: A critical overview,* ed. Rita James Simon, pp. 21–44. Beverly Hills, Calif.: Sage.

Inciardi, James A., ed.
1980   *Radical criminology: The coming crises.* Beverly Hills, Calif.: Sage.

Jackson, Donald D.
1974   *Judges.* New York: Atheneum.

Jackson, Robert H.
1940   The federal prosecutor. *Journal of American Judicature Society* 24:18.

Jacob, Herbert
1973   *Justice in America: Courts, lawyers, and the judicial process.* Boston: Little, Brown.

Jacobs, David
1980   Marxism and the critique of empricism: A comment on Beirne. *Social Problems* 27 (April): 467–470.

James, Marlise
1973   *The people's lawyers.* New York: Holt, Rinehart and Winston.

Jenkins, J. Craig
1979   What is to be done: Movement or organization? Review of
            Piven and Cloward, *Poor people's movements* in *Contem-*
            porary Sociology 8 (March): 222–228.

Jenkins, J. Craig, and Charles Perrow
1977   Insurgency of the powerless. *American Sociological Re-*
            view 42 (April): 249–268.

Jessop, Bob
1977   Recent theories of the capitalist state. *Cambridge Jour-*
            nal of Economics 1 : 353–373.

Jones, David A.
1981   *The law of criminal procedure: An analysis and critique.*
            Boston: Little, Brown.

Journal of Criminal Law, Criminology, and Police Science
1973   The right to appear *pro se*: The Constitution and the
            courts. 64 (June): 240–250.

Kadish, Mortimer, and Sanford H. Kadish
1973   *Discretion to disobey: A study of lawful departures from*
            legal rules. Palo Alto, Calif.: Stanford University Press.

Kahn, Journet
1966   Freedom in the Catholic Church. *Christian Century* (13
            April): 461–463.

Kalven, Harry, Jr.
1970   Chicago howler. *New Republic* (7 March): 21–23.

Kalven, Harry, Jr., and Hans Zeisel
1966   *The American jury.* Chicago: University of Chicago
            Press.

Kamisar, Yale
1969   The school desegregation cases in retrospect. In *Argu-*
            ment: The oral argument before the Supreme Court in
            Brown v. Board of Education of Topeka, 1952–1955, ed.
            Leon Friedman, pp. xiii–xxx. New York: Chelsea.

Karlen, Delmar
1971   Disorder in the courtroom. *Southern California Law Re-*
            view 44 : 996–1024.

Katzenbach, Nicholas
1969   Protest, politics and the First Amendment. *Tulane Law*
            Review 44 : 439.

Kessler, Joan B.
1975   The social psychology of jury deliberations. In *The jury
              system in America: A critical overview*, ed. Rita James
              Simon, pp. 69–87. Beverly Hills, Calif.: Sage.

Kifner, John
1973   8 acquitted in Gainesville of G.O.P. Convention plot.
              New York Times (1 September): 8.

King, Martin Luther, Jr.
1969   Letter from Birmingham city jail. In *Civil disobedience:
              Theory and practice*, ed. Hugo Adam Bedau, pp. 72–89.
              New York: Pegasus.

Kinoy, Arthur
1967   Brief remarks on *Dombrowski v. Pfister*: A new path
              in constitutional litigation. *The Guild Practitioner* 26
              (Winter): 7–11.

Kirchheimer, Otto
1961   *Political justice: The use of legal procedure for political
              ends*. Princeton: Princeton University Press.

Klapp, Orrin E.
1954   Heroes, villains and fools as agents of social control.
              American Sociological Review 19 (February): 56–62.

Kluger, Richard
1976   *Simple justice: The history of Brown v. Board of Educa-
              tion and black America's struggle for equality*. New
              York: Knopf.

Kolko, Gabriel
1962   *Wealth and power in America*. New York: Praeger.

Krisberg, Barry
1975   *Crime and privilege: Toward a new criminology*. En-
              glewood Cliffs, N.J.: Prentice-Hall.

Krislov, Samuel
1963   The *amicus curiae* brief: From friendship to advocacy.
              Yale Law Journal 72:694–721.

Kroll, Jack
1971   Morality play. *Newsweek* (22 February): 67.

Kucheman, Clark
1970   Churches and the Viet Nam issue. *Christianity Today* (23
              October): 15–16.

Kunstler, William M.
1961   Law and the sit-ins. *Nation* (4 November): 351–353.
1966   *Deep in my heart*. New York: William Morrow.

Kunstler, William M., and Arthur Kinoy
1964   Southern justice: Lawyers walk in fear. *Nation* (8 June): 576–580.

Langer, Elinor
1969   The Oakland 7. *Atlantic* (October): 78+.

Large, D. W.
1972   Is anybody listening? The problem of access in environmental litigation. *Wisconsin Law Review*: 62–113.

Laub, Burton
1964   The problem of the unrepresented, misrepresented, and rebellious defendant in criminal court. *Duquesne Law Review* 2:245.

Law Commune
1971   Insurgency in the courts. In *Radical lawyers: Their role in the movement and in the courts*, ed. Jonathan Black, pp. 289–297. New York: Avon.

Lefcourt, Robert, ed.
1971   *Law against the people*. New York: Vintage.

Levin, Martin A.
1977   *Urban politics and the criminal courts*. Chicago: University of Chicago Press.

Levy, Leonard W.
1960   *Legacy of suppression: Freedom of speech and press in early American history*. Cambridge, Mass.: Harvard University Press.

Lewis, Anthony and writers for the *New York Times*
1966   *The second American Revolution: A first-hand account of the struggle for civil rights*. London: Faber and Faber.

Lewis, David
1970   *King: A critical biography*. New York: Praeger.

Light, Charles
1978   Personal communication with the author from member of Clamshell Alliance Legal Committee.

Lipsky, Michael
1968   Protest as a political resource. *American Political Science Review* 62:1144–1158.

Lomax, Louis
1962   *The Negro revolt.* New York: Harper and Row.
1968   *To kill a black man.* Los Angeles: Holloway House.

Lukas, J. Anthony
1970   *The barnyard epithet and other obscenities: Notes on the Chicago conspiracy trial.* New York: Harper and Row.

Lukes, Steven
1975   Political ritual and social integration. *Sociology* 9 (May): 289.

Lusky, Louis
1964   Justice with a southern accent. *Harper's* (March): 62+.

Lyman, Christopher S.
1973   State bar discipline and the activist lawyer. *Harvard Civil Rights-Liberties Law Review* 5:301–309.

Mabee, Carleton
1969   *Black freedom: The nonviolent abolitionists from 1830 through the Civil War.* New York: Macmillan.

Major, Reginald
1973   *Justice in the round: The trial of Angela Davis.* New York: The Third Press.

Mankoff, Milton
1978   On the responsibility of Marxist criminologists: A reply to Quinney. *Contemporary Crises* 2:293–301.

Mannheim, Karl
1936   *Ideology and utopia.* New York: Harcourt, Brace, Jovanovich.

Marshall, Burke
1969   The protest movement and the law. *Virginia Law Review* 51:786.

Martin, Bob
1974   The account of the White House Seven. *Friends Journal* 20 (1 October): 484–499.

Martin, Yancey
1977   Interview with Yancey Martin. In *My soul is rested*, ed. Howell Raines, pp. 52–56. New York: Bantam.

Marx, Gary T., and Michael Useem
1971   Majority involvement in minority movements: Civil rights, abolition, and untouchability. *Journal of Social Issues* 27:81–104.

Marx, Karl, and Friedrich Engels
1947   *The German ideology: Parts I and III.* Edited and trans-
[1846]   lated by R. Pascal. New York: International Publishers.

Mathiesen, Thomas
1980   *Law, society, and political action.* London: Academic
            Press.

Mayers, Lewis
1964   *The American legal system.* Rev. ed. New York: Harper
            and Row.

McAdam, Doug
1982   *Political process and the development of black insur-
            gency, 1930–1970.* Chicago: University of Chicago Press.

McCarthy, John D., and Mayer N. Zald
1977   Resource mobilization and social movements: A partial
            theory. *American Journal of Sociology* 82:1112–1241.
1973   *The trend of social movements in America.* Morristown,
            N.J.: General Learning Corporation.

McLendon, Irmgard
1963   Pritchett plan succeeds. *Atlanta Journal and Constitu-
            tion* (18 July): 14.

Meier, August
1965   On the role of Martin Luther King. *New Politics* 4 (Win-
            ter): 52–59.

Meier, August, and Eliott Rudwick
1973   *CORE: A study in the civil rights movement, 1942–1968.*
            New York: Oxford.

Meltsner, Michael
1964   Twelve white men and true. *New Republic* (23 May):
            11–12.

Merton, Robert K.
1968   *Social theory and social structure.* Enlarged ed. New
            York: Free Press.

Michalowski, R. J., and E. W. Bohlander
1976   Repression and criminal justice in capitalist America. *So-
            ciological Inquiry* 46:95–106.

Milgram, Stanley
1975   *Obedience to authority.* New York: Harper and Row.

Miliband, Ralph
1969   *The state in capitalist society.* New York: Basic Books.

Miller, William R.
1968   *Martin Luther King, Jr.: His life, martyrdom, and mean-ing for the world.* New York: Avon.

Mills, C. Wright
1943   The professional ideology of social pathologists. *American Journal of Sociology* 49 (September): 165–180.

Minor, W. William
1975   Political crime, political justice, and political prisoners. *Criminology* 12 (February): 385–398.

Mitford, Jessica
1969   *The trial of Dr. Spock.* New York: Knopf.

Moore, Howard
1967   Black barrister at southern bar. *The Guild Practitioner* 26 (Winter): 27–30.

Moore, Lloyd E.
1973   *The jury: Tool of kings, palladium of liberty.* Cincinnati: W. H. Andrews.

Moore, Sally, and Barbara Myerhoff, eds.
1977   *Secular rituals.* Amsterdam: Van Gorcum.

Moore, Wilbert E., and Melvin M. Tumin
1949   Some social functions of ignorance. *American Sociological Review* 14 (December): 787–795.

Moran, Richard
1981   *Knowing right from wrong: The insanity defense of Daniel McNaughtan.* New York: Free Press.

Morgan, Charles, Jr.
1964   *A time to speak.* New York: Harper and Row.

Morris, Aldon
1981   Black southern student sit-in movement: An analysis of internal organization. *American Sociological Review* 46 (December): 744–767.

Morris, Richard B.
1952   *Fourteen who stood accused.* New York: Harper and Row.

Morrison, Samuel Eliot, and Henry Steele Commager
1962   *The growth of the American Republic.* Vol. 1. New York: Oxford.

Myrdal, Gunnar
1944   *An American dilemma.* New York: Harper and Row.

Nation
1964   Clipping in files of Meiklejohn Civil Liberties Institute, no title, n.d., n.p. Berkeley, California.

Nelsen, Hart M., Raytha Yokley, and Thomas Madron
1973   Ministerial roles and social actionist stance: Protestant clergy and protest in the sixties. *American Sociological Review* 38 (June): 375–386.

Newsweek
1967   The churches: "What shall we say?" (10 July): 81–82.
1973   Trials: Ellsberg on the stand. (23 May): 22–23.

New South
1963   Civil disobedience and the law. 18 (October-November): 24–28.

New York Review
1970   *Trials of the resistance.* New York: New York Review.

New York Times
1963   Lawyer in rights cases disbarred in Mississippi. (4 July): 38.
1974   Quaker sentenced in draft refusal. (28 April): 61.
1975   More seek to act as own lawyers. (9 December): 13.

Nixon, Ed
1977   Interview with Ed Nixon. In *My soul is rested*, ed. Howell Raines, pp. 27–30. New York: Bantam.

Nonet, Philippe
1969   *Administrative justice: Advocacy and change in a government agency.* New York: Russell Sage.

Oberschall, Anthony
1973   *Social conflict and social movements.* Englewood Cliffs, N.J.: Prentice-Hall.

O'Connor, Karen
1980   *Women's organizations' use of the courts.* Lexington: Lexington Books.

O'Dea, Thomas F.
1966   The sociology of religion. Englewood Cliffs, N.J.: Prentice-Hall.

Oregon Times Magazine
n.d.   Trials of Trojan. Clipping in files of Meiklejohn Civil Lib-
                      erties Institute, n.p. Berkeley, California.

O'Rourke, William
1972   *The Harrisburg 7 and the new Catholic left.* New York:
                      Crowell.

Packer, Herbert
1970   The conspiracy weapon. In *Trials of the resistance,*
                      pp. 170–188. New York: New York Review.

Palms, Charles L.
1966   Peace and the Catholic conscience. *The Catholic World*
                      (June): 145–152.

Parks, Rosa
1977   Interview with Rosa Parks. In *My soul is rested,* ed.
                      Howell Raines, pp. 31–33. New York: Bantam.

Pashukanis, Evgeny
1978   *Law and Marxism: A general theory.* Translated by
[1929]   Barbara Einhorn and edited by Chris Arthur. London:
                      Ink Links.

Peltason, Jack W.
1961   *58 lonely men: Southern federal judges and school de-
                      segregation.* Urbana: University of Illinois Press.

Perrow, Charles
1979   The sixties observed. In *The dynamics of social move-
                      ments,* ed. Mayer N. Zald and John McCarthy. Cambridge:
                      Winthrop.

Peterson, Horace C., and Gilbert C. Fite
1957   *Opponents of war, 1917–1918.* Madison: University of
                      Wisconsin Press.

Piven, Frances Fox, and Richard A. Cloward
1977   *Poor people's movements: Why they succeed, how they
                      fail.* New York: Pantheon.

Platt, Anthony
1974   The triumph of benevolence: The origins of the juvenile
                      justice system in the United States. In *Criminal justice
                      in America,* ed. Richard Quinney. Boston: Little, Brown.

Pollitt, Daniel H.
1964   Timid lawyers and neglected clients. *Harper's* (August):
                      81–86.

Porter, Russell
1949   Court Lets Dennis conduct own defense at red trial. *New
                    York Times* (March 18): 1+.

Poulantzas, Nicos
1973   *Political power and social classes*. London: New Left
                    Books.

Pound, Roscoe
1910   Law in books and law in action. *American Law Review*
                    44 (January-February): 12–36.
1921   *The spirit of the common law*. Boston: Marshall Jones.
1943   A survey of social interests. *Harvard Law Review*
                    57:1–39.

Powledge, Fred
1964   Lawyers aiding in rights drive. *New York Times* (28
                    June): 46.

Preston, William
1963   *Aliens and dissenters: Federal suppression of radicals,
                    1903–1933*. Cambridge, Mass.: Harvard University Press.

Pritchett, Laurie
1977   Interview with Laurie Pritchett. In *My soul is rested*, ed.
                    Howell Raines, pp. 398–404. New York: Bantam.

Quinney, Richard
1974   *Critique of legal order*. Boston: Little, Brown.
1977   *Class, state, and crime*. New York: David McKay.

Rabinowitz, Victor
1982   The radical tradition in the law. In *The politics of law*, ed.
                    David Kairys, pp. 310–318. New York: Pantheon.

Raines, Howell
1977   *My soul is rested*. New York: Bantam.

Redhead, Steve
1982   Marxist theory, the rule of law, and socialism. In *Marxism
                    and Law*, ed. Piers Beirne and Richard Quinney, pp. 328–
                    342. New York: Wiley.

Reed, Robin
1980   Jury simulation: The impact of judge's instructions and
                    attorney tactics on decision-making. *Journal of Criminal
                    Law and Criminology* 71 (Spring): 68–72.

Reed, Roy
1965   Jury in Alabama convicts Klansman in Liuzzo case. *New
                    York Times* (4 December): 1.

Reiman, Jeffrey H.
1979   *The rich get rich and the poor get prison: Ideology, crime, and criminal justice.* New York: Wiley.

Rex v. Shipley, 4 Doug 171 (1784).

Riley, David P.
1969   The challenge of the new lawyers: Public interest and private clients. *George Washington Law Review* 38:549.

Roberts, Dennis
1965   Diary kept while working as legal assistant to C. B. King, civil rights attorney, in Albany, Georgia, 1963 to 1965. In files of Meiklejohn Civil Liberties Institute, Berkeley, California.

Roberts, Steven V.
1971   Ellsberg: The goal—a new kind of political trial. *New York Times Magazine* (22 August): 6+.

Rockwell, David N.
1970   Controlling lawyers by bar associations and courts. *Harvard Civil Rights–Civil Liberties Law Review* 5:301–309.

Rodden, Bonny
1977   Hung jury in second protest trial. *Stanford Daily* (29 July): 1.

Rose, Arnold M.
1967   *The power structure.* New York: Oxford.

Rosett, Arthur, and Donald Cressey
1976   *Justice by consent: Plea bargains in the American courthouse.* New York: Lippincott.

Rothschild, Emma
1970   Notes from a political trial. In *Trials of the resistance,* pp. 106–124. New York: New York Review.

Rowley, Peter
1969   Blood and fire against the draft. *Nation* (15 September): 248–250.

Rudman, Norman G.
1963   Sittin-in on the omnibus—the 1961 segregation cases. *Law in Transition* 22 (Winter): 206–221.

Ryan, Mary Perkins
1966   The priest as witness. *America* (23 April): 587–589.

Ryan, William
1976   *Blaming the victim*. Rev. ed. New York: Vintage.

San Francisco Chronicle
1978   Arizona arrests Chavez. (14 June): 5.

Sarat, Austin
1976   Alternatives in dispute processing: Litigation in a small
               claims court. *Law and Society Review* 10:379.

Sarat, Austin, and Joel B. Grossman
1975   Courts and conflict resolution: Problems in the mobiliza-
               tion of adjudication. *American Political Science Review*
               69:1200–1217.

Sax, Joseph L.
1968   Conscience and anarchy: The prosecution of war re-
               sisters. *Yale Review* 57 (June): 481–494.

Schafer, Stephen
1971   The concept of the political criminal. *Journal of Crimi-
               nal Law, Criminology, and Police Science* 62 (September):
               380–387.
1974   *The political criminal*. New York: Free Press.

Scheflin, Alan W.
1972   Jury nullification: The right to say no. *Southern Califor-
               nia Law Review* 45:168–226.

Scheingold, Stuart A.
1974   *The politics of rights: Lawyers, public policy, and politi-
               cal change*. New Haven: Yale University Press.

Schneir, Walter
1971   Desanctifying the courts. In *Radical Lawyers: Their Role
               in the Movement and in the Courts*, ed. Jonathan Black,
               pp. 297–301. New York: Avon.

Schneir, Walter, and Miriam Schneir
1965   *Invitation to an inquest: A new look at the Rosenberg-
               Sobell case*. New York: Doubleday.

Schulman, Jay
1974   Judging jurors. *Time* (28 January): 60.

Schur, Edwin M.
1968   *Law and society: A sociological view*. New York: Ran-
               dom House.

Schwartz, Michael
1976   *Radical protest and social structure.* New York: Academic Press.

Scott, Glen
1962   If you can't get the law, get the lawyer. *Nation* (20 January): 51–53.

Searles, Ruth, and J. Allen Williams
1962   Negro college students' participation in sit-ins. *Social Forces* 40 (March): 215–220.

Selznick, Philip
1969   *Law, society, and industrial justice.* New York: Russell Sage.

Sheerin, John B.
1966   Who speaks for the Christian in Vietnam? *Catholic World* (November): 72–76.

1970   Tensions in a church alive. *Catholic World* (December): 115–116.

Shores, Arthur
1977   Interview with Arthur Shores. In *My soul is rested*, ed. Howell Raines, pp. 384–387. New York: Bantam.

Shuttlesworth, Fred
1977   Interview with Fred Shuttlesworth. In *My soul is rested*, ed. Howell Raines, pp. 166–176. New York: Bantam.

Simon, Rita James
1967   *The jury and the defense of insanity.* Boston: Little, Brown.
1975   ed., *The jury system in America: A critical overview.* Beverly Hills, Calif.: Sage.
1980   *The jury: Its role in American society.* Lexington: Lexington Books.

Simson, Gary J.
1976   Jury nullification in the American system: A skeptical view. *Texas Law Review* 54 (March): 488–525.

Sitton, Claude
1962   When a southern Negro goes to court. *New York Times Magazine* (7 January): 10+.
1963   The "Movement" in Albany, Ga. *New York Times* (11 July): 24.

Skocpol, Theda
1980   Political response to capitalist crisis: Neo-Marxist theo-
                ries of the state and the case of the New Deal. *Politics
                and Society* 10:155–201.

Skolnick, Jerome
1967   Social control in the adversary system. *Journal of Con-
                flict Resolution* 11 (March): 52–70.
1968   Coercion to virtue. *Southern California Law Review*
                41:588–691.
1969   *The politics of protest.* New York: Ballantine.

Smelser, Neil J.
1962   *The theory of collective behavior.* New York: Free Press.

Sourian, Peter
1978   Television. *Nation* (11 March): 285–286.

Southern Patriot
1960   Tallahassee judge gives his answer. June: 1.
1961   "Do-it-yourself court tactics." 19 (February): 3.
1962   Albany: An end and a beginning. October: 1.

Sparf v. The United States of America, 156 US 51 (1895).

Stein, Beverly, and Larry Hott
1978   Nuke protesters win one. *Guild Notes* (5 February): 1.

Sternberg, David
1972   The new radical-criminal trials: A step toward a class-for-
                itself in the American proletariat? *Science and Society* 36
                (Fall): 274–301.

Student Nonviolent Coordinating Committee
1963   Leaflet in files of Meiklejohn Civil Liberties Institute,
                Berkeley, California.

Student Voice
1963   6 freed in Americus vow to continue work. 4 (November
                11): 1.

Sudnow, David
1965   Normal crimes: Sociological features of the penal code in
                a public defender office." *Social Problems* 12 (Winter):
                255–276.

Sue, Stanley, Ronald E. Smith, and Cathy Caldwell
1973   Effects of inadmissible evidence on the decisions of simu-
                lated jurors: A moral dilemma. *Journal of Applied Social
                Psychology* 3 (March): 345–353.

Sumner, Colin
1979   *Reading ideologies: An investigation into the Marxist theory of ideology and law.* London: Academic Press.

Tatum, Arlo, ed.
1972   *Handbook for conscientious objectors.* 12th ed. Philadelphia: CCCO.

Taylor, Ian, Paul Walton, and Jock Young
1973   *The new criminology.* London: Routledge and Kegan Paul.

Teachout, Peter R.
1981   Light in ashes: The problem of "respect for the rule of law" in American legal history. In *Law in the American Revolution and the revolution in the law,* ed. Hendrik Hartog, pp. 163–225. New York: New York University Press.

Thayer, James Bradley
1898   *A preliminary treatise on evidence at the common law.* Boston: Little, Brown.

Thompson, E. P.
1975   *Whigs and hunters: The origin of the Black Act.* London: Allen Lane.

Thompson, Tom
1977   46 arrested at Diablo nuclear facility. *Open Forum* (Newsletter of California American Civil Liberties Union) (October): n.p.

Thompson, William C., Geoffrey T. Fong, and David L. Rosenhan
1981   Inadmissible evidence and jury verdicts. *Journal of Personality and Applied Social Psychology* 49 (March): 453–463.

Tides, R. Ed
1978   Schwartz jury boosts anti-nuclear forces. *Berkeley Barb* (17–23 February): 3.

Troeltsch, E.
1931   *The social teachings of the Christian churches.* Translated by O. Wyon. New York: Macmillan.

Trojan Decommissioning Alliance
1978   Trojan verdict: The nukes are guilty. *WIN Magazine* (19 January): 4–6.

Trubek, David M.
1977   Complexity and contradiction in the legal order: Balbus
               and the challenge of critical social thought about law.
               Law and Society Review 11 (Winter): 529–569.

Truman, David
1951   *The governmental process.* New York: Knopf.

Turk, Austin T.
1982   *Political criminality: The defiance and defense of au-
               thority.* Beverly Hills, Calif.: Sage.

Turner, Ralph H.
1970   Determinants of social movement strategies. In *Human
               nature and collective behavior: Papers in honor of
               Herbert Blumer,* ed. Tamotsu Shibutani, pp. 145–164.
               Englewood Cliffs, N.J.: Prentice-Hall.

Turner v. Memphis, 369 US 762 (1962).

Tygart, Clarence E.
1973   Social movement participation: Clergy and the anti-
               Vietnam War movement. *Sociological Analysis* 34:
               202–211.

UC Nuclear Weapons Lab Conversion Project
1978   U-Hall Six acquitted by jury. Newsletter (March): 1+.

Unger, Sanford J.
1973   The Pentagon Papers trial. *Atlantic* (August): 6–14.

United States of America v. Moylan, 416 F 2d 1002 (1969).

United States of America v. Steven E. Barkan et al.
1972   Transcript of testimony of Steven E. Barkan. United
               States District Court, Criminal Docket No. H–268,
               District of Connecticut: 1–16.

Useem, Michael
1973   *Conscription, Protest and Social Conflict.* New York:
               Wiley.

Vander Zanden, James W.
1963   The non-violent resistance movement against segregation.
               American Journal of Sociology 68 (March): 544–550.

Van Dyke, Jon M.
1970   The jury as a political institution. *Center Magazine* 2
               (March): 17–26.
1977   *Jury selection procedures.* Cambridge, Mass.: Ballinger.

Vose, Clement C.
1958   Litigation as a form of pressure group activity. *Annals of the American Academy of Political and Social Science* 319:20–31.
1972   *Constitutional change: Amendment politics and Supreme Court litigation since 1900.* Lexington, Mass.: Heath.

Walker, Wyatt T.
1963   Albany: Failure or first step? *New South* 18 (June): 3–8.

Wanner, Craig
1974   The public ordering of private relations. Part 1: Initiating civil cases in urban trial courts. *Law and Society Review* 8:421–440.
1975   The public ordering of private relations. Part 2: Winning civil court cases. *Law and Society Review* 9:293–306.

Wasserman, Harvey
1977   Tale of two trials. *New Age* (March): 33–40.
1978   Resistance gets set for spring. *Nation* (February 11): 137–140.

Wasserstrom, Richard
1971   Lawyers and revolution: In *Radical lawyers: Their role in the movement and in the courts,* ed. Jonathan Black, pp. 74–84. New York: Avon.

Watson v. Memphis, 373 US 526 (1963).

Weber, Max
1967   *Max Weber on law in economy and society.* Edited by
[1922]   Max Rheinstein. Translated by Edward Shils and Max Rheinstein. New York: Simon and Schuster.

Welsh, David P.
n.d.   Project Mississippi. Booklet published by National Lawyers Guild, Detroit. In files of Meiklejohn Civil Liberties Institute, Berkeley, California.

Weschler, Herbert
1959   Toward neutral principles of constitutional law. *Harvard Law Review* 73 (November): 15.

Winter, J. Alan
1977   *Continuities in the sociology of religion.* New York: Harper and Row.

Wittner, Lawrence
1969   *Rebels against war.* New York: Columbia University
            Press.

Wolfe, Alan
1971   Political repression and the liberal state. *Monthly Review*
            23:18–38.
1974   New directions in the Marxist theory of politics. *Politics
            and Society* 4 (Winter): 131–160.

Wright, Erik Olin
1978   *Class, crisis and the state.* London: New Left Books.

Yale Law Journal
1964   The changing role of the jury in the nineteenth century.
            74:179–192.
1970   The new public interest lawyers. 79:1070.

Yinger, J. Milton
1946   *Religion in the struggle for power: A study in the so-
            ciology of religion.* Durham, N.C.: Duke University
            Press.

Yngvesson, Barbara, and P. Hennessey
1975   Small claims, complex disputes: A review of the small
            claims literature. *Law and Society Review* 9:219–274.

Young, Andrew
1977   Interview with Andrew Young. *My soul is rested*, ed.
            Howell Raines, pp. 472–480. New York: Bantam.

Younger, Richard D.
1963   *The people's panel.* Providence: Brown University Press.

Zahn, Gordon C.
1966   The crime of silence. *Commonweal* (June 17): 354–356.
1970   The Berrigans: Radical activism personified. *Catholic
            World* (December): 125–130.

Zashin, Elliott
1970   Letter to Ann Fagan Ginger, 5 October. In files of Meikle-
            john Civil Liberties Institute, Berkeley, California.

Zeitlin, Irving
1968   *Ideology and the development of sociological theory.* En-
            glewood Cliffs, N.J.: Prentice-Hall.

Zinn, Howard
1962   *Albany: A study in national responsibility.* Atlanta:
            Southern Regional Council.

1965   *SNCC: The new abolitionists.* Boston: Beacon Press.
1973   Amazing grace: The movement wins in Camden. *Liberation* 18 (July-August): 4–5.

Index

Abernathy, Ralph, 62, 63–64, 65, 71, 72, 77, 80

Abolitionist movement, 4, 130–131, 138, 150

Adams, John, 137

Aiken, A. M., 75, 78

Alabama Christian Movement for Human Rights, 70

Alabama Supreme Court, 73

Albany, Georgia, civil rights campaign, 60–69; arrests, 60–62, 64, 65, 66–67; demonstrations, 61–62, 64–66, 67; negotiations, 62–63; success of, 65–66; trials, 63–64, 68–69

Althusser, Louis, 153

American Bar Association, 43, 90, 110, 139

American Civil Liberties Union, 46, 107

American Jewish Committee, 46

American Jewish Congress, 46

Anthony, Susan B., trial of, 4–5, 26, 108

Antinuclear movement, 12–13, 17–18, 20, 22, 23, 55

Arnold, Thurman, 134, 147

Arrests: in Albany, Georgia, 60–62, 64, 65, 66–67; in Birmingham, Alabama, 70; and civil rights movement, 32–33, 35, 38, 47, 53–55; in Danville, Virginia, 75, 79; of Martin Luther King, 35, 62–63, 71, 72, 80; and Mississippi Summer Project, 84; and

Vietnam antiwar movement, 88–89

Attorneys: availability of, 12, 39–41, 44, 46, 84–86, 89, 150, 151; black, 39, 41, 47, 48; civil rights, 39–51, 83–86; and defense strategies, 22–23, 41–46, 84–86, 99–101, 106–107, 150; harassment of, 46–51, 65, 75; and Legal Defense and Educational Fund, 41–46, 84; and National Lawyers Guild, 43–46, 84–86, 89; out-of-state, 40, 85; radical, 89–90; and Vietnam antiwar movement, 88–90, 99–101, 106–107

Bail: cost of, 54–55, 66–67, 72; denial of, 32; funds for, 70–72, 73, 84

Bailey, Harry A., 42

Balbus, Isaac, 8–9, 134, 157

Baltimore Four trial, 122, 124

Bannan, John and Rosemary, 144

Barkan, Steven, trial of, 104, 110–112, 113, 115–116

Batchelder, David, 111–112

Becker, Theodore, 3

Belafonte, Harry, 72

Belknap, Michal, 3

Berkman, Alexander, 108, 109

Bernstein, Ilene, 150

Berrigan, Daniel, 121–122, 123, 126

Berrigan, Philip, 19–20, 103, 108–109, 121–122, 123

Birmingham, Alabama, campaign,

Birmingham, Ala., campaign (*cont.*)
49, 69–74; negotiations involved
in, 72–73; use of children in,
71–72
Black Panthers, 91
Blumberg, Abraham, 134
Boutwell, Albert, 73
Brown v. Board of Education,
28–29
Bushell, Edward, 135

Camden Twenty-eight trial, 117,
143
Camil, Scott, 116
Campbell, Lawrence G., 42
Casper, Jonathan, 56
Catholics, radical, 119–131; antiwar
protest of, 121–124; and Baltimore Four, 122, 124; and Catonsville Nine, 92, 103, 122, 124–127,
140; and the Church, 120–121,
129; and Milwaukee Twelve,
92, 109, 110, 113, 115, 116, 117,
127–128
Catholic Worker movement, 123
Catonsville Nine trial, 92, 103, 122,
124–127, 140
Chambliss, William, 139, 147,
153, 154
Chavez, Cesar, 4
Chicago Eight trial, 24, 102, 109,
113, 117, 140, 142
Civil disobedience, 4–5, 7, 55–
57, 87
Civil Rights Act (1964), 65, 73
Civil rights movement, 28–86,
150–151; and Albany, Georgia,
demonstrations, 60–69; and
Birmingham, Alabama, demonstrations, 69–74; and civil disobedience, 55–57; and clerical
activism, 120; and Danville, Vir-

ginia, demonstrations, 74–79;
and defense attorneys, 39–50;
and defense strategies, 38, 41–46,
49–53; and federal courts, 28–31,
37, 47, 68–69, 73, 76–78, 80–81;
and injunctions, 33–34; and jails,
53–55, 61, 64, 66–67, 70, 73; and
judges, 30, 50–51, 75–77, 79–81;
and juries, 51–52; and legal harassment, 35–36, 46–51, 53–55,
66–67, 69, 75–78, 84; and lunch
counter sit-ins, 37–38; and Mississippi Summer Project, 83–86;
and Montgomery bus boycott,
34–37; and police, 53, 59–60, 61,
71–74, 75, 79, 82, 86; and Selma,
Alabama, demonstrations, 79–81;
and Southern legal system, 31–
33, 38, 47
Clark, Jim, 80–81
Clark, Joseph, 64
Cleghorn, Reese, 67
Clerical activism, 120. *See also*
Catholics, radical
Cloward, Richard, 66, 82–83
Committee to Assist Southern
Lawyers (CASL, later renamed
Committee for Legal Assistance
in the South [CLAS]), 43, 84. *See
also* National Lawyers Guild
Communist party, 24; and National
Lawyers Guild, 43–46; and Smith
Act prosecutions, 8, 12, 39, 43,
46, 89, 99, 115
Conflict theory, 7–8, 152–157
Congress of Racial Equality (CORE),
45–46, 53–55, 75
Connor, Bull, 70, 72, 73, 74, 80
Conspiracy charges, 98–99, 101
Constitutional arguments: civil
rights, 46, 49–50, 51, 56; Vietnam
antiwar movement, 13, 87, 101

Cooper, John S., 72
Costs, legal, 36, 39–40, 54–55, 61, 66–67, 88–89
Council of Federated Organizations (COFO), 44, 83–86
Council on United States Civil Rights Leadership, 44–45
Courts: as closed or open systems, 5–6; federal, 28–31, 68–69, 76–78, 80–81, 85, 87–88; as secular institutions, 129–131; segregated, 38, 64, 75–76; and Supreme Court, 28–31, 37, 47, 73, 87, 105 n, 106
Cox, Archibald, 29
Cox, William, 30
Criminal trials, 2–3, 134, 139

Dahl, Robert, 152
Danville, Virginia, civil rights campaign, 40, 42, 74–79; and arrests, 75, 79; negotiations involved in, 75, 78, 79; and police violence, 75, 79; success of, 78–79; and trials, 75–76
Danville Christian Progressive Association, 75
Darrow, Clarence, 98
Davis, Angela, trial of, 25, 26, 108, 109, 114, 116
Day, Dorothy, 123
Debs, Eugene V., 24, 33, 113–114, 116
Defendants: civil rights movement, 52–53; Vietnam antiwar movement, 87, 90–92, 109
Defense strategies: appeal-oriented, 41–42, 51, 84–85; of civil rights movement, 38, 41–46, 49–53; of defendants, 52–53, 87, 90–92, 109; disruptive, 91–92, 94, 102, 112–113; of draft resisters, 96–

97; and guilty pleas, 4, 56–57; and juries, 16–19, 51–52, 93–94, 97, 102–103, 112–116; of National Lawyers Guild, 41–46, 84–86; political versus technical, 15–17, 21–23, 49–51, 95–97; *pro se*, 105–118, 127–128; and publicity, 19–21, 71–72, 94–95, 99, 101, 102; and resource mobilization, 15–23, 117–118; and rules of evidence, 92–93, 99, 101, 112, 124–130 passim, 132, 155; of Vietnam antiwar movement, 16, 87, 95–103, 125–126
Democratic National Convention (1968), 93, 102, 125
Demonstrations, trial-related, 103–104, 125, 129
Disruptive courtroom tactics, 91–92, 94, 102, 112–113
Dombrowski, James A., 47
Dorsen, Norman, 3, 102
Draft files, destruction of, 92–93, 122–124
Draft resisters, 96–97
Due process, 96–97
Durr, Clifford, 46

Elliott, J. Robert, 30, 65
Ellsberg, Daniel, 100–101, 109
Engels, Friedrich, 152
External support, 11, 41–46, 58, 66, 72–73, 82

Faretta v. California, 105 n
Farmer, James, 55
Fifth Circuit Court of Appeals, 30, 32, 46, 65, 85
Fillmore, Millard, 138
Ford, Francis, 99, 139–140
Form, William, 134
Formal legal rationality, 8–9, 151

Forman, James, 44, 76
Fortas, Abe, 144–145
Fox's Libel Law, 136, 139
Friedman, Lawrence, 14
Friedman, Leon, 3, 102
Fugitive Slave Law, 138

Gainesville Eight trial, 4, 116
Garner v. Louisiana, 29
Garrow, David, 79, 82
Garry, Charles, 109
Gideon v. Wainwright, 106
Goldman, Emma, 109
Graf, Robert, 110, 115
Gray, Francine du Plessix, 125
Greenberg, Jack, 44, 45, 77
Greensboro, North Carolina
    sit-in, 37

Hagan, John, 150
Hamilton, Alexander, 137
Handler, Joel, 11–12, 14
Harassment, 46–51, 75–78, 98; of
    attorneys, 46–51, 65, 75; in jail,
    53–55; by judges, 40, 47, 49,
    50–51, 54–55, 75–78, 85; legis-
    lative, 47; by physical injury, 48,
    54, 75; by police, 35–36, 47–48,
    66–67, 69, 84; social, 46–47,
    48–49
Harris, David, 97
Harrisburg Seven trial, 108–109
Hartford, Connecticut, (author's)
    trial, 104, 110–112, 113, 115–116
Haymarket Square trial, 23–24
Higgs, William, 49
Hoffman, Julius, 24, 102, 140
Holt, Len, 42–44, 75–76
Hunt, Ward, 26

Ideological function of legal sys-
    tem, 133–134, 139, 140–141,

144–145, 149–157
Industrial Workers of the World, 1
Injunctions, 33–34, 64–65; Bir-
    mingham, Alabama, 70; Danville,
    Virginia, 75; Montgomery, Ala-
    bama, 36–37; Selma, Alabama,
    79–81
Interstate Commerce Commission
    desegregation order, 61, 70

Jackson, Harold, Jr., 128
Jackson, Robert, 98
Jails: civil rights movement policy,
    53–55, 64, 67, 70; overflow of, 61,
    66–67, 73
Jay, John, 137
Jenkins, J. Craig, 58
Johnson, Frank M., 30
Johnson, Lyndon B., 81
Judges, 23, 24–25, 149–150; fed-
    eral, 30, 76–78, 80–81, 85; and
    jury nullification, 139–146;
    Southern, 30, 40, 47, 49, 50–51,
    75–77, 79–81, 85; and Vietnam
    antiwar movement, 24–25,
    92–93, 97, 99, 101, 125, 127, 128
Juries, 16–19, 23–24; conversion
    of, 18–19; criticism of, 138–139;
    and social movements, 146–148,
    149; Southern, 51–52; and Viet-
    nam antiwar movement, 16–17,
    18–19, 93–94, 97, 102–103, 112–
    116. *See also* Nullification, jury

Kalven, Harry, Jr., 141, 144
Kennedy, John F., 30, 64, 73
Kennedy, Robert, 61, 64, 68, 72
King, C. B., 48, 65, 67, 68
King, Coretta, 64
King, Martin Luther, 82; and Al-
    bany, Georgia, demonstrations,

60, 62–67; arrests of, 35, 62–63, 71, 72, 80; and Birmingham, Alabama, demonstrations, 69–72; and Danville, Georgia, demonstrations, 77, 78; and "Letter from the Birmingham Jail," 57, 71; and Montgomery bus boycott, 34–37; and Selma, Alabama, demonstrations, 80–81; trials of, 53, 57, 95
Kirchheimer, Otto, 25
Klapp, Orrin, 112–113
Krisberg, Barry, 134
Ku Klux Klan, 48, 52, 81
Kunstler, William, 70–71, 76, 109, 140

Labor movement, 33–34, 36, 72, 98–99
Laws, Southern, 31–33, 38, 47; ante-bellum and Reconstruction, 32, 70, 76
Law Students Civil Rights Research Council, 84
Lawyers Constitutional Defense Committee (LCDC), 46, 84
Legal Defense and Educational Fund (LDF), 29, 41–46, 77, 84
Legitimatization of legal system, 13, 25, 26, 153, 156
Libel, seditious, 135–137
Lipsky, Michael, 10, 20
Litigation: costs of, 36, 39–40, 54–55, 61, 66–67, 88–89; ideological function of, 133–134, 139, 140–141, 144–145, 149–157; and resource mobilization, 11, 14, 117–118, 129; success of, 11–14, 25–27, 35, 65–66, 103–104, 127, 128, 129. *See also* Defense strategies; Political trials
Liuzzo, Viola, 52
Lomax, Louis, 63

Lovejoy, Samuel, 20, 23
Lunch counter sit-ins, 37–38

Magee, Ruchell, 109
Mannheim, Karl, 134
Marshall, Burke, 64
Marx, Karl, 134, 152
Marxist theory, 7–9, 152–157; class struggle (dialectical), 154, 156; instrumentalist, 8–9, 153, 155–156, 157; structuralist, 153–154, 156
McAdam, Doug, 58n, 59, 82–83
Merton, Robert, 145–146
Michie, Thomas J., 76–77
Milgram, Stanley, 144
Miller, David, 107
Mills, C. Wright, 134
Milwaukee Twelve trial, 92, 127–128; and *pro se* defense, 109, 110, 113, 115, 116, 117, 128
Mississippi Freedom Rides and Riders, 40, 48, 54–55, 56, 66–67
Mississippi Summer Project, 45, 83–86; success of, 85–86
Mitford, Jessica, 99, 116, 155
Montgomery, Alabama, bus boycott, 34–37
Moore, Wilbert, 112
Morgan, Charles, Jr., 49
Morse, Senator, 72
Mullaney, Anthony, 116

National Association for the Advancement of Colored People (NAACP), 11, 29; and Legal Defense and Educational Fund, 29, 41–46, 77, 84
National Conference of Catholic Bishops, 121
National Council of Churches, 46
National Lawyers Guild, 43–46, 84–86, 89

National Maritime union, 72
New criminology, 7–8, 134, 147
New York Times, 116
Nixon, Ed, 35
Nonet, Philippe, 6
Nuclear power and weapons. *See* Antinuclear movement
Nullification, jury, 132–148; historical development of, 135–139; and judicial instructions, 139–144; jury's right to be informed of, 94, 132–133, 138, 139–140, 143; and rule of law, 132–133, 137, 138, 141, 144–145, 154; and social control, 144–146, 155–156
Nuremberg Principles, 101, 127

Oakland Seven trial, 101, 142–143
Organizations, 11, 41–46, 58, 66, 72–73

Parks, Rosa, 35, 57
Pashukanis, Evgeny, 153–154
Pentagon Papers trial, 100–101
Perrow, Charles, 58
Piven, Frances Fox, 66, 82–83
Pluralist theory, 7–8, 152, 155
Police violence, 59–60, 71–74, 75, 79–81, 82, 86, 101; absence of, 61, 79
Political process theory, 58–59
Political question doctrine, 13
Political trials: definition of, 3, 90; formal and substantive justice, 157–158; history of, 1; and jury nullification, 139, 155–156; and resource mobilization, 11, 14, 25–27, 87–88, 103–104, 117–118, 129, 150; and social movements, 1–2, 6–9, 11–14, 150–151; types of, 3–5. *See also* Litigation

Poulantzas, Nicos, 153
Press, 19–21, 23, 149; and antinuclear power movement, 20, 23; and civil rights movement, 71–72, 95; and Vietnam antiwar movement, 19–20, 94–95, 99, 101, 102
Pritchett, Laurie, 61–64 passim, 66–67, 74, 77, 80
Privileged statute, 127
Prosecutors, 23–25, 149; and Vietnam antiwar movement, 24–25, 113, 127, 128
Pro se defense, 23, 105–118, 127–128; and jury sympathy, 112–116; and politicization, 109–112; reasons for, 106–112, 116–117; and resource mobilization, 117–118
Public response, 35, 149; and defense strategies, 19–21, 99, 101, 102–103; to police behavior, 59–60, 61, 71–74, 75, 79–81, 82, 86. *See also* Press

Quinney, Richard, 153

Rachlin, Carl, 46
Radical Catholics. *See* Catholics, radical
Reiman, Jeffrey, 134
Religion, 119–120, 129–131. *See also* Catholics, radical
Removal petitions, 70–71, 76–78, 85
Resource mobilization, 10–27, 103–104; and defense strategies, 15–23, 117–118; and litigation, 11, 14, 88, 129, 150; and movement morale, 17–18, 25–26, 29; and movement strength, 58–59, 82–83; and Vietnam antiwar movement, 88, 103–104, 117–118, 129

Rosenberg, Ethel and Julius, 24
Rules of evidence, 13, 23, 92–93, 99, 101, 112, 124–130 passim, 132, 155
Russo, Anthony, 100–101
Ryan, William, 134
Rytina, Joan, 134

St. Augustine, Florida, civil rights campaign, 82–83
Sax, Joseph, 139
Scheingold, Stuart, 14
Schlesinger, Arthur, Jr., 45
Schur, Edwin, 7
Seale, Bobby, 109
Seattle protesters trial, 143
Seditious libel, 135–137
Seidman, Robert, 139, 147, 153, 154
Self-representation. *See Pro se* defense
Selma, Alabama, civil rights campaign, 79–81
Shaw, George Bernard, 147
Shores, Arthur, 48
Shuttlesworth, Fred, 69–71
Simon, Rita James, 147
Smith, Benjamin, 47
Smith, Carl, 68
Smith Act, 8, 12, 39, 43, 46, 99, 115
Sobeloff, Simon E., 77–78
Social control, 1; and civil rights movement, 23–25, 28, 31–34, 36, 55, 58–86, 150–151, 155; and ideological function of legal system, 133–134, 139, 140–141, 144–145, 149–157; and jury nullification, 144–146, 155–156; and Vietnam antiwar movement, 103–104, 151–152, 155–156
Social movements: and juries, 146–

148, 149; and litigation, 1–2, 6–9, 11–14, 150; and morale, 17–18, 25–26, 29; and resource mobilization, 10–27, 87–88, 103–104, 129, 150; strength of, 12, 58–59, 82–83
Southern Christian Leadership Conference (SCLC), 60, 69–72, 75, 78, 79–81, 83–84. *See also* King, Martin Luther
Southern Conference Educational Fund, 47–48
Sparf v. The United States of America, 138
Spock, Benjamin, trial of, 24, 98–100, 106–107, 116, 139–140, 141–142, 155
Stokes, Rose Paster, 24
Student Nonviolent Coordinating Committee (SNCC), 32, 53–54, 75; and Albany, Georgia, demonstrations, 60, 61–62, 66–69; and Legal Defense and Educational Fund, 43–44; and Mississippi Summer Project, 83, 85; and Selma, Alabama, demonstrations, 79–81

Thompson, E. P., 154, 156–157
Thomsen, Roszel, 125
Tucker, Sam, 42
Tumin, Melvin, 112
Turner, Ralph H., 41

Ultra-resistance. *See* Catholics, radical
United Auto Workers union, 72
United States Department of Justice, 32
United States Supreme Court: and civil rights, 28–31, 37, 47, 73; and *pro se* defense, 105n, 106

Van Dyke, Jon, 142
Vietnam antiwar movement, 87–148; and defendants, 87, 90–92, 109; and defense attorneys, 88–90, 99–101, 106–107; defense strategies of, 16, 87, 95–103, 125–126; and judges, 24–25, 92–93, 97, 99, 101, 125, 127, 128; and juries, 16–17, 18–19, 93–94, 97, 102–103, 112–116; and jury nullification, 139–146, 155–156; and political justice, 150–152; press coverage of, 19–20, 94–95, 99, 101, 102; and *pro se* defense, 105–118, 127–128; and resource mobilization, 87–88, 103–104, 117–118, 127, 128, 129
Virginia Employment Commission, 77
Voting rights legislation, 81

Wallace, George, 73, 80
Waltzer, Bruce, 47
Ware, Charles, 68
Wasserstrom, Richard, 107
Weber, Max, 157–158
Weinglass, Leonard I., 140
White House Seven trial, 107–108
Willes, Edward, 133
Women's suffrage trials, 4–5, 26, 108
World War I trials, 1, 8, 19, 24, 146, 150, 157

Yinger, J. Milton, 119
Young, Andrew, 83
Young, Whitney, 45

Zeisel, Hans, 141, 144
Zenger, John Peter, 136–137, 140
Zinn, Howard, 66, 117